*Sanctifying Slavery and Politics in South Carolina*

*Sanctifying*

# SLAVERY & POLITICS

*in South Carolina*

THE LIFE OF THE
*Reverend Alexander Garden, 1685–1756*

FRED E. WITZIG

*The University of South Carolina Press*

© 2018 University of South Carolina

Published by the University of South Carolina Press
Columbia, South Carolina 29208

www.sc.edu/uscpress

Manufactured in the United States of America

27 26 25 24 23 22 21 20 19 18
10 9 8 7 6 5 4 3 2 1

Library of Congress Cataloging-in-Publication Data
can be found at http://catalog.loc.gov/.

ISBN 978-1-61117-845-6 (cloth)
ISBN 978-1-61117-846-3 (ebook)

*For Nancy*

# Contents

Preface  ix

Acknowledgments  xiii

*Chapter 1*
BIRTHPLACES  1

*Chapter 2*
ACQUAINTANCES  25

*Chapter 3*
FRIENDSHIP  52

*Chapter 4*
DALLIANCE  84

*Chapter 5*
ENGAGEMENT  100

*Chapter 6*
MARRIAGE  129

*Chapter 7*
TILL DEATH DO US PART  158

Notes  189
Bibliography  217
Index  233

# Preface

This is the story of an extraordinary relationship between the eighteenth-century colony of South Carolina and the Church of England minister Alexander Garden, the colony's chief representative of the official church of the global British Empire. These two partners were born a generation apart, Garden in "the valley of the Dee, on the southern boundary of Aberdeenshire" in Scotland, or so rumor has it, and the Carolinas in the investment and political offices of London. Initially skeptical of each other, they soon became fast friends and enjoyed a long and prosperous relationship until Garden died in 1756, approximately twenty years before South Carolina became one of the United States.

The man and the colony needed each other; certainly they seemed made for each other given the harsh realities of their time. Garden emerged out of historical obscurity in 1720—barely anything can be known of him before then—when he migrated from the British Isles to Charles Town. South Carolina at that time was recovering from the bloodbath of the Yamassee War of 1715–18 and experiencing political and economic adjustments that would convert it from an economy based on trade with Indians to one resting firmly on the backs of slaves laboring in rice and indigo plantations. For the next thirty-six years the two partners would weather monstrous hurricanes; the "Great Fire" of 1740; five outbreaks of yellow fever and periodic swells of malaria, smallpox, and typhus; a political revolution against colonial proprietors; the economic booms and busts of the Atlantic economy; and endemic strife with their Spanish neighbors in Florida. Internally relations between European settlers and Native Americans after the Yamassee War never relaxed entirely, and whites and blacks often came to blows, with colonial America's largest slave uprising erupting in South Carolina in 1739. In the midst of the particularly difficult years of 1739–42, the colony's religious affairs were convulsed by the evangelical Great Awakening that famously swept the Atlantic Seaboard. Through all of these travails, Garden provided steady leadership that not only helped guide the colony to prosperity but also bestowed upon him a considerable portion of that prosperity.

Alexander Garden was a minister in the Church of England and a husband, father, friend, religious administrator, and spiritual pastor. For these tasks he hardly needed a colony, or at least not specifically South Carolina. His homeland in the British Isles would have sufficed, as would any of the British colonies and particularly the baker's dozen along the coast of North America. There the Church of England struggled to fill its pulpits with ministers acceptable to independent-minded colonists and adaptable to the environmental vagaries of the New World. Garden, though, also nurtured dreams of material wealth, social power, and aristocratic privilege. To realize those dreams he became a slave master, a land speculator, a doyen of high society, and a pioneer in slave education. For those dreams and those tasks he needed the fresh and fertile soil of the slave colony of South Carolina, which, it turned out, badly needed someone with his administrative skills, his spiritual credentials, and the strength of his personality to impose religious legitimacy upon its more carnal pursuits. Together they accomplished remarkable feats of resilience, ingenuity, and force of will. Both achieved great fame while accumulating immense material wealth notable among their peers.

Yet one cannot help but wish that things had turned out differently for them, that they had charted some other course for their lives than the one they took. In retrospect, Garden and his white neighbors appear to have been blinded to a debilitating moral defect—slavery—that caused them immense struggles and even threatened their very existence. That Garden and his friends prospered anyway is the cause of any glint of admiration readers might feel for their resilience, ingenuity, and force of will, but that they refused to deal with the moral defect offends modern moral sensibilities and constrains approbation of their achievements. Perhaps, *perhaps,* upon hearing their story the reader will conclude that it is too much to expect them to have recognized their faults, that their failings were too much shared by everyone of their own era and of all of the ages before them, and that their posterity should therefore recognize their true greatness as forgers of a civilization and founders of a nation. Or perhaps the reader will reckon their story nothing but a tragedy, a horrific tale of exploitation and abuse. In the case of the latter, the true heroes will be found among those exploited and abused, who as such deserve admiration. In such a twist of the tale they become the protagonists, and Garden and his friends the antagonists. Or perhaps it is enough simply to tell the story and wonder at the dilemmas and complexities of human existence.

Telling Garden's story is not an easy task. Garden seldom spoke of his own life, feelings, or inclinations. Most of what he wrote that survives is in the form of personal correspondence related to his position as the leader of the Church of England in South Carolina. The writing style is businesslike in its efficiency, and the content is almost always about other people. Almost no correspondence between Garden and his friends or relatives survives, and no diary has been found. The sources that speak of his character and personality come almost exclusively from those who did not like him or his leadership. Their sentiments do match the images that can be teased out from his letters, the paper trail of legal documents concerning his business dealings, and bits and pieces of observations of Garden offered occasionally by his friends. However, if the historian wants to know the reasons for why he did anything, for instance the internal motivations for working hard to buttress the institution of slavery, he left little behind with which to work. It is difficult to give him the benefit of the doubt when he did bequeath the benefit of his thoughts. Some of his behavior seems to have been downright mercenary; for instance, he sided with wealthy parishioners and business partners, who could sabotage his career, when they slandered his ministerial colleagues, whom he was supposed to treat fairly. Without a better glimpse into his mind, it appears that he tended to be imperious in his role as the bishop of London's deputy in the Carolinas in order to advance his own interests. However, he also faithfully and selflessly served the poor and the sick in a deadly climate, nearly wore himself to physical incapacity traveling to fill empty pulpits, and started the first organized slave school in the South. He was the undisputed leader of a generation of Anglican ministers who turned a weak and culturally insignificant Church of England in South Carolina into a major social force, for good and for bad. The point is, little material exists with which to peer into his heart and soul and render a final judgment of the man, especially since he lived in a time very different from the twenty-first century in its labor arrangements, social hierarchy, and hazardous climate. Most of what is left to examine are the consequences, not the motivations, of his actions.

The biographer Roger Lundin offered something of a theoretical framework appropriate for dealing with the problem of understanding Garden using limited sources. Lundin rejected reductionist biographies that sought a single "key that will unlock the secret of a life," be it economic determinism, sexual drive, or some other factor or theory to be latched onto for its supposed explanatory power. Rather, the "meaning" of a life "is to be found in the whole of the life, from its beginning to its end," said Lundin, "and not only in the life itself but the life in the larger context, of its historical setting." Such sensitivity to the "competing claims" in any particular historical context "is a necessity for understanding fairly and creatively and justly another human life." In this light, making simple assertions about Garden's motivations and values, especially without attending to the cultural forces around him, appears particularly unwise and unjust. The fact that Garden left behind little self-reflection demands such a contextual approach.[1]

For these reasons the chapters that follow are something of a dual biography taking as its subjects the man Alexander Garden and his colony of South Carolina. Vignettes about his wife, his parishioners, and others at the end of each chapter, after the first chapter, seek to evaluate Garden's personal relationships from the perspective of each of the people with whom he interacted most intimately. Garden sometimes accepted the limited options available to him in the South. At other times he expanded them or used them to his advantage. He acted on his culture and not merely within his culture. The substance of his legacy has to do with the calculus of resignation and confrontation that governed his life. By accepting or pushing against cultural, economic, and political boundaries he both perpetuated and re-created his world while his world reinforced or reformed his character, habits, and predilections. His partnership with his colony was dynamic, at times strained and at times pleasurable, and always determinative and never guaranteed. When Garden's pen revealed little about the man, turning to the social and material conditions around him for plausible explanations of his behavior could be most fruitful.

In this book the metaphors of friendship and marriage are used to capture the intimate and evolving nature of the relationship between Garden and his society. Theirs was not love at first sight: soon after acquainting himself with the colony in the early 1720s, Garden spoke of his desire to leave for a more healthful climate and a parish less skeptical of ministers on the make. By the end of the decade, however, the colony had proved a willing partner to his ambitions, having provided him a wife with strategic social and financial connections and the highest seat of religious authority in the far South. When evangelical revivalists came courting his parishioners during the Great Awakening, Garden fended them off with a display of familiarity with and devotion to his colony's traditions, desires, and realities that sealed the relationship between Garden and the colony. These were foundational years in the colony's early history. Together, Garden and his friends built the Old South—the slave plantation economy, social politeness and hierarchy, and conformity to racial norms—that came to represent something of a founding myth comparable to New England's "City on a Hill." The Old South survived the American Revolution, and when it was struck down in the Civil War, the myth thrived well into the twentieth century.

## Acknowledgments

Research for this book began in the course of another project under the guidance of Lawrence J. Friedman, professor of history at Indiana University in Bloomington (IUB), whose conversation and encouragement have lasted many years. The research continued under the direction of Stephen J. Stein, now professor emeritus of religious studies at IUB, to whom I owe a tremendous intellectual debt. Thanks as well to Professors Sarah Knott and Wendy Gamber, both at IUB, and Marianne Wockeck at Indiana University—Purdue University Indianapolis, all three of whom have taught, encouraged, corrected, and inspired me in many ways. Jason Lanzter, now at Butler University, has been a good friend and support through and beyond graduate school.

I would be remiss if I failed to note the encouragement and support of Richard Gawthrop, professor of history at Franklin College, where I taught for many years. Rick's only official responsibility toward me was to oversee my teaching at Franklin, but being a uniquely generous person, he took great interest in my overall development as a professional historian, including my research. I still do not think it fair that he can be an expert in both European and American history. Are we not supposed to choose only one field of expertise? I greatly appreciate his mentoring and friendship.

The staff at the South Caroliniana Library and the South Carolina Department of Archives and History provided invaluable advice and service securing and interpreting primary sources. Chuck Lesser at the archives went above and beyond my expectations in recommending collections and interpreting legal documents. Some of the earliest research for this book was funded by the Sally Reahard Fellowship and the Donald F. Carmony Dissertation Award at Indiana University. The library at IUB and the staff of the Hewes Library at Monmouth College, under the direction of Rick Sayre, deserve special gratitude. Portions of chapters 2 through 6 were published first as "Beyond Expectation: How Charles Town's 'Pious and Well-Disposed Christians' Changed Their Minds about Slave Education during the Great Awakening" in the *South Carolina Historical Magazine* 114, no. 4 (October 2013). I thank the *SCHM* for permission to reprint those portions. Sincere thanks are due to the anonymous reviewers of this book in its manuscript version. Their suggestions and corrections improved the book significantly.

The history department at Monmouth College in Illinois has been a fantastic place to write this book. We are a teaching school with a love for research. My colleagues over the past several years, Tom Best, Simon Cordery, Stacy Cordery, Lynn Daw, Amy Caldwell de Farias, Lewis Gould, Tim Lacy, Christine Myers, Jeremy Pool, and Bill Urban, have been models of teacher-scholars. The idea for this book stems from a stimulating conversation at Bill's house. Bill, Stacy, Lewis, and Christine helped me work out a general framework for the book. Lewis, whose own work, like Bill's, spans many years and includes major books in history, gave me critical advice and encouragement during the book-proposal stage. Stacy has been a fantastic chair, working with the dean of faculty—thank you, David Timmerman—on a teaching schedule and work space that enabled me to fulfill my teaching responsibilities and still have large blocks of time dedicated to research and writing. She also provided the exact level of accountability to keep me on task without overburdening me, and she patiently counseled me at various stages of writing. Stacy and Christine carefully read each of the chapters, providing everything from editing corrections to insightful criticisms of the larger ideas. From day one Christine has been my consultant on all things Scottish. I have a shelf of books and articles that she not only recommended but also took the time to gather for me.

Many of the students in my Religion in America research seminar read the first two chapters of this book. I thought through some of my ideas in front of them and with their input. They also helped me understand how undergraduates might read what I was writing, allowing me to adjust my style and content accordingly. Thank you, Bill Bos, Kyle Dickson, Rebecca Eaton, John Fitzgerald, Henry LeCrone, Patrick McClain, Kalin McKean, Vickie Salyards, Andrew Shiakallis, Sara Stalter, Kyle Vestal, Toni Ward, Alex Waszak, and Madison Well. You dared to take me up on my plea to be critical and honest, and the book is better for it.

My daughter Rachel, who happens to be an outstanding English major at Monmouth College, read and commented on the first four chapters. I have never had the experience of critiquing my father's work, but I imagine that her efforts benefited me more than they did her. Thank you, Rachel! Where would I be without the love and encouragement of her and daughters Marta and Erica and the fun spirit of grandson Jaivyn? Thanks to all of you for making sacrifices necessary for me to finish this project, from its first kernel stage many years ago to this completed project.

To their mother, Nancy, I owe the most. She also has made numerous sacrifices of time and energy due to my unpredictable work schedule and frequent research trips. She read each of these chapters. More than that, her encouragement and optimism kept me at the computer when I felt like going back to writing lectures. Whatever else I could write here will never capture how much she has done for and meant to me throughout this writing project and our marriage of twenty-eight years.

Many years ago I read George Marsden's seminal book *Fundamentalism and American Culture*. I was struck by and admired his forthrightness in telling his readers that he wrote of fundamentalist Christians as an evangelical Christian who did not altogether agree with the people about whom he wrote. In that spirit, I should note that I am an evangelical Christian writing about a man, Alexander Garden, who had critical things to say about the evangelicals of his own day. On this I think the three of us would agree: we owe the largest debt to the One who gave us minds and the reasons to use them.

# Chapter 1

# BIRTHPLACES

South Carolina was born of the same dreams of wealth, power, and privilege that motivated Alexander Garden, although successful establishment by Europeans suffered through several false starts and multiple origins. European exploration and settlement of the Americas took many years, from 1492 until well into the 1700s, and involved tremendous investment and sacrifice, bad luck and providential serendipity, and wisdom gained only through painful experience. The intensity of misery and calamity that Europeans encountered in the Americas due to disorientation, disease, deprivation, weather catastrophes, and violence threatened settlers' very conception of themselves as civilized English men and women. In the early years of each colony, including South Carolina, a few people prospered, some gave up and returned home, others went insane, many suffered, and too many Indians, European colonists, and enslaved Africans died tragically.[1] The history of the founding of any one of the American colonies is not a simple story of merely transferring people and their culture from one location to another, and that of South Carolina is no exception. We could trace the founding of South Carolina to 1629, when the British king Charles I granted a charter for a colony, dubbed "Carolana" in his honor, to his ambitious and loyal attorney general Sir Robert Heath. Heath's biographer has judged him to have been "sometimes dishonest, always mean and consistently grasping" in his royal duties and even "less fettered by ethics" in his personal dealings. Such traits could prove useful to the task of cajoling European villagers to bobble four thousand miles across an unpredictable ocean in a boat's cargo hold to eke out an existence in a subtropical wilderness among native inhabitants of unknown sociability and next door to Spanish colonists aggressively resistant to English colonization.[2] However, preoccupied with sorting out Charles's legal problems at home, Heath failed to attracted enough attention to the endeavor among potential settlers. In 1632 Heath bestowed his rights to the colony upon Lord Maltravers, who also was unable to stimulate interest in the colony. It took more than mere ambition and cunning to get a colony started in the Europeans' New World; single-mindedness was crucial.[3]

All the character traits necessary for founding a colony existed in spades in men, and a few women, who had earlier settled in the Caribbean and were already accustomed to the otherworldly rigors of the tropical climates of the Americas. Of particular interest to the founding of the Carolinas was Barbados in the Lesser Antilles, a fourteen-by-twenty-one-mile patch of coastal, mostly arable plains; rolling, terraced hills; and central plateau. In 1627 enterprising Englishmen, usually younger sons of prominent families in England, planted an agricultural colony there. At home they had some wealth and plenty of models among their family and friends of how to make riches and spend them. Shut out of a meaningful inheritance by the practice of primogeniture, by which family estates passed down only to eldest sons, they needed a fresh landscape upon which they could build their own aristocratic estates. Barbados seemed a likely place for such endeavors, particularly when, by mid-century, great riches were being carried out of its planted fields.

Having found space, these sons of gentry needed labor. Some of the Barbadian settlers were men impressed into hard labor by war and by clever techniques frowned upon today, such as kidnapping and, by mid-century, enslavement.[4] Hundreds of Scottish prisoners of war during the British civil wars of 1642–51 were transported forcibly to Barbados, and elsewhere in the Americas, including 500 at the war's conclusion.[5] As the century wore on, they were outnumbered by African slaves. In the 1640s slave ships delivered to the colony's shores 18,700 African slaves, and in the last quarter of the century over 64,000 were transported there.[6] Dangerous work conditions, disease, malnutrition, and physical abuse from overseers took a dreadful toll on the slave population, preventing natural increase and demanding that planters account for a sizable annual expenditure on new slaves just to maintain a sufficient workforce.[7]

Meanwhile far more European men than women made the transatlantic journey, a situation amenable neither to natural increase nor natural happiness, and so the colony's boosters retrieved women from jails and brothels in the British Isles and sent them across the Atlantic to take up with the newly rich and restless in the Caribbean.[8] "This island is the dunghill whereon England doth cast forth its rubbish," wrote Henry Whistler when he visited in 1655. "Rogues and whores and such like people are those which are generally brought here."[9] This was an unfortunate and condescending description, to be sure, but one that gets at the social strata in the old country from which many emigrants fled.

Over the next several decades these hapless souls, white and black, planted tobacco of insufferable quality and then sugar of insatiable quantity, producing fabulous riches for the landlords. Wealth accumulated in Barbados—at least for the plantation owners—faster than in any other British colony. Even the Scottish prisoners of war fared well: one Barbadian promoted the Scots in a letter to King Charles II as "the chief instrument of bringing Barbados to perfection."[10] An observer who happened to pass by the island at mid-century wrote in amazement that "the riches of the Island far exceed English apprehension."[11] Planters built ever bigger houses—out of wood imported from hundreds and thousands of miles away as plows deforested the island—outfitted them with fine furniture, and turned to some, but not all, of the pleasures of the aristocratic life.[12]

Too much indulgence might distract from the real business of the island, which was business. Richard Ligon, a gentleman of sorts who spent three years on the island and published his *True and Exact History of the Island of Barbados* in 1673, admitted that English settlers would not find all of the "Pleasures of Europe" on the island. He faulted the hot climate of the "Torrid Zone" for the absence of some of the outdoor sports of English gentry, such as horse racing and hunting, while noting that Barbadians enjoyed all of the indoor pleasures, such as "Chess, Tables, Cards, Dice, Shovel-abord, Billiards; and some kinds of Dances." The island's singular pursuit of profit seemed to be more to blame: there were those "whose souls were so fixt upon, and so riveted to the earth, and the profits that arise out of it, as their soals were lifted no higher." Ligon contented himself, however, to "leave them to their own earthly delights."[13]

Planters had to move quickly to enjoy their luxuries; noxious and fatal diseases, insurrection among laborers, and persistent warfare with competing empires created a colony perched on the precipice of calamity. Families were extraordinarily small because the death rate was extraordinarily high. Out of this forge of adversity emerged a planter class of immense determination and rapacity. In the words of the historian Richard S. Dunn, "they lived fast, spent recklessly, played desperately, and died young."[14] The island was no place for the "sluggard" or the "Sleepie man," wrote Richard Ligon, and the men "whose minds are not overballanc'd with avarice and lucre" would likely prefer to "settle themselves quietly in England" than to labor against the rampant disease of the islands, regardless of the fortune to be made.[15] Pottery produced locally for sugar processing provides a tangible metaphor for the easy-come, easy-go nature of the colony: archaeologists have described Barbadian sugar jars as strictly functional, half-baked, and "chalky and friable," but the goal was to make money, not impress later generations of art historians.[16]

This account should not be misunderstood to say that religion counted for nothing on the island. English settlers may have prospered materially, but they were also aware that they lived in a sort of cultural exile from their homeland. Thus many of them worked to re-create the spiritual comforts of home by building churches and following the religious practices with which they were familiar in England. They used church space for communal activities that could be religious, but sometimes not, and liturgy and the sacraments as binding for social cohesion in a racially volatile setting by distinguishing communicants—always white—from others—often black. Such rituals as baptism, marriage, and burial were performed in ways that drew racial lines and economic distinctions. For instance, only whites could enjoy the sacrament of marriage, and the varying qualities of funeral materials, such as casket palls, reflected the benefits, or lack thereof, of social class. Some of these practices and the symbolism attributed to them contradicted or at least went beyond the intent of the church, but the laity guarded jealously the levers of control of the church; the establishment of the Church of England was for the benefit of the laity, not the prerogative of the clergy. Church practice and authority had to yield to the economic and racial realities of the island. Rather than abandoning religion for secularism, inhabitants used elements from their previous lives in England for personal comfort while infusing them with new social vitality that bolstered their power over blacks and other supposed inferiors.[17]

By the mid-1600s so many people, now most of them African, had crowded onto the small island that its population density exceeded that of "any comparable area in the English-speaking world, except London." Barbados proved too small and the soil too depleted just a few decades after its founding, so its white fortune seekers searched elsewhere for land upon which they could force their slaves to produce riches. When they found Jamaica and other Caribbean islands, they looked back to Barbados as a model to emulate in all its economic, slaveholding, religious, and social features. Barbados was in many ways a "cultural hearth" for the British New World.[18] By 1670 they had also discovered the coastal plains, called the lowcountry, of the land now called South Carolina. The region's warm and humid subtropical climate and its fertile soil bore some resemblance to Barbados.

In 1663 King Charles II issued a new charter to settle a colony in the Carolinas. The charter vested authority over the endeavor in eight proprietors, all of them ambitious men with going concerns in both the Americas and England: John Colleton, a fierce defender of the Stuart thrones—he was knighted for his loyalty—and a Barbadian planter who probably did the most work securing the charter; Anthony Ashley Cooper, the future Lord Shaftesbury, who owned a plantation in Barbados and did the most to get the new colony settled—the Ashley and Cooper Rivers by Charleston are named for him; William Berkeley, governor of Virginia; and five more noblemen of great wealth, political influence, and interest in Atlantic trade, several of them members of the royal Council on Foreign Plantations.[19]

The proprietors depended on Barbadians to get their lowcountry colony on the ground. After a small group of New Englanders settled in the Cape Fear area only to leave discouraged within six months, assurances of interest in settling the region among planters in Barbados rescued the colony from negative publicity. By 1665 the proprietors reached an agreement with the self-styled "Barbadian Adventurers," led by the Barbados planter, judge, and councilman Sir John Yeamans. Yeamans proved a likely candidate in terms of determination and resourcefulness, and there were plenty more like him who followed his lead.

Ambition had its flip side, however; he and his cohort could prove difficult to handle, pursuing their own interests rather than that of the proprietors. At least one of the proprietors caught on quickly to Yeamans's character, remarking, "If to convert all things to his private profit be the marke of able parts Sir John is without a doubt a very judicious man."[20] Yeamans allegedly murdered his business partner, Benjamin Berringer, who also happened to be the husband of his lover; Yeamans married Margaret Berringer ten weeks later.

Yeamans's first attempt to establish a colony in North America soon fell apart, through little fault of his own. The Barbadian Adventurers' efforts failed when the Anglo-Dutch War broke out in 1665, followed by the Great Fire of London in 1666, both of which diverted the Lords Proprietors' attention, money, and shipping resources. In 1670 the Lords Proprietors tried once more, this time successfully and again with Yeamans and the Barbadians in the lead. Yeamans served as governor of Carolina from 1672 to 1674 before retiring to the grave.[21] In his wake he left behind the powerful Goose Creek faction, dominated by Yeamans's Barbadian friends, which dominated Carolinian politics into the eighteenth century.[22] Although most of the settlers aboard the first ship to reach the colony hailed directly from England, over half of the white settlers who arrived in the colony in the 1670s and 1680s were from Barbados, mostly small planters and free laborers. A few of the island's elites migrated to Carolina, while others chose only to send their investment cash. Additionally over half of the African slaves who came during these early years were from Barbados.[23] The ambitious and impetuous men and women from Barbados left a deep social and cultural imprint on the Carolinas during the first several decades. They also turned Carolina into an "adjunct to the Barbadian economy," trading food and other natural resources for island sugar and slaves.[24] Indeed a significant part of their influence on Carolina included a penchant for using slave rather than free labor.

Thus another place and time to trace the birth of South Carolina is West Africa in the early sixteenth century, when Portuguese merchants began purchasing slaves from the ancient African slave market to toil on slave plantations on islands off Africa's coast. All of the European empires in the Americas constructed similar labor regimes in their colonies across the Atlantic. From the sixteenth through nineteenth centuries approximately 12.5 million Africans were crowded onto ships bound for the Americas, and after the weeks- or months-long journey across the ocean, not even 11 million of them disembarked on American soil, the rest having succumbed to the hosts of diseases plaguing slave ships. Fewer than 400,000, or less than 4 percent, of these men, women, and children ended up in the British North American colonies. The Caribbean Islands, including Barbados, received almost 45 percent of the slaves, and the remainder went to Brazil and the rest of the South American mainland. The

Carolinas did not receive African slaves in any large numbers until the 1720s, more than half a century after Barbados turned to slavery as a primary form of labor. In the slave trade and slave labor, as in the ambitions and business of the master class, the Carolinas followed the Caribbean precedent, Barbadian especially.[25]

The Carolinas turned to African slavery because an earlier form of forced labor had failed to produce expected gains. Far more Indian than African slaves passed through ports in the North American Southeast before 1720. Early European settlers in the Carolinas busied themselves not with cotton, which had to wait until the late 1700s, or with indigo, which was not grown profitably until the 1740s, or even rice, a crop that emerged simultaneously with the triumph of African slavery over Indian slavery in the 1710s and 1720s.[26] Rather, the Barbadians who arrived in the Carolinas relied on partnerships with Native Americans in the realms of trade, defense, navigation of the terrain, foodstuffs, marriage and companionship, and slaves. Long before Europeans arrived on the American shores, Native Americans had integrated various forms of what is now called slavery into their social systems and intertribal relationships. Indian slaves—not unlike those in Africa before the transatlantic trade—served as markers of wealth and power more than as sources of labor. Imagining themselves not as some cohesive ethnic set called "Native Americans" but rather as separate peoples with competing interests and allegiances, Indians in rather small numbers fell prey to slavery as part of the long-simmering intertribal conflicts that plagued North America. For those in South Carolina, the purpose and magnitude of slavery changed with the arrival of European settlers. It did not take long for Indians to discover that in trading with Europeans it could take them two years of hunting deer to make the same profit as when they traded one fellow Indian into the Atlantic slave market.[27] The trade in Indian slaves escalated quickly, seemingly beyond what either side could control. The result was disastrous for everyone.

In the first fifty years of the colony's existence, the Indian slave trade overwhelmed all other dimensions of southern trade, politics, and culture in importance for European settlers and Native Americans alike.[28] As is true for so much in early colonial American history, exact numbers of Indians enslaved and merchandized in the Atlantic slave trade system are impossible to reconstruct, but these had to have been in the tens of thousands and certainly more than the number of African slaves traded through the Charles Town port.[29] Add to that number those who were killed in the brutal process of enslavement, which often involved wars and bloody raids. Entire tribes disappeared and others migrated out of their homelands, political alliances shifted, and cultures dissipated, amalgamated, and assimilated.

The trade in slaves was the worst practice among many employed by European settlers in their relentless drive for wealth. Sometimes they encouraged Indians to drunkenness before they began trade negotiations. Dubious negotiations and commodity pricing schemes and a diminishing deer population pushed Indians deeper and deeper into debt, a problem aggravated by the European practice—foreign to Native American culture—of selling debts at a discount to other traders, whereby a debt changed hands and was modified in the process without Indian consent. Indians found it increasingly difficult to meet the seemingly insatiable and evidently unscrupulous demands of the European commodity trade. Frustrated, many of them turned to the slave trade to extricate themselves from their precarious economic dilemmas.[30]

In the early 1700s the slave trade, having already decimated Native American populations, independence, and culture, nearly wiped out the young Carolinian colonies. Competing factions of colonists ruthlessly pursued any advantage they could, turning Indian tribe against Indian tribe, always seeking better deals and intriguing to capture a larger share of the market. An attempt by the colonial legislature to reform the trade in 1707 ended up being for naught, rather predictably considering the title of the act, which completely ignored the needs of the Indians: "An Act for Regulating the Indian Trade and Making it Safe to the Public," which, the act made clear, meant white communities. Colonial traders, of the same moral ilk as John Yeamans and his band of Barbadian Adventurers of the founding generation, cared more for personal gain than public safety. The law addressed the concerns of the colonists for proper Christian behavior and their own survival. Indian welfare and the greediness of Anglo traders were ignored: "Whereas the greater number of those persons that trade among the Indians in amity with this Government, do generally lead loose, vicious lives, to the scandal of the Christian religion, and do likewise oppress the people among whom they live, by their unjust and illegal actions, which if not prevented may in time tend to the destruction of this Province," traders were to purchase licenses from the government—opportunities for cronyism if there ever were any—and bonds for good behavior. Then they should behave themselves.[31]

They did not. Periodic legal attempts to improve or better enforce the 1707 reform failed as well. Eventually colonists dared to pit their Indian allies against each other. Fed up, various tribes surrounding Charles Town united militarily in 1715 and sought justice through war. Led by the Yamassee, a coalition of Indians that represented one of the most impressive and powerful Indian alliances in colonial America pushed the European colonial settlements to the brink of annihilation. Indians burned plantations and sacked villages. Some four hundred colonists and untold hundreds of Native Americans died. "The Southern parts . . . of the Province are entirely depopulated" by the depredations of the "Savages," the colony's clergy reported to the bishop with horror, "and the whole must have undoubtedly fallen a Sacrifice to their Barbarity" were it not for divine intervention and the colonists' courage.[32] At one point European settlement was clustered within a few miles of Charles Town. The Yamassee, however, appreciated the trade opportunities brought by the European newcomers, and so they sought not to extinguish the colonists but to teach them a lesson they could not forget. Within a year the colonists had convinced the Cherokee to join the fight on their side. With this crucial assistance, the colonists ultimately prevailed. By 1718 the war was over, but nobody had won. It ended in exhaustion, not triumph.[33]

The consequences of the conflict, however, were enormous for the development of the South. Native Americans moved westward to create a safe space between themselves and colonists. Trade with colonists continued, but now, chastened by war, both sides acted with greater circumspection and caution, aware of the dangers of out of control, ruthless competition. The colonial government gave gifts—tributes really—to Indians and issued trading licenses to colonists much more strictly. Most important, while trade in hides and food continued, the trade in Indian slaves declined precipitously. On both sides trade assumed much more importance in the realm of imperial and continental diplomacy, with governors and tribal leaders using trade accommodations as incentives for political and military alliances. Wary authorities reined in renegade fortune seekers. Meanwhile space created by Indians' westward movement enticed colonial settlement. Agriculture, not trade, became the basis of the colonial economy, and for labor, colonists turned to that same source that had served them so well in the Caribbean. Practical considerations motivated by fear of another awful war, not some process of moral soul-searching, birthed the postwar settlement. African slaves converted South Carolina into a plantation economy on the magnitude of the West Indies. Annual importation of slaves jumped from fewer than two hundred before the war to thousands after the war. The population transformed from mostly Indian with an important European contingent to mostly African with a small but powerfully wealthy European ruling class. Ruthless exploitation of African slaves replaced ruthless exploitation of Indian slaves, although now with considerable government inspection and regulation. "The Yamassee War was thus an end and a beginning," wrote the historian Alan Gallay. "It reconstructed the South in a way that few events have—only the end of the Civil War compares—for this war marked the birth of the Old South, just as Appomattox marked its death."[34]

South Carolinians sought better leadership for the new colony. Historians have labeled this search the "Revolution of 1719," for in that year colonists banded together to unseat their governor and demand transfer of authority from the proprietors to the Crown. To be sure, problems other than the war also prompted the revolution. Far away and distracted by more immediate concerns, the proprietors had proved incapable of dealing with the pirates plaguing Atlantic shipping and using the Carolina coastline as a refuge from the British navy; Blackbeard anchored his flotilla off the Charles Town harbor in 1718, stopped ships, took hostages, and demanded medicine for his crew.[35] It was up to Carolinian colonists to root out the pirates enough to carry on with their trade. Wars with the Indians and the Spanish spawned massive debt and innovative funding techniques that led to oppressive inflation and more wrangling with proprietary policy makers. Laying all blame for the colony's troubles squarely on the shoulders of the "confused helpless and negligent government of the Lords Proprietors," the petitioners "renounce[d] all obedience" to their legal lords and aimed to "throw [them]selves at the foot of the throne."[36] The king complied, setting in motion the royal assumption of control over the colony that would be complete in 1729. Colonists succeeded in achieving royal colony status, with a more pliable royal governor resident in Charles Town.

As a result, on April 24, 1720, when Alexander Garden arrived in the port of Charles Town, he found a colony reeling from inflation, piracy, war and rumors of war, and with a population only beginning to venture beyond the safe confines of the town's fort. With their main trading partners removed west, many of their frontier settlements pillaged and burned, and hundreds of their friends killed, colonists faced the daunting process of rebuilding their economy, their homes, and as it would turn out, their government. But Garden was a minister, and he came armed with a Bible, not guns, wealth, or political decrees.

Garden served the Church of England, the established—government-supported—Protestant denomination. The king was the head of the church and exacted taxes to be used on the church's behalf. Some, including Presbyterians, Congregationalists, and Quakers, rejected the Church of England. At home and abroad such dissenters could worship only with the government's permission. However, after paying a horrific cost in gold and blood during religious wars in the 1600s, many exhausted European rulers concluded that there were limits to the price they were willing to pay for religious conformity. They developed a tendency toward religious toleration at home and throughout their global empires. In North America colonists and those who ruled them in England, whether the Crown or proprietors, worked out policies of varying religious toleration that they believed worked best in their own colonies. Most colonies maintained established churches, so colonists were required to pay taxes used for the established church even if they did not affiliate with it, and in some cases political privileges were open only to members of the established church. Some colonists practicing religious traditions deemed too theologically distant from accepted Protestant Christian norms—Jews and Catholics come to mind—endured violence or the threat of violence, but outright coercion in the cause of religious conformity was arguably rare and became even less common in the 1700s, especially outside Puritan New England. Even today many American schoolchildren know of the Salem, Massachusetts, witch trials of the 1690s only because the scope of their violence was so anomalous in North America; their representativeness of colonial culture can be easily exaggerated. The point is, "establishment" was interpreted and enforced differently across time and space.

The bishop of London sent Garden to Charles Town after Garden served a brief stint at the Barking Church in London, but the bishop may have been acting at the request, officially or unofficially, by the Society for the Propagation of the Gospel in Foreign Parts (SPG). The name speaks concisely of its mission.[37] Formed as early as 1701 with the assistance of Archbishop of Canterbury Thomas Tennison and Bishop of London Henry Compton, the SPG sent Anglican, meaning Church of England, missionaries around the British Empire upon colonial requests for religious instruction.[38] The society vetted ministers for proper education and acceptable character and often helped support them financially after they settled in their parishes. The Church of England at the time owed much to this organization, as do the historians who make use of the extensive collections of correspondence and other records left behind by its missionaries.

The SPG hoped to recruit converts from among European transplants, African slaves, and Native Americans. The king chartered the SPG in response, he said, to the demands of his far-flung imperial dependents for "Learned and Orthodox Ministers" who could "instruct [his] said Loving Subjects in the Principles of True Religion," but when the SPG issued "Instructions for the Clergy Employed by the Society," they included "Directions to the Catechists for Instructing Indians, Negroes, &c."[39] In South Carolina none of these populations proved to be particularly enthusiastic students. Population estimates for the religious groups in South Carolina are difficult to come by, but members of the Church of England were certainly in the minority. Native Americans preferred their traditional religious beliefs, and slave masters were reluctant to allow missionaries to distract their chattel property from their all-important earthly labor. Among the white population, a 1710 estimate put the number of Presbyterians and Congregationalists at a slight numerical advantage over the Anglicans, 45 percent to 42.5 percent, with the rest Baptists and Quakers.[40] In 1725 the Anglican missionary Francis Vernod, sometimes spelled Varnod, identified 48 percent of the families in his parish as "dissenters" from the Church of England and 52 percent as "non-dissenters."[41]

Denominational diversity began at the founding of the colony in the seventeenth century and persisted through the first half of the eighteenth century. The eight proprietors to whom King Charles granted the colony were all Anglicans, but they intended to make money in the New World and quickly saw the utility of a generous policy of religious toleration as an incentive to attract settlers and did not impose Anglicanism on their colony by establishing the Church of England there in any meaningful way. Some of the first governors of their colony were non-Anglicans. Aside from a bitter dispute over establishment in 1704–6, for which political power more than religious conversion was the coveted prize, religious diversity took root largely in a climate where interdenominational friction occurred as socially benign competition among church leaderships.[42] Denominational differences remained largely tangential to social and political conflicts after the first couple of decades. For instance, Anglicans led the way in the tugs of war with the proprietors during the revolution of 1719, but the association they formed to counter the proprietors and demand a royal coup received widespread support from all religious quarters.

This is not to say that denominational boundaries counted for nothing. Anglican ministers frequently bemoaned the presence of so many dissenters, deists, and infidels—their labels. Ministers reporting to the SPG or the bishop of London, both of whom provided supervision in the absence of a local bishop, often boasted of how many dissenters they had been able to attract to Sunday services. Vestries, lay leadership, frequently noted the necessity of a good Anglican minister to combat heresy and nonconformity. When dissenters did attend Anglican services, they often pressured the minister to allow practices common among dissenters that sometimes rankled Anglican clergy; in 1713 the commissary, the bishop's representative or deputy in the colony, Gideon Johnston, reprimanded a minister for allowing some of his dissenter parishioners to stand while taking communion.[43] Often ministers relented, knowing that insisting on conformity would divide their congregations.

These examples of competition suggest at least two realities of religious culture in eighteenth-century South Carolina. First, religious diversity was a fact of life for which no religious authority seeking conformity to any tradition had an answer.[44] Second, laity of all denominations refused to give up control over their religious life. Because of the number of religious options that existed around them, they could conform to official Church of England practices and beliefs only when they wanted to, and there was precious little that Anglican clergy could do about it. As a result, a general religious toleration prevailed in South Carolina, and even Anglican ministers came to accept that fact. The religious culture that Alexander Garden encountered included an Anglican establishment that counted for little in practical terms, especially in comparison to the Puritan establishments in New England.

The few Baptists in the colony represented an excellent example of the way a religious minority could enjoy a considerable level of spiritual autonomy in South Carolina in spite of their markedly distinct—and, to other Carolinians, annoyingly intense—religious habits. Baptists distinguished themselves by their refusal to baptize infants, a cherished practice among virtually all other Christian denominations.[45] Baptists appear to have been a numerically and economically unremarkable sect in the colony, and except during the Great Awakening, they left a light imprint on colonial Carolina history. One historian has counted four Baptist churches and 117 members in the entire colony in 1740, equaling approximately one quarter of 1 percent of the population, but this is almost certainly an undercount. The historian Leah Townsend estimated the Baptist population in 1724 to have represented up to 10 percent of the population, or 1,400. Considering the frequency and urgency with which Anglican missionaries reported Baptists in their midst, Townsend's is likely the more accurate estimate.[46] Politically they allied themselves with other dissenters—and lost—against the effort by Anglicans in the early 1700s to establish the Church of England in the colony. Otherwise they carried little weight in South Carolina government until the disestablishment controversies of the revolutionary era. Only 15 Baptists can be identified as members of the colonial assembly from the 1600s through the 1750s. No Baptists can be identified from the lists of South Carolina politicians in 1789. If their later political situation is any indication of previous importance, they had little.[47]

Economically a few Baptists appeared to have done well in South Carolina. William Elliott Sr. owned a "great wharf" in Charles Town and bequeathed to his three sons ten thousand pounds currency and valuable pieces of property.[48] Only a few other Baptists could boast of wealth anywhere close to that of Elliott. With the exception of Charles Bealer of Euhaw, who held a remarkable total of 179 slaves, none is notable for large slaveholdings, a key signifier of wealth. However, Baptists probably made use of slaves as often as other groups did. Townsend estimated that two-thirds of the Baptists in 1790 held no slaves but that seven-eighths of those nonslaveholders lived in the backcountry. Since dissenters had flooded into the backcountry mostly in the second half of the century, it is reasonable to conclude that the Baptist families extant earlier in the century were the primary slaveholders in 1790 and that Baptists, though not building up large slaveholdings, were neither ignorant of nor inimical to the economics of slaveholding.[49]

If Baptists were numerically and economically unremarkable, they did achieve distinction for their religious zeal. Baptists were among the first settlers in the late 1600s, and many of them, including the founder of Carolina's first Baptist church, the Reverend William Screven, fled from the rigid church establishments of New England to Carolina's climate of religious toleration. Screven came from Maine, where his preaching against the established norms of baptism got him imprisoned and then expelled. However, such "great ardor and energy in spreading and maintaining Baptist principles" not only garnered Baptists difficulties in New England but also made them stand out as particularly noxious dissenters to established Anglican clergy in South Carolina.[50] Anglican ministers and their vestries, when reporting to their superiors in England the numbers of Anglicans and dissenters in their parishes, often singled out Baptists or Anabaptists among the dissenters. The vestry of St. George's Dorchester Parish urgently requested a full-time Church of England minister because of their "Apprehension of some weak people being seduced and drawn of[f] to joyn with the Anabaptists or other dissenters whose Teachers are officially Industrious in coming among us and Seeking to gain Proselytes."[51]

Other dissenters perceived that cooperation with Anglicans could better serve their own interests. French Huguenots—Protestants in mostly Catholic France—moved to South Carolina as early as the 1670s, and within the span of several decades they became reliable allies of Anglicans in the colony. Although they numbered only in the hundreds during the colonial period, by the turn of the eighteenth century they represented a minority sufficiently wealthy and influential to sway elections and government policy and were thus courted by the English Anglican minority. Outnumbered and without ecclesiastical support from France and a reliable source of educated French clergy, Huguenots yielded to Anglican wooing. Other dissenters, mainly Presbyterians and Congregationalists, recognizing the power of an Anglican-Huguenot coalition, worked to disenfranchise Huguenots, many of whom, having recently migrated to the Carolinas to escape persecution after the revocation of the Edict of Nantes and religious tolerance in France in 1685, were not fully naturalized Englishmen. These efforts, though, worked only to drive Huguenots into a full alliance with Anglicans to the extent that Huguenots supported the colonial Church Act of 1706 establishing the Church of England in South Carolina.[52] Eventually many converted to Anglicanism.

Presbyterians and Congregationalists resisted the lure of Anglicanism longer than French Huguenots did. Despite a population at least as large as that of the Anglicans, these two groups left a record that is difficult to track. Hurricanes and war destroyed most of their records. Surviving evidence indicates that members of these traditions, though at a political disadvantage to Anglicans, achieved economic prosperity and by the mid-eighteenth century became fairly comfortable with Anglican social leadership. Proprietors actively courted their migration with promises of religious toleration and material prosperity, particularly in the 1680s, when proprietors tried to balance the power of the increasingly independent-minded Barbadian, and Anglican, "Goose Creek" faction by building a proproprietary coalition of dissenters grateful for the opportunity to live freely in South Carolina. By 1706 an Anglican missionary had described Presbyterians as "the soberest, most numerous, and richest people of the province."[53] Some of these men achieved high office, as proprietors replaced first-generation Anglican magistrates with new dissenter immigrants. These new, relatively more scrupulous dissenters willingly tried to implement proprietary policies aimed at ending the collusion of pirates and Carolina officials and reforming the Indian slave trade, both lucrative enterprises long cherished by Barbadian settlers. This was easier said than done—by 1685 the Presbyterian governor Joseph Morton had given up and joined in both trades, going so far as to suspend a sheriff who tried to prevent the infamous buccaneer Henry Morgan from resupplying his ship in town—but the effort temporarily stoked antiproprietary and antidissenter feelings.[54] Political friction with prominent Anglicans together with protests over taxation led largely by dissenters gave rise to the establishment controversies that resulted in the establishment of the Church of England and the disenfranchisement of Presbyterians in 1706.

Anglicans did not press their political advantage to the point of permanently alienating Presbyterians and Congregationalists. That religion played a secondary role in the establishment controversy is demonstrated by the fact that the minister in the St. Philip's pulpit in Charles Town, the Reverend Edward Marston, protested the political machinations of his coreligionists in the legislature. Marston preached against the act because he believed that the Anglican political faction wanted to take control of the colonial church away from clerical leadership. For this impertinence the assembly refused to pay him his salary, and he left the colony. The writer Daniel Defoe of *Robinson Crusoe* fame reported in London, with questionable veracity, that the Anglican governor James Moore chased Marston around the streets of Charles Town with a whip. Meanwhile, having proved unable to beat the Anglicans in politics, some wealthy Presbyterians and Congregationalists eventually joined them in their pews.[55]

Denominational fidelity to Congregationalism or Presbyterianism did not necessitate complete estrangement from Anglicans. One estimate has asserted that of the 179 members of the assembly whose religious affiliations can be determined, almost 52 percent held some sort of dissenting persuasion.[56] Dissenters often were elected to such local town offices as fire master and commissioner for the workhouse and the market. Of over 100 men listed in the records of the Congregational Church from 1729 to 1759, 25 were elected to the assembly.[57] Clearly the legal establishment of the Church of England did not stand in the way of dissenters' political participation. In sum, Presbyterians and Congregationalists occupied a social and political position close enough to that of Anglicans to allow fraternization and cooperation without abandoning their religious identity altogether.

Thus it is fair to say that the religious establishment bore lightly on the daily lives of most non-Anglican Carolinians. Roman Catholics were perhaps the sole exception, although any social and political disadvantage they experienced probably stemmed more from Protestant backlash against Catholic Florida than any structural political animosity.[58] The mild establishment of the Church of England occasionally irritated dissenters, particularly when they struggled to fund building projects of their own and realized more keenly their dual financial responsibilities toward both the Anglican establishment and their own religious institutions. Otherwise religious toleration successfully attracted numerous Anglicans, Baptists, Quakers and dissenters of various sorts, and those for whom religion mattered little. They found enough space in the colony to live out their distinctive denominational and sectarian visions.

Religious difference had always been subsumed into the more lively and critical political factionalism, even during the heated establishment dispute in the first decade of the eighteenth century. Like most controversies, that dispute was much more about political power than any attempt to convert the population to any particular religious persuasion. Divisions between Anglicans and dissenters melted away among the public, reducing the potency of Anglican establishment. In 1715 Commissary Johnston attempted to address the "senseless and ridiculous Schemes of Church Government in America, and more especially in this province" through what amounted to a letter-writing campaign to the bishop of London, but apparently nothing came of it. In fact just days before the outbreak of the Yamassee War, Johnston had nothing more to report to his superior in London during those "times of Danger and difficulty" than the annoyances of his obstreperous assistant.[59]

In the years before Alexander Garden arrived, religious concerns in the colony gave way almost entirely to the problems of the Indian trade and the Yamassee War. The Church of England in Carolina suffered through the war like everyone else, and once again practical concerns, not efforts at imposing Anglican conformity, captured clerical attention. The commissary Reverend William Tredwell Bull, Johnston's successor after his death in 1716, reported on the condition of the Church of England in the colony in 1718. He noted the absence of clergy in the now "thinly inhabited" St. Bartholomew's and St. Helena's Parishes, both "having been almost ruined by the Calamityes of our late unhappy Indian War." The other clergy suffered under minimal salaries owing to rampant inflation, and Bull went so far as to list the high prices of such staples as wheat, cheese, shoes, and black cloth as examples of "the hardships to which such of your Clergy must be necessarily exposed." Bull blamed "the unavoidable Calamyties of our late unhappy Indian War (which hath greatly embarrass'd the Publick Affairs, & Credit of the Country)" rather than "any unkind Dispositions of the People." Johnston then asked for permission to return to London, notwithstanding he felt "extremely sensible of the great want of more ministers at present in this Province."[60] He had lost hope that the Church of England could advance against the worldliness of the lowcountry.

In the years after the Yamassee War, the Church of England needed skilled leadership if it was going to hope to strengthen Anglican authority in the reeling white and black populations. The eminent nineteenth-century Episcopalian historian Frederick Dalcho saw affairs clearly when he noted dryly that however pious the early generations had been, "the restraints of religion soon grow weak unless regularly enforced."[61] In 1713 Gideon Johnston complained to the bishop of London that even Anglican clergy in the colony were lukewarm in their attachment to Anglican traditions, doctrines, and practices, especially compared to dissenters. "For us to be less zealously affected" than the dissenters, though "in a much better cause," he wrote, "is shamefull and Scandalous to the last degree." Worse, "open prophaness and Immorality" in the church provided ample excuse for dissenters to form their own congregations.[62] In 1717 the Anglican missionary Francis Le Jau told the secretary of the SPG how much he wished he could "give a satisfactory and Comfortable account of the flourishing state of" the colony, but, he wrote, "to my great Sorrow I have no ground for it." It seemed that God's hand lay heavy on the colony "for the punishment of our Sins, and the Impenitence of too many of us." There were too few missionaries for so great a mission and too many "ennemyes" who "use all their Endeavours to discourage the Clergy . . . and delude many poor people."[63]

If the Establishment Act of 1706 accomplished anything, it provided for the outward means of Anglican worship. The act mapped out ten parishes in the colony, each to have a church building and a minister. Further legislation provided government salaries for the clergy.[64] Stone structures replaced temporary houses of worship. As in Barbados, many Anglicans found spiritual sustenance within the church and its liturgy and sacraments. However, also as in Barbados, much of the governance of the parish lay in the hands of the laity, not the church. Parishioners elected the vestry, who in turn selected the clerk and sexton and were responsible for the process of electing a minister, by which he was given or denied permanency in the pulpit after a trial period. Laity did care for religion but often in ways that undermined and controverted the teaching, counsel, and ethos of the Church of England. South Carolina had no resident bishop of its own, falling instead within the jurisdiction of the bishop of London, thousands of miles away.[65] This distance could not be overcome by the bishop's representative in South Carolina, the commissary, whose legal powers were vague and whose authority depended more on personal social status and reputation than on the force of law. Protests in Charles Town and in London and efforts to strengthen the establishment by increasing the authority and autonomy of Anglican clergy repeatedly met with frustration.[66]

Establishment, in other words, did not confer any particular social, political, or economic benefits upon Anglicans. However much attracted individual adherents may have been to Anglican worship or doctrine, they did not join the

Anglican Church out of any deference to Anglican prerogative or because they felt coerced or compelled in any way to follow Anglican dictates. Carolinians picked and chose their religious affiliations from among a menu of equally viable options. Prior to the Yamassee War, to declare oneself Anglican or Presbyterian or Baptist did not say anything about one's political, social, economic, or cultural standing. Neither did identifying as Anglican imply significant loyalty to Anglican tradition. Conformity, which in historiography usually refers to adherence to official tradition and doctrine of the religious establishment, meant in the Carolinas clerical adaption to lay demands. Such was the religious climate in South Carolina before Alexander Garden arrived in 1720.

Compare this religious situation in the Carolinas, and Barbados, to that in New England, often depicted in historiography and in popular culture as the archetype of colonial religious devotion. The religious establishment of Puritanism from the beginnings of the colonies in the 1620s and 1630s was socially and culturally defining, although from the beginning Puritan adherents were challenged numerically by "strangers," as Puritans called them, whose attachment to the church was rather tenuous. While not a theocracy, the church in New England wielded powerful cultural and political authority, with church and state often working in tandem to make New England into a "city on a hill" for all the world to see and marvel at its Christian piety and harmony. Although this arguably failed to materialize, this vision soon became a mythical touchstone that guided future generations of New England clergy. Ministers in the late 1600s and early 1700s compared their seemingly decadent and godless culture to the glories of the founding generation that had purportedly succeeded in achieving the city-on-a-hill vision. Preachers bemoaned worldliness in jeremiads, sermons consisting of summaries of present sins and their inevitable awful consequences and calls to repentance and forgiveness. Ministers could recall the pieties of the founding generation and scourge their listeners for their failure to live up to the founders' hopes and dreams for the colony.[67]

The point here is not that New England had ever been more righteous or even religiously devout than South Carolina, but that the city-on-a-hill vision provided New England a model against which ministers could hold up contemporary culture for scrutiny and correction, and the establishment often succeeded in its task of persuading political figures to govern consistently with the doctrines of the Church of England, the guardian of that vision. No similar vision or myth ever existed in the Carolinas, or at least none ever animated the culture of settlement as it took place on the ground. Hence no jeremiads were ever preached in South Carolina, no compelling tales of falling from the grace enjoyed by the founding mothers and fathers of the colony. The Church of England, even after legal establishment in 1706, never was able to propagate such a myth in South Carolina, and that failure weakened the authority of the establishment culturally, relative to New England, until at least 1720, when Garden arrived. Indeed if anything from the founding generation was recalled in the political battles of the late 1600s and early 1700s, it was the religious freedom guaranteed to the first settlers by the colony's proprietors. Pluralism, not Puritanism, was the closest thing to a city-on-a-hill vision in the South, and it worked against the authority of the Church of England, not for it.

It was Garden's task to rectify the anemic situation of the Church of England in South Carolina. Those who preceded Garden had succeeded in legally establishing the Church of England in Carolina, but it would now be up to Garden to give that establishment cultural meaning. Garden could not use the past to recall the colony to some mythical holiness that purportedly obtained in the colony's early years, but he could and did elevate the church to a place of visibility and authority in the cultural life of the settlement. As a minister of St. Philip's Church, the most important congregation in the colony and located in the heart of Charles Town, he possessed a bully pulpit of sorts. He would find that, like everything else in the lowcountry, Carolinian pulpits were rather wobbly pillars upon which to rebuild church and colony.

Fortunately for the Church of England, Garden came equipped with a keen sense of propriety, tradition, and opportunity. He figured out quickly that, according to the moral compasses of his fellow colonists, great gain with just enough godliness to avoid calamity was the path to contentment preferred by his parishioners. Cultivating that measure of godliness among a white population whose desire for wealth was tempered only by the very real threat of destruction proved a formidable task. Garden would need to draw the finest of lines between personal greed and lawful pursuit of profit, and another fine line between church teaching and individual preference. He soon realized that planters preferred that he err on their side when drawing those lines, so he did. Garden became adept at drawing lines that preserved his social and economic standing. Historians today speak of the concept of "lived religion," which refers to the way laypeople practice their religion in real time, often in distinction from and even opposition to the doctrinal statements of their official leadership. How laypeople perceive God and their duty to him is most often different from how they are taught by learned theologians. Garden would have been quite comfortable in such a conversation. He knew that in the eyes of slave masters, slave traders, merchants, and even common laborers God appeared different depending on whether one was looking at him from a pew or from, say, a rice field. In addition, it was thought, God would have to make accommodations to the realities of the rice business if he expected planters to accommodate to the realities of the Church of England. Garden became an expert in this business of lived religion, for his survival as a minister depended on his ability to know exactly how much he could push his parishioners to conform to church teaching. In fact he became an expert in the many other sorts of business that occupied the time and attention of his parishioners, but this is getting too far ahead in the story. Suffice it to say here that Garden proved himself a perfect candidate for the job of civilizing the renewed colony with the tools of refined Christianity. He was economically perceptive, politically aware, religiously informed, and socially astute.

How Garden got these character traits is a matter of a debate that has yet to be argued, historians having shown little interest in his precolonial life. Tradition has it and records of the University of Aberdeen corroborate that he graduated with a master of arts degree from the University of Aberdeen in either 1706 or 1711.[68] There he would have imbibed latitudinarianism, a rather awkward-sounding word for a simple concept that the Christian tradition is broad enough, or is of wide enough latitude, to include all sincere followers of the teachings of Christ regardless of doctrinal peculiarities. Latitudinarianism deemphasized doctrinal specificity in favor of "holy living." Biblical morality, discerned through a rational approach to the scriptures, not theological sophistication, was the thing to be had. Following the wildly popular preacher and Archbishop of Canterbury John Tillotson, many Anglicans of the turn of the eighteenth century preferred this more ecumenical approach to the religious bickering and wars of the seventeenth century. A consensus on proper moral behavior seemed to them something far more attainable than theological uniformity. Christian morality commended itself both to human reason and social harmony. Historians have misinterpreted Alexander Garden as a stickler for Anglican canon and doctrine. He was not, and this should come as no surprise, given his educational background in liberal latitudinarianism.[69]

Ancestry and upbringing may also explain Garden's savviness and social skills. A Carolinian artisan carved his time of birth, merely "1685," into his gravestone and his date of death as "the 25th day of Sept anno domini 1756 age 71 years."[70] Aside from where he attended college, precious little can be known about the years between 1685 and 1720, when he stepped ashore in Carolina. It is unclear even where he came from beyond the general area of Scotland. His genealogy is hopelessly entangled in a crowd of Alexander Gardens of seventeenth- and eighteenth-century Scotland and buried by inadequate record keeping and a curious reticence on his part to speak of his past. Had he won a glorious battle, as did John Paul Jones in the American Revolution, or written a seminal book that influenced American thinking for centuries, as Adam Smith did, or even lent his name to a popular American icon, as Samuel "Uncle Sam" Wilson did during the War of 1812—all of these men were of Scottish ancestry—his mysterious past would have been perfect for the amalgamation of banal fact and heroic myth that people often enjoy building up around their cultural ancestors. But since he was vastly underrated by those who came after him, his early biography has been ignored and probably mistaken.

As a result historians have made only a few passing remarks about Garden's precolonial past. Indeed, Garden's name is most often mentioned only in relation to the heroic Gardens who came before him and after him and may or may not have been his kin. This seems to have been his lot in history: Alexander Garden has gained importance only for his relationships to other, more famous people. A "George A. Gordon" described Garden in an early history journal as of "the third generation" from the "Protestant hero" and officer in the Scottish army Maj. Alexander Garden, a son of "Lord Garden of Banchery." Gordon also briefly characterized Garden as a charitable but scrupulous man who sued the famous transatlantic evangelist George Whitefield in ecclesiastical court for behavior unbecoming of a minister. That depiction is debatable but plausible, as is the observation that Garden gained notoriety for educational reform, mainly for establishing a "negro school." However, contra Gordon, the school was not "the earliest known among the English," and he was likely not descended from a hero in the Scottish army. Neither was his son the prominent South Carolina botanist Dr. Alexander Garden or his grandson the notable Revolutionary War officer and memoirist Benjamin Garden.[71] James Barney Hawkins repeated some of these misleading claims in his 1981 biographical dissertation on Garden, the only attempt by a scholar to take the measure of the man. It is no doubt true, as Hawkins said, that Garden came from a "distinguished family in Scotland," but the nobility of their distinction is questionable.[72]

Alexander left no record of his parentage, and his birth was not recorded anywhere in Scotland. Nobody claimed him as his or her son, and he did not identify his parents. It is possible that Alexander Garden was the son of the Reverend Dr. George Garden, minister at Aberdeen, Alexander's supposed birthplace, at the time of Alexander's birth. David Bertie, editor of the encyclopedic *Scottish Episcopal Clergy,* listed all of George's offspring, but no Alexander. There is, however, a gap between the births of George Jr. in February 1684 and James in September 1686 just wide enough to allow for another birth. George had a daughter named Anna, likely named after George's wife Anna Crichton.[73] Curiously, while Alexander and his wife, Martha, named their sons after men in Martha's family, they named this daughter Anne, or Ann, as it is sometimes given, who would have been namesake to nobody in her mother's family. Was Alexander born out of wedlock to George's wife and was Alexander's naming of his daughter Anna an indirect reference to his mother?

If Alexander were born to Anna, there would have been other reasons for Alexander to distance himself from George. George Garden achieved some fame, or notoriety, depending on one's religious, spiritual, and political perspectives. He enjoyed a close enough relationship with Henry Scougall, the author of the immensely popular Christian devotional *The Life of God in the Soul of Man,* that he preached at Scougall's funeral. George translated into Latin and published the works of John Forbes, a man of considerable theological influence in his time. George earned his doctorate of divinity at King's College in Aberdeen and became minister at the venerable Cathedral of Old Machar and then at St. Nicholas, the parish church. He came into political difficulty, however, when he refused to pray for the new monarchs William and Mary after the Glorious Revolution of 1688–89. In fact he continued to pray brazenly for the deposed King James VII.[74] For this his ministry lost official sanction, after which he preached with the strong backing only of his parishioners. George threw his support behind Queen Anne, daughter of James VII, when she ascended the throne in 1702, and he tried to curry favor with her by dedicating to her his edition of Forbes's works. In 1713 his Episcopalian colleagues at Aberdeen chose George and his brother James to present a letter of congratulations to Queen Anne upon the achievement of the Peace of Utrecht ending the War of the Spanish Succession. His troubles worsened after Queen Anne's death brought about the ascension of the Hanoverians to the British throne and he backed the Jacobite rebellion to restore the Stuarts. Scottish Episcopalian colleagues chose the Garden brothers to present a letter of support to the earl of Mar, leader of the rebellion. The rebellion was thwarted in 1715, and George was thrown into jail. He managed to escape to the European continent, returning only in 1720, the year Alexander reached South Carolina.[75]

Yet George Garden's religious temperament and convictions may have sealed his legacy more than his political judgments did. George led a small but notable movement of Scottish mystics attracted to continental quietism, including the teachings of the French Catholic Jeanne Marie Bouvier de la Mothe Guyon, or "Madame Guyon." Quietism is an apt name for a movement that taught passivity and silent, surrendered prayer through the emptying of one's mind and the abnegation of one's will. Most famously, Garden translated and prefaced copies by the French Catholic mystic and apocalypticist Antonia Bourignon, and then in 1699 he published *An Apology for M. Antonia Bourignon.* Garden asserted that the *Apology,* as a representation of Bourignon's teachings, contained "the essentials of Christianity" while leading believers to the "great end of Christianity, which is to bring us back to the love of God and charity." Scotland's Presbyterian General Assembly disagreed, judging the book's "dangerous, impious, blasphemous errors" as damnable, and so they damned it forthrightly. Using them as justification, they barred Garden from the ministry, a sentence which Garden summarily ignored.[76] However, Garden's defense of his *Apology*—that the end of Christianity was love—pointed to a possible effort to transcend the religious and civil politics that so easily beset him. Perhaps with this in mind, Donald Macmillan, who wrote a sketch of Garden's life for the Scottish Episcopal Church in the nineteenth century, wondered if Garden's attraction to Bourignon could be found in Garden's weariness with religious and political factionalism, with the French mystic providing spiritual relief from more worldly troubles.[77]

George Garden certainly was not an uncritical follower of the mystics; he worried that quietism could lead to spiritual arrogance and deception. In a 1709 letter to one of his disciples, James Cunningham of Barns, Scotland, he warned his younger colleague of relying too much on the "prayer of silence" advocated by quietists as the means to spiritual vitality and understanding. According to Garden, Cunningham was taking things too far when he relied on such prayer to negate self and enable God to communicate directly to the human soul. Rather than providing a path to spiritual purity, prayer of silence done wrong could "make way" for delusion. Garden gave, as an example, the case of the Reformation era, when the church was split into "many contending parties" excited by Satan himself "to strife and envy against one another." Zealous reformers fought "against the errors and corruptions of the contrary partys, without taking care to deny themselves and to be followers of Jesus in humility and charity."[78]

George Garden's political and religious troubles suggest a connection between him and Alexander. Alexander demonstrated considerable political shrewdness throughout his career in South Carolina, although he, unlike George, chose to utilize his attentiveness to factionalism to navigate away from political shoals that detained other ministers of his time. Likewise, Alexander repeatedly warned against overheated spiritual "enthusiasm" that could lead to religious anarchy and social fragmentation. Alexander, chief minister of the established Church of England in South Carolina, came to value religious toleration in the colony, but like George he remained a strong partisan of Episcopalianism until his death. George may have encouraged Cunningham to "live in the midst of partys without being of a party" and to follow Jesus, "not either of Luther or Calvin or A.B. or J.B or the prophets," the latter two being references to Bourignon and Jacob Boehme, another mystic, but his political actions delineated the limits to which he would take religious toleration.[79] In similar fashion, Alexander came out strongly against any threat to the religious and social order. In addition if Alexander were George's son biologically, temperamentally, and religiously, he would not have been the first Scot in his family or in his community to flee religious intolerance in his homeland, this being a chief instigator of Scottish immigration to the Americas, including Barbados and the Carolinas, in the late 1600s and early 1700s.[80]

Although the case for George and Anna Garden as Alexander's parents seems particularly strong, there are plenty of other options to choose from when drawing his genealogy. As is the case with George, their attractiveness as ancestors is debatable. In 1555 "George of the Ilk," the Ilk being the "very ancient and highly respected" Garden family, acquired the land of Banchary in the valley of the Dee River and adjacent to Old Machar Parish. In 1585 King James I sent this George to Denmark to celebrate James's marriage arrangement to Princess Anne. George's grandson Alexander enlarged the landholding in 1618 only to lose it five years later when he became "embarrassed in circumstances."[81] There were well-to-do Gardens of Midstrath and a Reverend Alexander Gardyn at Deir.[82] The Presbyterian George Gardyn ministered at Clatt and an Alexander Garden ministered at Forge, and both were regularly consulted by their sessions.[83] The daughter of the minister at Forge married the Reverend John Cockburn, who, like the mystic George Garden, was rebuked for not praying for William and Mary and jailed for authoring politically injudicious pamphlets.[84] John Gardyne of St. Andrews lost his pulpit after being "accused of immorality."[85] In another place a minister brought complaint against the wife of "George Garden, sometyme in Hopshill" for marrying another man without sufficient evidence that George, who had run off thirteen years previously, was indeed dead as rumored.[86] An Alexander Garden born just a few years before ours pastored a church in Kinerny. His son became a wealthy merchant in London, and his grandson, the famed naturalist Alexander Garden of Charles Town, South Carolina, arrived in the Americas shortly before our Alexander passed away."[87]

Only one remark penned by our Alexander concerning his ancestors survives, and it indicates that perhaps he felt some embarrassment. Sometime around 1742 Alexander received a manuscript written, he thought, by his "grand Uncle, a 4th son of the Family, & a Schoolmaster in Elgin." This is not enough information to trace, especially since it may be a maternal ancestor. He did note that a grandfather had "fooled away" the "Title and Estate" of "Blackford."[88] That reference too turned out to be too cryptic to trace, perhaps because of its rather ignominious connotations. In the mid-1700s the genealogist William MacFarlane noted that sometime in the early to middle 1700s an Elizabeth Lesley "married John Gairden of Bruckles[,] Brother to Alexander Gardin of Blackfuird." This Alexander would have been about the right age to be our Alexander's grandfather, but no descendants can be found.[89] Could these be the "Alexander Garden of Blackfourd" and his brother "John Garne" recorded in the Register of the Privacy Council for being accused of murdering a James Leslie in an argument over the sale of an ox at a fair?[90] Then again, the dates work out, with the murder occurring around 1633, likely after a marriage into the Lesley family would have taken place, and the incident may have arisen from or contributed to the "foolishness" that cost the Gardens Blackford. Besides, it was unlike MacFarlane to make mention of the brother-in-law of a Lesley daughter. Perhaps "of Blackfourd" was enough of a clue to alert his readers to the dishonorable connections and sufficient of a stain on the family to warrant a bit of reticence on the part of our Alexander.

This much is clear: there were no doubt compelling reasons why Garden hazarded settlement in the tumultuous colony of South Carolina in 1720. He most likely had personal motives for leaving Scotland, motives that were a bit less glowing than Gordon and Hawkins would have it, motives that might have included an escape from a socially despised parentage or a father whose political problems and religious preferences made a successful career in Scotland difficult. If so, Garden joined many other Europeans fleeing into the anonymity of the Americas, clear as it was from the entangling webs of public rumor in the old country shires. Gossip had a difficult time crossing the Atlantic in those technologically primitive days. Or maybe he shared the mystic George Garden's adventuresome and independent spirit and, like many other sons of the almost-gentry, saw opportunity written all over the reports of Carolina's near demise at the hands of the Yamassee. Or maybe, to retreat to the simplest explanation, he sensed that Scotland was just too crowded with other Gardens, or with educated professionals who looked outward at a prosperous British Empire, or with Episcopalians, who had an increasingly difficult time of it in Presbyterian Scotland.[91] Colonial law fixed the annual salary for the minister of St. Philip's at the attractive sum of 150 pounds.[92] If this was his motive, Garden shared much with his future neighbors transplanted from Barbados. Like theirs, Garden's island had grown too small; he too looked elsewhere for solid ground to build his own empire, and he too found it in South Carolina. So in 1720 the good minister stepped off a ship and onto the shores of the Carolina lowcountry. Thus began the historic relationship between Alexander Garden and the Carolinas, a partnership of opportunism, industry, and ambition that would last for almost four decades.

# Chapter 2

# ACQUAINTANCES

By 1720 South Carolina had begun to undergo a remaking. The colonists emerged from the Yamassee War chastened but determined to recapture the urgent optimism of the colony's early years. Plantation agriculture displaced trade with and in Native Americans who, by moving west, remained close enough to bargain with but far enough away for colonists to again venture into the backcountry. The clearing of forests and draining of swamps required the type of labor few whites relished, and since nobody moved to the colony dreaming of slogging through snake- and disease-infested rice fields, ongoing labor demands seemed to justify the importation of thousands of African slaves to claim the land for Atlantic commodity markets. Like their profit-thirsty predecessors in Barbados, whites forced blacks to chop trees and clear fields at a tempo that bordered on the vicious.[1] The walls of the fort protecting Charles Town were dismantled, allowing the town to stretch across and up the Charles Town peninsula between the Ashley and Cooper Rivers. Internally laborers began repaving streets and improving the crude colonial buildings.

It was an opportune time for Garden to establish himself as a cleric and for South Carolinians to establish a permanent and prosperous colony in British North America. White residents of all ages in Charles Town and its nearby surroundings barely numbered twelve hundred in 1722. They were joined by at least that many slaves and several hundred sailors and other transients at any given time, making it easy for a keen mind such as Garden's to take the lay of the social land.[2] Despite floods, drought, and a flattening hurricane in 1728, ships left port with barrels full of rice for the West Indies and Europe and returned with coffers full of money for planters and merchants as well as skilled immigrants, both men and women, to help them spend it. Charles Town would not reach its peak of affluence and luxury for at least two more decades, but the foundations were reset in the 1720s.[3] Politics remained a problem, with the usual wrangling exacerbated by a contest of wills among country planters, Charles Town merchants, and the English government over imperial trade policy and the local printing of paper money. Garden's merchant friends wanted the stability of a predictable money supply, while planters wanted the flexibility of an expansionary monetary policy. Rice planting was proving highly lucrative, although planters felt unnervingly vulnerable to the vacillations of the Atlantic market. The political crisis that grew partly out of the uneven economy ended in 1729 with the official transfer of proprietary rights to the Crown, more favorable relations with Parliament, and the arrival of a governor, Robert Johnson, sympathetic to the colonists' concerns.[4] This decade of economic growth and political tension meant that economic opportunity and social power were there for the making and the taking. In 1720 the concrete for the colony's new foundation was being poured. By the end of the decade, its most important features had hardened. It was committed to slavery, to rice agriculture, and to local government.

The decade of the 1720s for Alexander Garden was therefore a period of figuring out how to stake his claim in this bustling port city, entrepôt for the Atlantic World and the frontier. Garden, now in his mid-thirties, immediately set about finding a pulpit, some useful friends, a wife, and a comfortable place for himself in Carolina's increasingly hierarchical society. It was not easy; nothing in the lowcountry was, for Garden or for anyone else in the colony. In a way Garden and the colony were in similar stages in their lives, too experienced to be labeled adolescents but having plenty of development ahead of them. The years leading up to 1720 had been something of a crisis for them, fraught with introspection that led first to disillusionment and then to hope for a better future. If Garden and the colony entered the 1720s vulnerable and grateful for surviving the journey that had brought them to this point, they emerged from the decade on sure footing, having had core questions about their labor, their family, their friends, and their enemies answered. The process of redefining their identity was well under way by the 1730s, and in the process emerged other possibilities for a long and fruitful friendship.

First, Garden had to figure out how to survive the challenging physical environment. The colony's beautiful visage, with its Edenic quilt of forests, savannas, and marshes, could distract a person from the periodically inclement weather and disease that could take down even the strongest of human bodies. Garden's boss, the commissary and reverend William Tredwell Bull, described Garden in 1723 as "of a sickly & weak Constitution," which is virtually the only description of his physiognomy left today.[5] It seems unlikely that Garden would have ventured across the ocean with this natural frailty; more likely the difficult climate had weakened him after his arrival. Winters could be surprisingly cold. "I assure you that I have felt as Cold Weather here as in England and seen Ice at Least an Inch Thick," wrote the young Margaret Kennett to her mother not long after settling in Charles Town.[6] Garden had arrived in Charles Town in April 1720 during what one colonist described as the "freshness and gayity" of the spring season.[7] Summer was just a couple of months away, though, when the weather would turn hot and muggy.

Disease was always a problem. One colonial doctor blamed "pituitous asthma," "suffocating or catarrhal peripneumony," "serous quinsy," "spurious pleurisy," and "hooping cough," among other maladies, for his patients' suffering.[8] Historians have identified smallpox, dysentery, typhoid, malaria, and yellow fever as the worst culprits.[9] Results were devastating. One estimate put the annual crude death rate in the "charnel house" of colonial Charles Town at more than fifty per one thousand population; that is more than six times the death rate in the United States today and approximately three times worse than those in some of the most deadly places in the world, such as Somalia and Sierra Leone.[10] The mortality rate in colonial South Carolina was probably higher than anywhere else in British North America. In Christ Church Parish, which neighbored Charles Town, 86 percent of colonial children "whose births and deaths are recorded in the parish register died before the age of twenty."[11] Americans today justifiably bemoan the horrible death rates among Native Americans upon their encounter with Old World diseases—in some towns the entire populations died within months—but it should not be forgotten that white settlers too died in unimaginable numbers from those same diseases.

Disease took a dreadful toll on lowcountry ministers. Fewer than half of the Anglican missionaries made it through their first ten years in the colony without suffering debilitating or mortal illness.[12] Archibald Simpson, a mid-century Presbyterian minister, described South Carolina as "truly a grave for Ministers."[13] Garden often complained of sickness and weakness. In 1724 Garden came close to abandoning his mission in order to save his life. "Your Lordship will, I hope, excuse the trouble of acquainting you," he wrote to the bishop, "that for the most part I've been so bad and precarious of my Condition's being ever reconciled to this Climate, and am afraid that at last I shall be obliged to quit the Country and return to Great Britain." However, he had recovered a bit, and as he wrote the letter he thought that he would "venture the Tryal for sometime longer."[14] In 1732 Garden and his family suffered from an outbreak of "great Sickness . . . but thro' His Mercy and Goodness, not" the "Mortality" in Charles Town.[15] In 1736 he sought refuge for five months in New York, Massachusetts, and Rhode Island, having been beset by a curious set of afflictions: "a violent Headach, Flatulance, Lowness, Oppression, Watchfulness, and Indigestion."[16]

Garden sought the best medical advice available in his battle against disease and death. In the midst of a smallpox outbreak in the summer of 1738, he submitted to the *South Carolina Gazette* "Doct. Pitcairn's Method of curing the Small-Pox," particularly for use by "those who cannot have the Assistance of a Physician." As one of the town's most educated citizens and its foremost champion of Christian charity, no doubt Garden felt obligated to enter the realm of medicine on behalf of his suffering countrymen. To do so he turned to the celebrated Scottish physician Archibald Pitcairn, who, although suspected of atheism by his critics, remained an early eighteenth-century authority on healing. Pitcairn recommended the usual sorts of treatments for his era, beginning with letting blood, doses of "Syrup of white Poppies" and "Zedoary-Root," "Figgs," and "Scruples of Theriac or Dialcordium," which nurses could "sweeten" with "Syrup of Kermes and white Poppies," accompanied by the application of "a large Blistering Plaister between the Shoulders." If an afflicted child could not clear his lungs of infection by coughing, a parent should "to the Throat apply, in a double linnen Cloath, a Pultess of Cow's Dung boil'd with Milk, and soft white Bread," mixed with some brandy. If Garden had tried these remedies himself, they may explain his own problems with headaches and indigestion. Still, Pitcairn's guide was the *Merck's Manual* or WebMD of his age for medical knowledge. Garden's extensive and verbatim quoting of Pitcairn strongly suggests a familiarity with his works and indicates that Garden had either brought with him a copy printed immediately after it was first published shortly before 1720 or imported a copy after it was republished in London in 1727. Garden clearly was interested in the latest medical trends as a means to combat the maladies affecting him in his adopted home.[17]

The lowcountry ecology was difficult, but the social climate could be even worse for young ministers seeking permanent church homes. Alexander Garden settled in St. Philip's Church, the only Church of England congregation in Charles Town, and the story of how he achieved that pulpit reveals some of the social hazards of being a minister in colonial South Carolina. The lessons he learned from the experience proved a blessing in disguise, for he discovered what mattered to his parishioners and how tending to those matters could make or break a career for a minister. More important, he learned the power of wealth and the need to ally with those who had it.

Garden arrived in Charles Town at a moment both serendipitous and inauspicious. It was serendipitous because the SPG, the vestry, the governor, and the legislature had just fired his predecessor in the pulpit, the Reverend William Wye, and were anxious to fill the position quickly and with someone of Garden's character and ability, a "man of Parts & temper," in the words of one colonial observer.[18] It was inauspicious because the SPG, the vestry, the governor, and the legislature—an unprecedented coalition whose mere coalescence signaled that something important had gone awry—were also anxious to fill the position quickly to keep one of Wye's predecessors, Edward Marston, from trying to retake the pulpit. Telling Wye's story demonstrates just how fortuitously Garden entered the colonial stage and foreshadows the difficulties he experienced averting an early exit.

Reverend Wye arrived in the colony in 1717 and presented several letters of recommendation from his home country of Ireland, including one signed by the bishop of Rapho and the bishop of Kittaloe in Ireland. These impressive certificates vouched for his "unblameable Character" and reported that he had achieved a "batchelour and master of Arts with the deserv'd Credit and reputation of a sober Man and a good Scholar." He was "a Good Christian" all around.[19]

The people of St. Philip's Church in Charles Town received Wye kindly and with some relief. After less than three months in the pulpit—in record time for a Carolina parish—they elected him their rector, mainly because Edward Marston had returned to the colony.[20] Marston had a reputation as a loud-mouthed, opinionated, and argumentative preacher.[21] He had left the colony, or had been "turned out," before 1708, and according to the Reverend William Tredwell Bull, he failed in St. Philip's because of "his Temper and so impudent his behavior that the Church there is almost empty."[22] Recall that Marston had dared to challenge some of his own parishioners—Anglicans who took pews in St. Philip's assembly on Sunday and seats in the legislative assembly the other days—when they established the Church of England in the early 1700s, and he got fired in consequence. Marston left behind a congregation in a rather bitter mood.

Shaking that mood by hiring a permanent replacement took time, due to the hazards of the colonial South Carolina environment. The Reverend Gideon Johnston assumed Marston's pulpit in 1708 and served it well, but he drowned in an offshore boating accident in April 1716, leaving behind a "Widow, two daughters and a niece all young women left here in sad Circumstances," according to Reverend Le Jau of neighboring St. James Goose Creek Parish.[23] Johnston, the only casualty of the accident, had taken ill and "through weakness of Body could not come out of the Hold" when a squall hit the coast.[24] John Whitehead, Johnston's assistant, took his place, but he died in December 1716. The Reverend William Guy, rector at St. Helena's Parish, agreed to fill in temporarily when possible with the assistance of other surrounding ministers. According to Le Jau, the congregation "neglected" to ask the SPG for another minister because of "some disagreement" regarding clergy in general.[25] Nonetheless in August 1717 the leaders of the SPG informed the church in St. James Goose Creek that they intended to move Le Jau to Charles Town.[26] It was a good plan, Le Jau being a man of experience and esteem in the colony, but he died in September 1717 "after a long and tedious sickness which had deprived him of the use of his Limbs and speech."[27] Fortunately, within weeks of his death his intended replacement in St. James Goose Creek, William Wye, landed in Charles Town.

Wye quickly made known his preference for Charles Town over St. James Goose Creek. Governor Johnson reported that Wye "behaved himself with all emaginable Sobriety and good conduct" and "his Preaching is very well aproved of."[28] But it was not long before his story of being a well-recommended minister began to unravel. Shortly after he left Britain, the bishop of London received a petition from John Smart and William Ordnay from Bedfordbury in England complaining that Wye had rented from them three horses, saddles, and a "Shaise," or small carriage, and traveled to Bristol. There Wye sold the horses and the saddles and pocketed the proceeds, loaded the carriage onto a ship, and sailed for South Carolina.[29] The SPG leaders investigated and judged the petition legitimate, so they sent a letter of warning to Governor Johnson telling him that they were removing their support for Wye.[30] Wye denied the allegations, although Bull noted that the accusations dampened his congregation's enthusiasm for his preaching.[31] In the meantime the SPG also inquired of Bishops Raphoe and Kittaloo, wondering about their letters of recommendation of Wye.[32] "I have not seen Mr. Wye to my knowledg, these past five or six years," Bishop Raphoe shot back, "and he is one of the last Clergymen I know whom I would recommend for a Missionary, being more likely to obstruct the Gospel by his Immoral life than to promote it." His letter of recommendation had been a forgery.[33]

The SPG sent another letter, dated July 21, 1718, to the church wardens and vestry of St. Philip's and to Governor Johnson, this time telling them of the forged letters of recommendation.[34] The recipients of the letter must have assumed that the colonists would deal promptly with Wye, but at this point the problem of not having sufficient local church authority on hand became acute, there being no bishop resident in the colonies. This rendered the church vulnerable to political meddling in the months leading up to the revolution of 1719. Several councilmen and assemblymen moved to "eject by an Act of Assembly" the problem minister, but according to the Reverends Thomas Hasell, Gilbert Jones, and William Guy, all reputable and experienced ministers in the colony, the clergy persuaded the governing gentlemen to wait for the bishop to move first against Wye. They were concerned that a good pastor would "hereafter suffer by such a precedent, if he should be soe unhappy, as through inadvertently to fall under the displeasure of any leading Gentleman of the Province."[35] Experience had taught these men that the assembly could be a dangerous place to adjudicate ecclesiastical disputes, so they pleaded with the bishop to act expeditiously to preserve the church's independence and integrity.

Unfortunately, Wye continued to dig himself into a hole. A few days after Jones, Guy, and Hasell wrote to the bishop asking him to intervene against Wye before members of the assembly made up their own minds, Jones sent another note to the SPG, this time reporting that Wye had married a young man to the young man's aunt. The couple had asked Jones to officiate, but he admonished the pair for the "Unlawfulness" of such an "Incestuous Marriage."

Wye performed the wedding at the bedside of the bride as she gave birth to the couple's son. Wye just wanted the money for officiating, Jones alleged. He warned the SPG that "many are much Scandalized at this Wedding, and if there be not some Severe and speedy resentment shew'd against such an enormity," Jones wondered "what he [Wye] will not dare to commit, and what Mischievous effects may be produced from such Actions."[36] In November 1719 the SPG sent a letter to Governor Johnson, with the approval of the bishop of London, asking him to "assist the Revd Mr. Bull his Lordship's Commissary in removing Mr. Wye" from St. Philip's.[37] It is unclear exactly what action was taken, but in September 1720 Hasell reported to the SPG that Wye had been expelled from St. Philip's and had moved to Virginia.

Alexander Garden took Wye's place and no doubt was keenly aware of the conditions surrounding his predecessor.[38] He had good reason to fret over his own prospects, and his first years in the parish probably gave him few reasons for optimism. Garden took over the pulpit in 1720, but it was not until December 1724 that the vestry saw fit to elect him as their permanent rector.[39] As late as July 1723 another minister predicted to the SPG that Garden "in all probability will not be elected."[40] Perhaps the vestry hesitated after their sour experiences with William Wye and Edward Marston, or maybe Garden had gotten tangled up in the political matters that plagued the transfer of power from the proprietors to the Crown as a result of the revolution of 1719. After the rebelling colonists deposed Governor Johnson, they selected Colonel Moore as their acting governor. Moore was not Anglican and resented the legal restrictions that assigned marriage rights solely to Anglican ministers. The Anglican clergy had chosen to support Johnson's claim to the governorship, believing that until the king approved of the transfer of power, they were legally and spiritually obliged by their oaths of allegiance to the king, the head of their church, to obey his government representatives, and they refused to marry anyone without Johnson's signature.[41]

Already annoyed with the establishment of the church, Moore attempted to intimidate its clergy into supporting the revolution. The colony suffered in the midst of a drought, and so Johnson, still claiming legal authority, declared that July 22 would be a "Day of Fasting and Humiliation." Moore upstaged Johnson by declaring a fast day for July 20. Colonists were to attend church that day, which meant that the clergy had to declare publicly their support for one government or another by conducting services for their parishes on one day or the other. On the Sunday before the declared fast days, when the Reverend William Tredwell Bull arrived at his church, he found himself confronted by one of Moore's supporters. In a letter to the bishop of London, Bull wrote, "Colonel John Fenwick, Chief Officer of the Militia of Colleton County, & one of my Parishioners, raised a very great Disturbance in the Church Yard both before

& after Divine Service the Lords Day before the Fast was to be observed, & very rudely insulted me, taking upon him to command me to observe the Day appointed by Colonel Moor & strictly forbade the People to repair to Church on the Fast Day, & treated me Further with scurrilous & abusive Language in the Face of my whole Congregation." In the same letter Bull lamented that Garden and Peter Tustian of St. George's Dorchester Parish could not persuade their vestries to elect them permanently even though everyone in their churches, including the vestrymen, did "not object anything against the Abilityes, the Lives, & conversations either of Mr. Tustian or Mr. Garden, Their Abilityes being unquestionable and their lives and conversations unblameable."[42] Vestries jealously guarded their powers over their clergy, and it is highly probable that they wanted to see how Garden played his politics before they made him their permanent minister. While still a newcomer, Garden experienced firsthand the weakness of the church relative to the economic and political priorities of his parishioners.

Bull accurately linked the political troubles to Garden's delay in getting elected, but Garden told the story in a way that made him out as less of a victim and more of a man in charge. In early 1724 Garden told the bishop of London that the reason he had not yet been "induct'd into this Living" was because he was not sure he wanted to stay in South Carolina as long as the government was so unstable. "The Government's being unhing'd . . . prevented my desiring or accepting" election, he wrote, and he noted that the rules of election seemed to be equally "unhing'd."[43] This explanation placed the blame squarely on Garden's parish, as though he were holding election at bay because his parishioners could not get their business in order, in spite of their eagerness to keep him. Garden did have reason to pause. He had endured anticlericalism caused by the revolution. Worse, Francis Nicholson, the new governor who had replaced both Moore and Johnson in 1721, had tried to force the clergy to write letters to the king on behalf of the revolutionary government. The clergy resisted, but Garden's frustration over the matter lingered for years. In 1727 he complained to the bishop about such pressure from the governor and grumbled, "I heartily wish that Stop was put to that Humor of his perpetually hazing the Clergy about Addresses."[44] No doubt in the first few years after his arrival Garden worried about this sort of pressure and wondered if he had the fortitude or the ambition to navigate the political and social system of this newly reborn and cantankerous colony.

In truth, the delay in Garden's election probably had to do with all of these factors. The vestry hesitated to move quickly both because of Wye and Marston and because of the political controversies surrounding the church, and Garden was reluctant to force the issue, wondering if election in such a climate of turmoil was worth the fight. Like strangers eyeing each other warily, Garden and the colony's population would need time to warm to each other enough to make any formal contract.

Peter Tustian gave up within a year and moved northward, where he enjoyed a long career as the minister of St. James' Parish, Anne Arundel, in Maryland.[45] Garden decided to wait it out, perhaps because of the choice location of his assignment. Garden reported to the bishop in 1724 that only "three hundred and fifty Families" lived in the parish, but it was still by far the largest town and the social, economic, and political hub of the colony.[46] Not until after 1750 did the backcountry develop towns of any considerable size, and even then they were merely centers of local exchange that counted on trade of goods in and out of Charles Town.[47] Garden's keen mind no doubt grasped the potential inherent in such a parish if he could learn to work the political, economic, and social systems. Besides, the St. Philip's rectorship carried a salary of £150, fully 50 percent more than the country parishes paid.[48]

The St. Philip's Church building too was worth waiting for. Construction began in 1711 but was not completed until at least 1723. It replaced a comparatively crude wood-frame structure, and the contrast must have been breathtaking, both in beauty and in the connotations of temporality versus permanence. The new design suggested an attempt to reflect the permanence of the Church of England in this unsteady colony while drawing one's attention, slowly, from the ground from which the colony drew its sustenance to the heavens. Built out of somewhat dark-hued, rough brick, the surface of the church expressed an earthiness dispelled only by the towering pillars that supported the porticoes and the nave ceiling and by the immense bell tower that rose some eighty feet into the air. The main building was rectangular in its outline, but porticoes extending outward in front of and on each side of the belfry created the impression of a Christian cross. Inside the building a semicylindrical roof ran along the seventy-four-foot length of the nave and descended from its peak into a series of arches supported by, in the words of an appreciative early nineteenth-century observer, "Tuscan Pillars . . . ornamented on the inside, with fluted Corinthian Pilasters, whose capitals are as high as the Cherubim, in relief, over the centre of each arch, supporting their proper Cornice."

Ominously, as far as the unelected Garden would have been concerned, artisans had memorialized the revolution of 1719 in the St. Philip's sanctuary by carving into the middle arch on the south side "some figures in heraldic form, representing the infant colony imploring protection of the King," accompanied by an inscription quoting Virgil's *Aeneid* from the passage where the Trojans call upon Jupiter to spare their city. Recall that the clergy openly resisted the revolution and sided with the proprietary governor, who was Anglican and worshiped at St. Philip's; one can imagine a wealthy donor angrily directing sculptors to carve the relief to spite the minister and the governor. It was a permanent reminder that the Anglican vestry, not the clergy, held the reins in the church, and Garden, perched in his pulpit on the northeast corner of the nave, had a clear view of it whenever he looked out upon his congregation.[49]

Nonetheless, by all accounts St. Philip's was magnificent for its era and a fitting throne from which Garden could govern the religious life of the colony. Before the church was even completed, William Tredwell Bull praised it as a "large, regular, & beautiful Building, exceeding any that are in his Majesty's Dominions in America."[50] Another eighteenth-century visitor from England recognized St. Philip's as "a grand church resembling one of the new churches in London." Frederick Dalcho, an early nineteenth-century historian and visitor to St. Philip's, penned a paean to the building's spiritual utility: "Its heavy structure, lofty arches and massive pillars, adorned with elegant sepulchral monuments, cast over the mind a solemnity of feeling, highly favourable to religious impressions." In 1777 the great British political philosopher Edmund Burke wrote of its beauty as "exceeding everything of that kind which we have in America."[51] The leading nineteenth-century architect Robert Mills said that "the effect produced upon the mind in viewing this edifice is that of solemnity and awe." Simply put, it had no peer anywhere along the coast. More important, it was buried so deeply in the city's psyche that when it burned down in 1835—from a fire that started in a brothel, ironically—the congregation insisted on rebuilding it just as it had been.[52]

The building dominated the landscape from a location in the center of the city's hustle and bustle. In fact, it interrupted that hustle and bustle by jutting out into Church Street, a major thoroughfare, causing passersby either to alter their course or run into the monumental building; the church could not be easily dismissed. A 1739 engraving depicts its tower watching over the city, with the port in clear view down the hill from the church; an array of ships is anchored in the water just off several piers that lie waiting to receive the ships' cargoes. (See figure 1.) Tending to affairs in the church building, without the modern muffling noises of trucks and automobiles, Garden could hear the shouts of the sailors conducting the Atlantic business that made the town relevant. He could also hear the cries of slaves being sold at the slave auction just two blocks away.[53] Upon leaving St. Philip's and turning east, he would in a couple of minutes have reached Bay Street, where, turning right, he could walk along the high-rent district where the most prosperous merchants lived and worked. He could also look to his left as he walked and see the wharves, crowded with boats and warehouses. Continuing two blocks on Bay Street, he would have reached Broad Street, another major thoroughfare of commerce. As he strolled up Broad Street away from the bay, he could view in the distance the homes and shops of the poorer sort, but within two blocks of Bay Street he would have found Church Street again, where many of the wealthier artisans lived and kept shop. Turning

FIGURE 1. *An Exact Prospect of Charlestown, the Metropolis of the Province of South Carolina,* by W. H. Toms, after Bishop Roberts; engraving on paper; 6 ¾ x 20 inches; museum purchase; 1940.014.0005. © Image courtesy of the Gibbes Museum of Art / Carolina Art Association, Charleston, S.C.

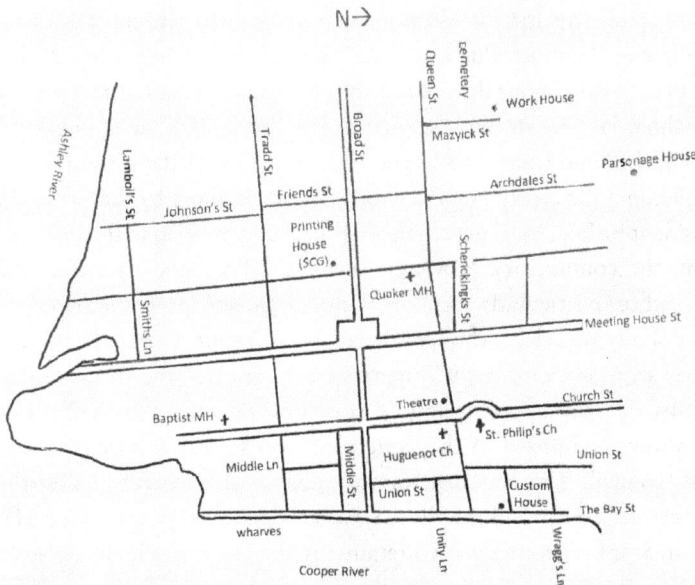

FIGURE 2. Map of Charles Town, circa 1740

right and going north would have taken him past the Huguenot church and returned him to St. Philip's. In just a ten-minute walk from his church home, he would have passed through the heart of Charles Town's commercial district. (See figure 2.)

Along the way he could also observe craftsmen, white and black, building beautiful homes that mimicked the Georgian architectural style popular in England—the attainment of aristocratic status always being in the foreground for Charles Town's gentry—for those who made the most of the colony's Atlantic trade. Bricklayers busied themselves setting down sidewalks, engineers improved the town's sewage system, and other laborers built fences to keep the local livestock from fouling the streets. Charles Town emerged from the Yamassee War in a mode of production and public improvement, and Garden witnessed all of it. As he was acutely aware, the friends to whom he doffed his hat along the way were the ones who paid for his salary and for the grand edifice that reminded everyone of the source of his power. His power and theirs were intertwined and interdependent. For more than a century his church would represent both the earthly power and the luxury of the upper echelons of Charles Town's social hierarchy and the other world to which they were supposed to aspire. If St. Philip's bell tower stood sentinel over the town, pointing everyone's attention to God, whose blessings and protection they sought and signaling piety to immigrants and visiting sailors, the church's roots lay deep in the everyday buying and selling that often distracted the pious from their prayers.[54]

By waiting patiently for his election, Garden gained the most socially prominent pulpit in the most illustrious and prosperous city in the South. He also learned a key lesson about the relationship between the church and society in South Carolina. He was in town in time to see Guy, Hasell, and Jones—all of whom would become friends to Garden—work to expel the objectionable Wye while defending the clergy and the church from meddling by the assembly. Without a resident bishop, local governance of the clergy resided in the bishop's representative, the commissary. However, such was the vague nature of the commissary's office, particularly vis-à-vis the prerogatives of the local church vestries, that nobody was clear who had the authority to fire a minister. Hasell, Guy, and Jones were aware of the willingness of the vestries and the assembly to step into this vacuum of power and exert control over the church. Vestries were almost always composed of the same men who sat in the assembly and the governor's council. Thus the first lesson available to Garden was that the relationship between clergy and the church wardens and vestrymen was crucial if the church in South Carolina was to retain any dignity and relevance. More personally, it became clear to Garden that his relationship with church wardens and vestrymen was crucial if he were to survive as a minister in Charles Town. The second lesson to be learned was that the office of the commissary needed to be more than merely a reporting agency for the bishop of London. The political and social powers in Charles Town did not eagerly recognize the authority of any bishop and were all too willing to step in and manage the church to their own liking. Somehow the office of commissary had to be remade into a meaningful and authoritative institution respected in all quarters.

Garden learned these lessons early and well. He quickly set about making friends among those who controlled the purse strings and the seats of political power in Charles Town. In 1722, when Garden pressed a lawsuit against a man for failing to pay a debt, he retained the services of Benjamin Whitaker, who at the time was already well on his way to becoming one of the most powerful attorneys in the province.[55] In 1721 Whitaker had presided over the vice admiralty court. He later became attorney general, chief justice, and speaker of the Commons House of Assembly, sometimes simultaneously.[56] By the end of the decade, Garden had befriended others among the richest and most influential men of the South, both in the town and in the countryside. These included Capt. Thomas Boone, a vestryman, churchwarden, commissioner of the high roads, Berkeley County justice of the peace, future assemblyman, and son of a Barbadian immigrant who participated in the Indian slave trade; George Logan, a merchant and planter, ofttimes assemblyman, commissioner of the Indian trade before the Yamassee War, and holder of many other political posts; Andrew Allen, "one of the first great Charleston merchants," assemblyman, planter, and holder of many political offices; and Charles Hill, a merchant, chief justice, and assemblyman.[57]

Arguably, Alexander Garden's greatest achievement socially and economically in his personal relationships was his marriage to Martha Guerard on June 8, 1725.[58] Generally speaking, a man assumed control of, or at least benefit from, his bride's property upon marriage, and Martha was a wealthy woman.[59] Her paternal grandfather, Jacob Guerard, was one of the first Huguenot settlers in South Carolina, having been granted 4,000 acres of land by the proprietors in return for organizing Huguenot settlement in the colony. One historian conjectured that he was included in the venture because of his financial resources.[60] Martha's father, John Guerard, became a leading merchant in Indian and African slaves and in deerskins. Martha inherited some of his property, and in 1725, the year of her marriage to Alexander Garden, she received another tidy sum of cash when her oldest brother, David, died.[61] She also brought at least 842 acres to the marriage as part of her dowry.[62]

Martha's connections to the centers of economic production in the colony, particularly planting, merchandizing, and slave trading, presented opportunities for Alexander. Her uncle Peter Jacob Guerard, a planter, goldsmith, and the "Collector of the Port of Charles Town," was in addition something of an inventor, patenting a rice-husking tool that contributed to the development of the rice trade that brought so much fortune to the colony.[63] Martha's brother John Jr. continued the family tradition of affluence and enterprise, becoming one of the most prosperous merchants and slave traders in the colony; eventually he and a business partner—Richard Hill, son of the previously mentioned Charles Hill—owned one of the eight wharves on the bay.[64] In marrying Martha, Garden befriended some of Charles Town's most powerful men and women and created family alliances that would serve him well in negotiating Charles Town's social scene. Garden must have been socially adept enough to warrant such an arrangement in the first place, but no doubt the partnership represented for him a significant step up in society. He married Martha just fourteen months after he complained to the bishop that he might leave the colony because of the political and religious turmoil and just six months after his election to St. Philip's. One wonders if Martha played a role in convincing him to stay and if his attachment to her and the Guerards made his stay acceptable in the eyes of his vestry. If, in fact, Garden had been born out of wedlock, his memories of his ignominious beginnings may have driven him to the security of wealth and public approbation that he found in Martha.

This is not to say that this marriage was purely mercenary from Garden's standpoint. The record is largely silent about their relationship, but there are a few indications that they enjoyed a warm companionship. Martha was approximately twenty-two years old at the time of their wedding, and Alexander was about forty, not an uncommon age difference for their time. Within a little over ten years, their family had grown to include three daughters and two sons, although they also shared the pain of losing a young child. Their first daughter, Martha, was born in October 1726; Anne in September 1729; Mary in November 1731; John in November 1733; and Benjamin in December 1736. When mother Martha died in July 1737, probably of one of the diseases that plagued the hot Carolina summers, her obituary in the *South Carolina Gazette* noted, "Her removal is a sore Loss to an afflicted Husband and four small Children she left behind her"; Mary had died at the age of four and less than a year before her mother passed away.[65] Alexander Garden was approximately fifty-two years of age, with children ages six months, five, seven, and ten, and it would not have been unusual for him to remarry.[66] He never did, suggesting that Martha had claimed his heart while he claimed her property. Perhaps memories of his shamed mother inspired greater love for and loyalty to Martha. He seems to have become somewhat estranged from his oldest son, John, on whose behalf he made a disheartening journey to England in order to sort out financial problems and to whom he bequeathed only a small gift of money from his estate.[67] His will provided much more wealth to his younger son, Benjamin, and to Martha and Anne, each of whom he identified as "my loving daughter."[68] In sum, Garden appears to have been an affectionate husband and father.

One other element of Garden's marriage proved formative. The rise of Alexander Garden to prominence in South Carolina coincided with that of slavery, and his marriage to Martha inserted him into a family whose complicity in the slave trade and the lowcountry slave plantation economy made it unlikely that he would challenge the institution on any level. Records indicate that before the Yamassee War the colony never imported more than 500 slaves in a year, and most years the total did not exceed 100. In 1720, 601 African slaves were sold into the colony, and for the next two decades seldom did the total fall below

1,000; in 1736, 229 ships transferred over 3,000 slaves to South Carolina.[69] Already in 1720 about half of Charles Town's population was enslaved, not counting the temporary presence of black sailors who idled in the taverns waiting for their next cargoes. Town slaves performed skilled labor, manual labor, and housework. Black women, enslaved and free, traded with country slaves to import vegetables into the town, and slaves manned the small river vessels that conducted cargoes and passengers to and from the country plantations.

The black presence in Charles Town must have been remarkable. A Swiss settler incorrectly estimated the black to white population ratio as twenty to one, but the exaggeration is telling: "Carolina looks more like a negro country than like a country settled by white people," he wrote.[70] Whites perceived a wide range of threats from and misbehaviors among their racial others. Blacks disrupted proper Christian practice with their "Meeting in such Numbers in the Streets of Charles Town on the Lords Day" that they caused a "great Noise and Disturbance" with "prophane cursing and swearing and other enormities to the Great Scandal of Christianity and Offense of all sober and well disposed persons," protested members of a grand jury that investigated such things in 1734. Such complaints should not be casually dismissed. The scholarship on slave resistance and resilience has brilliantly documented the creative ways that Africans, held against their will, nevertheless made room for themselves among their oppressors. Blacks also competed with whites for jobs, and their savvy business practices, according to several gentlemen, swayed the market: "Negroes are suffered to buy and sell, and be Hucksters of Corn, Pease, Fowls &c. whereby they watch Night and Day on the Wharves, and buy up many Articles necessary for the Support of the Inhabitants and make them pay an exorbitant Price for the same."[71] How tragically ironic that many of the very people who forced Africans to live among them could barely tolerate their presence.

Alexander Garden was geographically and socially positioned to observe this rapidly expanding slave trade and increasingly interracial community. In the years leading up to Garden's arrival, Virginia received more slaves than did the Carolinas or any other colony in British North America, but the momentum in the slave trade was already shifting perceptibly toward South Carolina and Charles Town specifically. In the first decade of the 1700s, Virginia imported more than twice as many slaves as South Carolina did. In the 1710s and 1720s South Carolina lagged behind its northern neighbor by only about 10 percent, and by the 1730s it imported approximately a third more. By the 1750s, the last decade of Garden's life, South Carolina's numbers almost doubled Virginia's. Ships arrived most often in the summer months in both colonies, but because Charles Town was far more likely than Virginia to receive slaves throughout an entire year, the presence of Africans and the slave trade was more prolonged in the southernmost town. By 1740 Charles Town easily ranked as the single largest slave port in North America. Perhaps most important, slavers sold their human cargo in multiple ports in Virginia, so the intensity of the slave trade presence was felt less acutely there than in the Carolinas, where a large majority of slaves entered the colony through Charles Town. In addition, because Charles Town so dominated the trade in the Deep South, buyers from all over the countryside traveled to the town to make their purchases. Such transactions united the merchants and the planters, the suppliers of slaves and the users of slaves, in a fraternity of slave exploitation whose core lay within Garden's neighborhood and church.[72] In other words, Garden could not have selected a better vantage point in British North America from which to witness and contribute to South Carolina's descent into African slavery.

Garden's choice to settle in the heart of this booming trade in human beings and his choice of a marital partner suggest that he was morally disposed to approve of and maybe even profit from the business. By marrying Martha, Alexander committed himself to the institution of slavery, both the ownership of slaves and the transatlantic slave trade. Martha's father participated in both the Indian and African slave trades and almost certainly owned slaves to work his plantations. Her brother John became the third-largest slave trader in South Carolina in the 1730s and 1740s, if not before—unfortunately, records do not tell enough about individual merchants before 1735 to make reliable rankings—and by the time he died he owned over 150 slaves, a considerable number. When in 1723 William Tredwell Bull resigned the office of commissary and returned to England, he granted power of attorney to Garden and Edward Brailsford Esq. "to Give such orders and Directions to my Overseer or Overseers upon my Plantation or Plantations," including the right to hire and fire overseers, who bore the bulk of the responsibility for the failure or success of plantations.[73] If Garden had any qualms about taking up such a responsibility, he never made it known, and when he married Martha, he signaled his willingness to affirm his colonial colleague's decision to sink the post–Yamassee War economy ever deeper into the practice of African slavery. There were a few important voices in the British Empire critiquing slavery, particularly in its southern form, by the 1720s. Garden chose not to heed their warning.

By the end of the 1720s Alexander Garden could look with considerable satisfaction upon his first decade in South Carolina. He had weathered the political upheavals of the revolution, the economic disruptions of droughts, a scarcity of paper money and fluctuating prices on the international rice market, a hurricane, and disease. In the process of securing a pulpit he had learned lessons about the religious power of wealth in the colony. He had made strides toward holding and expanding the influence of his ministry by making friends in high places, the crowning achievement of that endeavor being his marriage to one of the most prominent young women of his time and place, with whom he had begun a family. In short, he had prospered right along with South Carolina as a whole. Making acquaintance with this new colony had not been easy—it was hardly a welcoming place. But he had endured and achieved a significant level of stability in his social and financial situations. His neighbors liked him and appreciated his ministerial abilities.

Yet one senses from the records that Garden had his eyes set higher than mere survival and security. For him, as for many others in South Carolina, wealth and social power went hand in hand, and both proved temptations difficult to resist for this aspiring minister. By mid-decade he already had plenty of wealth, but he lacked power. St. Philip's was grand, but it was controlled by the vestry, and the Church of England had merely limped out of the turmoil of the Yamassee War and the revolution. Conveniently, William Tredwell Bull resigned the office of commissary in 1723, leaving open an office that a man of ambition, acumen, and social skill could exploit on his own behalf and for the welfare of the church, if not the society.

Garden was not in every way the obvious choice to replace Bull, and in fact it took him six years to be chosen for the position by the bishop of London. Garden had arrived in the colony relatively recently, several years before Bull resigned. Gideon Johnston had assumed the office immediately upon his arrival in 1708, and Bull had become commissary with only four years' experience in the colony. In Garden's case, though, in 1723 he still had not been elected, and it was not at all certain that he could be, which must have given the bishop of London pause. By 1729, however, Garden had to his credit nearly ten years of experience leading the most prominent congregation in the Carolinas and in the most central location among the parishes.

Just as important to the bishop's confidence in him was that in at least two separate incidents Garden had shown himself to be a bold leader who had earned respect from a large minority of society; there is no indication what slaves thought of him, and they were in the majority in the South Carolina population. One episode concerned a schoolteacher and the other a young minister who got crosswise with the elites in his congregation and got fired by his vestry. Both were newer to the city than Garden, and both felt the force of Garden's aggressive personality.

In 1726 the schoolmaster in Charles Town, Thomas Morritt, wrote to the bishop of London complaining of his treatment at the hands of Alexander Garden. The pulpit in the adjacent parish of Christ Church was then vacant, and the vestry had invited Morritt to fill in. The minister could cross the harbor on Saturday night or Sunday morning and return again to Charles Town on Sunday evening in plenty of time to resume his school duties. However, he had been assisting Garden in St. Philip's, something with which his Sunday excursions across the bay conflicted. Garden told Morritt that he had made a motion before the Board of School Commissioners to prohibit such extracurricular activity. Later, Garden tried to prevent the colonial treasurer from paying Morritt for his services at Christ Church.

According to Morritt, this was just one more episode in a history with Garden that had started before Morritt even left England, where he had heard rumors about Garden's overbearing ways. He had tried to back out of taking the schoolmaster position but, upon application to the bishop for that purpose, had been persuaded to try out Charles Town anyway. Once he arrived in South Carolina, he found the school project in much disarray, but because his "Wife was with Child," he attempted to "get me appointed to a parish," probably as a minister, rather than make the return journey to England. When Garden found out about this, he worked behind the scenes to prohibit Morritt from backing out of the schoolmaster position, lest his doing so "reflect upon some Gentlemen that Subscribed to the Letter to invite me over" from England, Morritt wrote. According to Morritt, Garden wanted not merely to protect the reputation of his gentlemen friends' hospitality and integrity but also to keep Morritt in town as his personal assistant, with the formal title of lecturer. Morritt concluded, "I know the Grudge is because I will not undertake what he calls the Lectureship which in plain terms is to be his Curate, his Underling and do on all occasions the Drudgery of the Parish that he may live at Ease." Consequently, "I find every Step is narrowly watch'd and every motion I make is rather hindered than forwarded."[74]

Morritt's story comported with Garden's own letter to the bishop two years earlier, even in its attitude toward Morritt. Garden had complained to the bishop about his own poor health and the harsh climate, certainly legitimate concerns, claiming that he badly needed an assistant. His workload, he wrote, "is indeed rather too weighty for any one person in this Climate." His understanding had been that the schoolmaster was supposed to double as Garden's assistant, but since the bishop had not licensed Morritt to preach in the colonies, Garden had proposed making him a lecturer. Instead, Garden wrote, "I am still in the same Condition as before; and he presuming the Liberty to supply any vacant Cure he thinks fit, at the Rate of the Country Salary allow'd any regular Incumbent, over and above the like Salary allow'd him as School Master."[75] Morritt had correctly identified Garden's desire for an assistant as the root of his bitterness toward the schoolmaster, although it appears that Garden also resented Morritt's ability to collect double pay. In this Garden had accurately detected a less godly motive in Morritt's itinerancy. Morritt later became minister in Prince George Winyaw Parish, where he built up a significant landholding as a prosperous planter, busying himself so much with earthly affairs that his parishioners eventually asked him either to resign his pulpit or to quit his commercial pursuits. He resigned his pulpit.[76]

In this conflict with Morritt, Garden expected some sort of deference to his needs and desires, but Morritt was unwilling to show the unelected rector that sort of respect. Garden's failure to bring Morritt to heel suggests that he had not yet attained enough access to the levers of social power, although he knew where that power resided. Garden perceptively styled his case against Morritt's leaving his schoolmaster post and becoming a minister in terms of the wishes of the gentlemen to protect their good names. He felt bold enough with the treasurer to try to prevent payment of Morritt's ministerial services. Yet when Morritt told the president of the Board of School Commissioners of Garden's claim that Garden had petitioned the board to prohibit Morritt's activities outside the parish, the president denied ever receiving any such motion from anyone. He "wonder'd Mr. Garden wou'd buisy himself so much as he did with affairs that do not Concern him, who allways shew'd himself busy medling in acting ungratefull offices toward those that no ways deserv'd it at his hands." By 1727 Morritt was so fed up being schoolmaster that he quit and moved to the countryside, assuming the pulpit in Prince George Winyah Parish the next year. It does not appear that the two ever mended fences. Ironically, Morritt performed Alexander and Martha's wedding ceremony in 1725, probably because he was the only available clergyman.[77] One wonders how cheery that ceremony was.

Garden displayed his assertiveness in the Morritt controversy, even though he failed to manage the young minister effectively. In a contest with another minister, Brian Hunt of St. John's Berkeley Parish, Garden triumphed. In 1727 Hunt performed a midnight marriage ceremony for a young man, Robert Wright, of Dorchester Parish and a teenage girl, Gibbon Cawood, of Charles Town, whose wealthy father had died before giving consent to the marriage. Hunt should have deferred to the local clergy, but when the couple informed him that neither the Reverend Vernod of Dorchester nor Cawood's legal guardians would consent to the marriage, Hunt agreed to perform the ceremony, and in Charles Town, Garden's territory. Individual letters of complaint were dispatched to the SPG by Vernod, the "Clergy of South Carolina," the vestry of St. John's, Alexander Garden, and the two guardians, Andrew Allen and Charles Hill, who together had initiated the proceedings against Hunt. For his part, Garden wrote a detailed account of Hunt's misdeeds for the bishop and recommended that Hunt be suspended from the ministry.[78]

Garden had personal reasons to oppose this marriage. Hunt had violated parish boundaries by performing the marriage within Garden's jurisdiction but without Garden's consent. Perhaps as important, Charles Hill, one of Cawood's guardians and a rich merchant in town, sat in his pews on Sunday. Garden's brother-in-law John Guerard would later enter a business partnership with Hill's son Charles and marry Hill's daughter Elizabeth. Those unions were yet to come, but clearly Hunt had offended those within Garden's social circle. Or perhaps by taking Hill's side, Garden perceived that he could ingratiate himself with the wealthy slave trader, a move which paid off in time. Allen was a Presbyterian, but his wealth and prominence in the community probably incentivized Garden to move on his behalf. William Tredwell Bull defended Allen's character in the dispute by depicting the merchant as "a Person of fair character as to business and reputed at least worth 20,000 pounds sterling, so cannot reasonably be suspected to be against the Match purely on account of" concern for his personal estate. Besides, according to the guardians' petition to the bishop of London, Hill and Allen worried that they had not been able to "procure a marriage Settlement," a prenuptial agreement, protecting Cawood and that before long her inheritance would be "ruined and Begard Notwithstanding her great Fortune whose father left a legacy of 3000 pounds this currency for adorning the Church of this Parrish."[79] St. Philip's Church stood to benefit from Cawood's inheritance, a point the guardians wanted to bring to the bishop's attention and which, no doubt, did not escape Garden's.[80]

Hunt did not dispute the basic facts of the case, and it was not the first time he had united a couple under dubious circumstances: Garden claimed that Hunt had married a couple after Garden and Governor Nicholson had both forbidden the marriage in light of widely known and incontrovertible proof that the groom already "had a wife living in England."[81] Hunt defended himself by attacking Allen's and Hill's integrity. He claimed that the young woman's guardians, neighbors to the Cawoods, had had no regard for the family before hearing of a "great Estate falling to Mr. Cawood" shortly before he died, after which they "caress'd him and he dying soon after on the meer force of necessity" made them executors of his will. Having secured the estate, these "pretended Eminent Merchants" refused to consent to the marriage, not wanting to lose control of the "young woman's fortune." Hunt portrayed his detractors as deceptive frauds motivated only by material gain. "One was a Scots pedlar: the other a broken Dutchman; the one a virulent Presbyterian, the other a cruel Wretch, an opposer of Widows and orphans," and both were "now contriving to cheat mother and daughter."

Hunt, in his desperation, had likely gone off the rails in describing his critics this way, but in his frustration he illuminated for posterity an instance of Garden siding with merchants against a fellow minister. More important, the story indicates the extent to which Garden by mid-decade was willing to assert his prerogatives. The story also reveals something of his overbearing character. Hunt claimed that Garden rallied the clergy: they were "stir[red] up" by him into signing a joint statement protesting the marriage. Garden "domineer[ed] over the Missionaries," who were "by Mr. Garden's Malice aw'd."[82] Hunt was fired as minister and imprisoned for a time before leaving his impoverished wife and children behind to seek work in the Bahamas. Fortunately for him and his family, he found good success in a pulpit in Barbados.[83] Meanwhile, Garden and his vestry used some of Cawood's estate to purchase an organ for St. Philip's.[84]

Hunt's testimony against Garden failed to damage the bishop's esteem for Garden, perhaps because Bull countered Hunt with his own positive character reference. The bishop had given Hunt's petition to Bull, now settled back in England, and asked for his opinion. Bull judiciously hesitated to comment on people he did not know, including Hunt, claiming that there had been too much turnover in the clergy since he had lived in the colony. Nonetheless he criticized Hunt for violating established church practices regarding marriages and then announced his surprise at Hunt's portrayal of Garden as some sort of ministerial tyrant: "I have often declared otherwise, & do solemnly again, that I am firmly p[er]suaded Mr. Garden is a person worthy of your Lordship's favour & the most proper of any in the Province to represent your Lordship, as one that will not be guilty of an unjust ac[tion] either out of prejudice, favour, or affection, or any other motive."[85] The bishop agreed, no doubt seeing in Garden the makings of a firm leader who could forge stability and conformity out of disorder. Within a year he appointed Alexander Garden commissary of North and South Carolina and the Bahamas.

Garden received his letter of commission with humility and a promise of faithfulness in the discharge of his duties. "I am really diffident, my Lord, of my Abilities for this Service," he wrote, "& Yet such as they are," he vowed to employ them "with all Diligence, Circumspection, and Fidelity." He expressed concern that the commission had been printed on regular paper and lacked the bishop's official seal. Because of the "bareprinted" nature of the commission, he wrote, he would desist from carrying out any disciplinary action. Apparently the Hunt case had precipitated the commission, nudging the bishop finally to appoint a successor to Bull six years after his retirement and convincing him that Garden was the reliable choice, for directly after refusing to engage in any "judicial" action, Garden hastened to point out that none would be necessary anyway, "for Immediately on my Receipt of the above Dispatch from your Lordship, Mr. Hunt embarked & saild hence for Barbadoes."[86]

Being commissary provided Garden with a seat of power that would prove vital for his own ambitions and the security of the Church of England in South Carolina. Garden had security in his pulpit, an office commensurate to the sort of social influence that would bode well for the Church of England in South Carolina and for his own standing among the colonial elites; considerable money and other financial resources; and a wife who not only played an important role in securing these material benefits but also proved a loving companion.

Alexander Garden gained much by marrying Martha Guerard, but what did the marriage look like from her perspective? How did she experience life as the wife of an ambitious and domineering minister soon to be chosen commissary by the bishop of London? She no doubt consented to her marriage to the frail, middle-aged Scottish minister; women did have the final say in responding to marriage proposals. But did she approve of it deep in her soul? Was it a marriage that provided what she likely thought of as the necessities of life: companionship; children; and respectability as a wealthy married woman? Men outnumbered women by a considerable margin in the colony, which probably meant that she had choices.[87] What did she think of him as a person? Who was Alexander Garden to Martha Garden?

Unfortunately nothing remains in Martha's own words that would afford a glimpse of her feelings and beliefs. She survives in the historical record primarily because of the men in her life: her grandfather and father; her brothers; and her husband. From them it can be assumed that she lived a life of relative material ease and social respectability. Wealth and status opened for her opportunities less accessible to poor, immigrant, or enslaved women and made her a suitable partner for an aspiring minister just arrived from Britain and looking for female companionship. Her training as a young girl would have equipped her with the skills for and sensitivities to the proper conduct and deportment necessary for a woman of high society. She likely attended dances and banquets and occupied a seat of some honor in St. Philip's. Social grace, informed but deferential conversation, and fashionable clothing enabled her to move comfortably through the process of her courtship with Garden. While such practical considerations as securing a living and a respectable social rank still governed the process of matchmaking, women and men of the eighteenth century aimed increasingly to marry for love, or at least for intimate companionship. The latter can be inferred by Garden's words at the end of his life when he remembered her as "his truly amiable consort."[88]

Martha's coming of age coincided with the colony's plunge into and emergence from the Yamassee War. One can easily imagine her telling her new husband suspenseful stories of death and destruction and the collapse of civil society as she and her family and friends huddled behind the Charles Town walls. Her tales must have contributed to Garden's perceptions of the colony's instability in the years before his arrival and sensitized him to the need for strict adherence to the demands of social order and authority. Such concerns became guiding lights for Garden in the next three decades, ordering his priorities and conditioning his personal and professional relationships. As a result her concerns became his and his career became hers, and together they formed a partnership grounded in companionship and sympathy and reaching upward toward what they believed was a godly social order.

Martha came of age during the beginning years of the industrial and consumer revolution of the British Empire in the eighteenth century. Print culture expanded, transportation networks thickened, and mass-produced consumer goods, especially fabrics, became available to middling and wealthy people. South Carolina's recovery began in just enough time for Martha to enjoy the fruits of this revolution. The new pieces of furniture, tableware, fine clothing, and other luxury goods needed to be cleaned, repaired, and properly stored or displayed, but for that, Martha almost certainly had house slaves. Alexander Garden's will confirmed that they personally owned slaves. Slaves probably came early into her life, given her family's role in the transatlantic slave trade. These laboring people would have done the most menial and distasteful—and socially disdained—work around Martha's house, freeing her to indulge in more comfortable activities. At the same time, she took on the role of slave mistress, enjoying slave labor on her behalf but with all of the watchfulness, sternness, and imposition of discipline that attended the use of slaves.[89] Garden's work, especially as commissary, kept him busy with counseling, meeting with vestries, transatlantic correspondence, preaching, and traveling to settle problems between ministers and vestries or temporarily filling vacant pulpits. This would have left Martha to manage the business of the house, an appreciable contribution to Garden's career.

Running the household supported another dimension of Garden's public stature and enhanced the social importance of Martha's work in the home. In the eighteenth century, as colonies became increasingly prosperous, hospitality became one way for wealthier colonists to distinguish themselves from the lower strata of the socioeconomic scale. As a woman of wealth, Martha would have been expected to host and attend lavish parties that reflected the Gardens' social class as much as it facilitated friendships among women. The quality of the food and drink—women shared recipes and assembled cookbooks—the finery of the table settings, and the grace and manners with which mistresses and servants attended to their guests implied proper training and discipline. When Garden hosted a visiting minister, Martha would be responsible for making his stay as comfortable as possible. Her success conferred dignity upon Garden and demonstrated her own worth as a virtuous woman.[90]

Virtue took on unique importance for Martha as the wife of the rector at St. Philip's. Men and women of Martha's time considered spiritual and moral sensitivity to be especially pronounced in the female sex. To them, women were more emotional and men more rational, and this was a good thing for both society and marital happiness. Supposedly women's heightened emotional tendencies rendered them more cheerful, compassionate, and capable of religious experience. Their moral conscience and feminine beauty and grace enhanced social interaction by refining men, who would otherwise tend toward crude and violent behavior. Virtuous women also lifted the tenor of conversation, both in a crowd and between them and their husbands. As companionship became increasingly important to individuals looking for marriage partners, women and men granted greater value to these feminine virtues for the sake of the husbands' comfort at home and for the women's ability to teach virtue to their children. As a minister's wife and a model for other women in St. Philip's Parish, Martha must have felt these expectations more acutely than many other women did.[91]

Martha engaged the community outside of her home as well. The lives of comparable women of her time suggest possibilities of how Martha may have exerted herself in her marriage and community. Henrietta Johnston, wife of the first commissary, Gideon Johnston, successfully lobbied the SPG in London for financial support and kept an eye on colonial affairs for him while he visited England to report on the status of the church in South Carolina. In her letters to her husband she informed him of the behavior of recalcitrant ministers. When a minister's "patient temper was not for acquainting" Johnston of a problem with a French Huguenot turned Anglican minister, the Reverend Claude Philippe de Richebourg, she "begg'd leave to let you know all that comes to my Ears while you are where perhaps you may take better measures for the redress of Errours, than you coud here." She did more than simply convey news. Her letters included her advice for resolving church disputes. Of Richebourg she opined that "no doubt that Mungrell sort of Clergy does a great deal of hurt, and greatly foment the differences, and widen the Breaches, between our Church and the French. I fancy it woud be much for your case as well as the Good of the Church in this Province, if they coud be provided elsewhere, and sound Men put in their Stead."[92] Neither did Henrietta shy away from arguing policy with her husband's detractors. When congregants complained to Henrietta of Gideon's insistence that Richebourg and other French clergy scrupulously follow Anglican customs, she "Justifyed" her husband's policies, after which the protesters warned her that he would lose their "Love and esteem."[93]

Remarkably, Gideon relied on Henrietta's judgments to the point of using them as evidence in his written report on the church. In the report he quoted her at length and verbatim and referred to it as "my wifes Letter" in three different sections of his account, using it as decisive evidence in the case he was making for strengthening the Anglican establishment in South Carolina. He assumed that the bishop would give her words the same credibility as his own. When the French parishioners—Henrietta called them "headstrong Fools"—of the Anglican Reverend LaPierre took their complaints about LaPierre's insistence on Anglican conformity to the minister of the French Protestant Church, Paul L'Escot, and were rebuffed by his ardent support of Anglican prerogatives, Henrietta commended L'Escot to her husband. "This [Henrietta's words] sufficiently speaks the worth and merit of this good Man," wrote Gideon of L'Escot to the bishop, believing his wife's words good enough to establish L'Escot's reputation. In sum, it appears that Henrietta enjoyed her role as counsel to her husband, the commissary, a role that Gideon seems to have appreciated as much as President John Adams did Abigail's later in the century. Henrietta also helped support her family financially by painting, becoming quite an accomplished portraiture and "the first professional woman artist in America."[94]

Other women took active roles in the Charles Town community. In 1707 the minister Francis Le Jau lamented political wrangling and legislative grid-lock and then noted the "singular" instance of women in Charles Town who "turned Politicians . . . and have a Club where they meet weekly among them-selves." They must not have resolved issues any better than the men did, for Le Jau wrote that "they meet weekly among themselves, but not without falling out among one another."[95] Martha Guerard's mother, also Martha, involved herself in the public affairs of Charles Town. In 1719 South Carolina's House of Commons directed tax assessors to meet "at the house of Madam Martha Guerard, in Charlestown, or at such other house as the said assessors shall think fit to meet at."[96] Martha was by then a widow, so it was not on account of her husband's political activities that they chose her house. One wonders if she observed the proceedings from a distance or if she interjected her opinions now and then, and if her daughter, then just sixteen, took notice.

Meanwhile advertisements in the *South Carolina Gazette* in the 1730s and 1740s—the newspaper commenced printing in January 1732—revealed a wide range of commercial activities available to women. "Madame Peter Precour" painted fans; Jane Voyer "undert[ook] the mending of Laces, and drawing Patterns for any kind of Needlework"; Nathaniel and Mary Gittens taught drawing; and Elizabeth Anderson was a music teacher. Mrs. Eldridge hosted cockfighting at her home.[97] Mrs. Mary Price rented "lodgings . . . by the Year, Quarter, or Week"; and one of Martha Garden's neighbors, Mrs. Hammer-ton, let "a Parlour, two Chambers," and a "Storehouse . . . with the Use of a Kitchen, Garden, Well of very good Water, and other Conveniences." Catharine Joor ran a dry goods store and Mary Bedon a tavern, while Hellen Govan sold textiles, shoes, and sugar from her shop. Rebeccah Pollard had such "great Suc-cess" treating victims of smallpox in Charles Town that she took her medical "business" into the countryside. As her absence from town lengthened, people in town worried that smallpox had claimed her life, so when she returned she posted a notice in the *Gazette* to "inform all Persons that I am always ready . . . to wait on any sick Persons or Lying-in Women."[98]

Women in the countryside too realized various commercial opportunities. Eliza Lucas achieved fame more for her pioneering work in growing indigo, after 1750 the most lucrative crop in colonial South Carolina besides rice, than for her marriage to the prominent merchant and politician Charles Pinckney. As a teenager she managed three plantations assigned to her care by her father. She consulted men in the area, but she made the final decisions regarding virtually everything to do with the plantations, including the choice of plant varieties, the management of slaves, and the purchasing and selling of farm goods and crops. In her free time she studied music, French, and poetry; taught children—some of them African—to read; and dabbled in political gossip. She even studied law and drafted wills for several neighbors.[99]

It is evident, then, that opportunities for involvement in public and economic activities existed for Martha, particularly as a woman of considerable financial means.[100] No indications in the extant records suggest that she did so, but certainly she participated in the daily economy of her household. Likely she found contentment in her life as mother to five children, wife to the leading pastor and commissary, companion to a man who loved her, sister to men active in political and mercantile affairs, and friend to other women working to establish themselves on the edges of the British Empire. In a culture and an era where so much depended on personal relationships, Martha had plenty. That may have been enough for her.

Or was it? On the one hand, colonial laws and social customs placed her under the permanent authority of her husband and other men in her life. Upon marriage a woman almost literally disappeared into the social reputation, legal standing, and economic prerogatives of her partner. Typically the husband owned the property, pursued legal remedies on behalf of his family, and determined the disposition of his estate in his own will. Perhaps Martha chafed under these restrictions and was a person to be pitied in our more progressive age. On the other hand, economic customs allowed her opportunities to serve her community in marketable ways, and another, secondary set of social customs, admittedly less reputable and desirable than the first, could have granted her de facto freedom from her husband: Mary Wood ran away from her husband; and Hannah Barbara Lee and Sarah Davis both eloped from their mates. Abandoned husbands often posted announcements in the *Gazette* that they would no longer pay debts incurred by their departed spouses.[101] The practice of coverture, whereby men took full legal responsibility for the financial activities of their households, and not some attempts at public shaming by bitter husbands provoked such advertisements. At any rate, Martha did not leave Alexander, nor did she leave behind any clue that she ever wanted to do so.

It may be reasonably concluded that Martha lived a contented life in the shadows of her increasingly prominent husband. Perhaps one might read too much into the description of Martha as Alexander's "amiable consort," and perhaps her five children were not testament enough to loving relationships within their home. However, if in fact they did evidence a warm marriage and if the stories of Henrietta Johnston and Eliza Lucas were at all representative of white women of means in South Carolina, then it might be assumed that

Martha Guerard Garden lived a pleasant life and that marriage, to her, was as much an opportunity for her to achieve her own dreams as a wife, mother, and friend as it was a step up in the social world for her husband. From her perspective, Alexander Garden was a friend, lover, spiritual confidant, and father of her children.

# Chapter 3

# FRIENDSHIP

The bishop's letter appointing Garden as commissary arrived at a most opportune time. At that time Garden was coincidentally involved in another contest with another unfortunate victim of South Carolina's elite slaveholding class, a minister who in important ways bore resemblance to the Reverend Brian Hunt, the minister of St. John's Berkeley Parish whom Garden worked to expel in 1728. John Winteley had been preaching in Christ Church Parish, right next door to St. Philip's Parish and Charles Town, since he arrived in the colony in 1727. (See figure 3.) From early on, Winteley clashed with his church vestry and wardens over behaviors he considered immoral, and from early on they accused him of all sorts of heinous behaviors. They finally forced him, disgraced, from the pulpit in 1729. Throughout the controversy Garden publicly and aggressively sided with the vestry and wardens. If Winteley's testimony can be believed—and there is good reason to take him seriously—Garden took pains to humiliate his young colleague openly and acted in concert with the planters in the parish to expel him from the pulpit. However, Garden and his lay colleagues had purposes that were quite reasonable for their times. Those purposes were inextricably linked to the institution of slavery.

In turning from Indian to African slave labor after the Yamassee War, white Carolinians plunged from one danger to another, daringly hopeful that they could finally attain for themselves the level of aristocratic power and wealth they had left behind in the West Indies and Europe by harnessing the labor of yet another group of supposed inferiors. They already possessed a slave code, which could easily be modified to adapt to changing demographic and social realities and which they could use to control this burgeoning population of the exploited, but they realized that more would be required than a legal code and a desire to succeed. White colonists would need to re-create southern society to conform in every way to the dangers and opportunities inherent in keeping others in a condition of abject servitude. Managing this feat of social and economic engineering, attaining the glories of wealth and public esteem so admired by their families and friends back home without getting themselves killed in the pursuit, would require unity of purpose and an imposition of social norms carefully designed to secure social harmony on a foundation of racial and economic

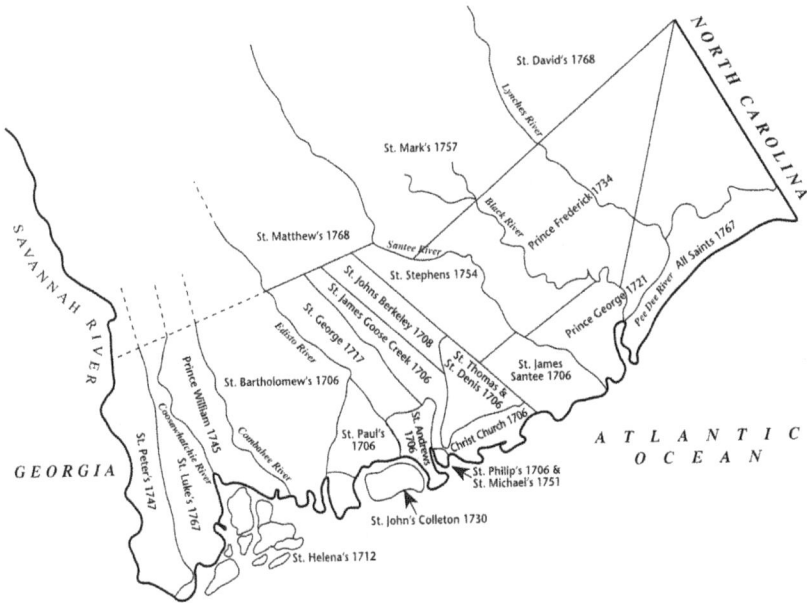

FIGURE 3. Parishes of the Anglican Church, colonial South Carolina. Courtesy of South Carolina Department of Archives and History, Columbia, South Carolina.

hierarchy. Members of Charles Town's elite fraternity, or what people then and historians now call "polite society," took it upon themselves to create and maintain this social hierarchy, a project they believed sincerely was in the best interest of the entire colony.

Garden, having achieved membership in this fraternity through marriage and other calculated alliances, did his part to uphold the hierarchy. Together with the laity, Garden used the Church of England to buttress the stability and durability of this young and volatile slave society. In the process, in the 1730s the commissary and the colony became more than acquaintances. They forged a partnership, a close friendship of interdependence and intimate familiarity. Understanding slave resistance, Garden's views of it, and the utility of eighteenth-century politeness in stifling it reveals why Garden worked so hard against Winteley and others like him whose criticisms of polite behavior threatened social order. He understood that the very survival of the white population in the lowcountry depended on maintaining racial solidarity. So he labored to secure a place for the Church of England in the upper echelons of the social hierarchy. By succeeding, he empowered the office of commissary, turned the Church of England into a symbol and instrument of white authority, and blessed the earthly pursuits of Charles Town's laity. It was a masterful accomplishment owed almost entirely to the ambition, energy, and keen intuition of Alexander Garden. Of course, if Garden aimed to make a name for himself, South Carolina proved to be a splendid place of opportunity. The colony needed someone of his abilities to squash spiritual disapproval with polite behaviors and paint a veneer of godliness over the decidedly carnal business of slave exploitation.

Unsurprisingly, slaves resisted exploitation. Leaving aside the moral question of whether or not a slave could steal from a master—was it stealing if a slave took a chicken, for instance, that he raised but that his master intended to use himself?—slaves appropriated for themselves livestock, household items, jewelry, cash, food, and clothing. Some made the most daring choice and stole their own bodies away from their masters, choosing to seek freedom in Florida rather than allow their sweat and strength to be exploited another day. From the late 1600s Carolinian settlers complained to the Spanish of the steady stream of slaves who, as Gov. James Colleton put it to his Spanish counterpart, "run dayly into your towns." In the 1730s hundreds of slaves successfully responded—sometimes with the assistance of the other population in the South resistant to British control, Native Americans—to Spanish offers of freedom to British slaves who reached Florida.[1] The back pages of the *South Carolina Gazette* were replete with advertisements placed by masters whose slaves had run away and by authorities who announced they had caught runaways. Those ads revealed the brutal measures masters had employed to subjugate slaves: "Run away from Mrs. Elizabeth Dill, on James's Island, a young Negro Wench named Orinda, having a Scar in her Cheek and Forehead"; "Brought to the Work-house in Charlestown . . . Booba A Negro says he belongs to Mr. Ball at Wando, two Toes upon each Foot seem as if they were cut off"; and "A Negro Boy, named Billy, has a Chain and Padlock on his Neck."[2] Often they took with them expensive dishes, fine clothing, weapons, and other emblems of white power. Not only did these slaves represent lost investments for the slaveholders, but in addition these runaways were no longer under any white person's supervision, making them a particularly dangerous threat to white existence.

Slaves resisted in other creative ways. They feigned illness, broke tools, left barn doors open, and committed other acts of sabotage to slow down work production. They told lies and gave incorrect directions to befuddle whites. They poisoned masters, and even those who did not know how to use poison effectively or had no intention of actually carrying out the deed could use to their advantage the fact that many whites considered most Africans to be experts in poisoning; intimidation could be a potent weapon. Other individuals, in fits of desperation, lashed out physically at their abusive masters. Resistance turned violent when slaves fought back with weapons, including axes and other tools of their exploitation reconceived as means of retribution. Whites continually watched out for slave arsonists, a particularly dangerous problem in a town crowded with wooden houses and lacking modern firefighting capabilities. More benignly slaves illegally chose to wear white people's clothing rather than the "negro clothing" allotted to them by their masters. No wonder the eminent historian of slavery Philip D. Morgan introduced his seminal study of slavery in the lowcountry and the Chesapeake, a book that reached almost seven hundred pages, with a preemptory explanation: "Readers may be surprised that there is no chapter on resistance. In a sense, the whole book is a study of resistance. In work and in play, in public and in private, violently and quietly, slaves struggled against masters."[3]

In addition there was the specter of mass slave rebellion. Whites hesitated to record details about slave conspiracies in public places, such as the newspaper, but it appears that slaves regularly planned uprisings involving a fearful number of slaves. One colonist wrote to a friend in 1720 that whites had just uncovered "a very wicked and barbarous plott" among slaves to "destroy all the white people in the country and then to take the town in full body." Perhaps this explains why it was reported in London that the "whole Province was lately in danger of being massacred by their Own slaves, who are too numerous in proportion to ye White Men there." The *Boston Weekly News-Letter* reported in 1730 that a "great Body" of slaves gathered outside of Charles Town and "had a great Dance" in hopes that country slaves would join their conspiracy. News from the Caribbean only stoked white fears. Carolinians learned from the pages of their own *Gazette* about massive uprisings in the Virgin Islands in 1734 that resulted in the slaughter of hundreds of black and white families, including "all the white People on that Island."[4] Whites actually did survive, some by escaping to other islands, but it must have seemed like a complete annihilation. In July 1739 the *Gazette* printed news of a slave uprising in Jamaica, and later that year South Carolina experienced the Stono Rebellion, the largest slave uprising in the British North American colonies.

For these reasons, maintaining social control over the slave population required more than mere legal stipulations. It required vigilance and virtually any force necessary for suppression of blacks' initiative. Whites stayed constantly alert to any sign of resistance and demonstrated willingness to crush subversion with a force that exceeded the bounds of regular morality. "Discipline and Correction must be observed among every Parcel of Slaves," wrote Alexander Garden, "which . . . may be, and often is misrepresented" as "Cruelty and bad Usage."[5] However, whites needed more than mere physical violence in their arsenal, especially since a slave injured by "the Rod" of discipline turned less profit. Controlling slaves, stifling resistance, and preventing the destruction of white society at the hands of black rebels required a comprehensive code of conduct that reached into every nook and cranny of southern society, including its mental habits and spiritual conscience. This code functioned as a web of trip wires woven through the very fabric of colonial society. When this web operated effectively, African slaves could not glance toward resistance without setting off alarms. This web was imposed and maintained by elite society using the tools of eighteenth-century politeness.

"Politeness" is a term with broad applicability, from politics to the economy, from social organization and religion to personal morality.[6] Although they are not entirely synonymous, the term is often used alongside or in place of "gentility" and "civility." In colonial South Carolina, politeness was an attitude, an aptitude, and a social altitude. It involved worldliness and cosmopolitanism, fashionableness in clothing and home furnishing, and an ability to dance, converse, and play at games with an ease and amiability that made deliberate condescension to the impolite unnecessary.[7] One young Carolinian woman described her model of a true gentleman, the celebrated British admiral George Anson, as "generous without Profusion, elegant without Ostentation; and above all of a most tender humane Disposition."[8] A polite person could enjoy entertainments, discern quality wine, read Virgil, converse about the latest scientific discoveries, and gift money to a degree and with a liberality and sense of modesty that awed others without humiliating them. At its most basic level, politeness was manifested in one's comportment and an aura of presence that, in a way not unlike what today is called "stage presence," had to be witnessed, rather than linguistically defined. In fact the exhibition of politeness in the eighteenth century was not unlike playacting, for politeness was, above all, performed. The historian Richard Bushman has drawn attention to the "theatricality" of the "elaborately staged performances" of the "great ball." "People did not attend such events to relax, but to present their most beautiful, gracious, and pleasing selves."[9] Assemblies such as balls, dances, card playing, and banquets were indispensable locations where claimants to politeness were observed, judged, and ranked, and where, under their watchful eyes, their offspring could meet and court others of similar respectability.

By the 1730s South Carolina could boast a surprisingly wide array of such forums. Soon after arriving in South Carolina, Thomas Dale, author, wit, doctor, and man-about-town, announced to a friend that "we live very gaily and pleasantly here and find much more good Company and Conversation" than elsewhere.[10] In 1735 a theater opened across the street from St. Philip's Church, and there wealthier colonists could see some of the same plays and concerts as experienced by their English counterparts in London. Horse races also began that year, one of them offering a prize of "a handsome Sadle and Bridle of Twenty Pounds Value." On March 11, 1732, a Mr. Salter, "organist," advertised in the *South Carolina Gazette* the opening of "an Assembly of Dancing

and Cards, for the Entertainment of Gentlemen and Ladies." Two years later
a William Sterland posted "notice to all Gentlemen that he ha[d] a fine new
Billiard-Table with new sticks and balls at their service."[11] The historian Richard Waterhouse estimated that "a total of 34 [public] balls were held in the
period 1732 to 1770," along with others held by invitation only.[12] For those with
expendable money but who lacked social graces, teachers of dancing, drawing,
foreign languages, music, fencing, and even of how "to blow the French Horn"
advertised for students throughout the 1730s.[13] Colonists founded numerous social clubs in the late 1720s and 1730s, including such charitable organizations as
a St. George's Society, a South Carolina Society, and a St. Andrew's Society. The
latter became a model for similar societies elsewhere, including one in Georgia
for whom the goal of its annual festivities was to inebriate as many people as
possible.[14] By 1748 a Library Society was formed, apparently the first of the
societies intended for more intellectual pursuits. The *Gazette* in 1747 noted the
presence of a "Loyal Society vulgarly called the Laughing Club" and in 1736
extended an invitation to "Gentlemen, Ladies, and others" from "Samuel Grice,
Sugar Refiner from London" to "come and partake of the largest Plum Pudding
(gratis) that ever was made in this Country."[15]

That this social world of wealth, entertainment, fashion, and revelry sprang
up so quickly in Charles Town, scarcely two decades after the apocalyptic
Yamassee War of 1715 and in the midst of continued upheavals of disease,
hurricane, and threats of war with other imperial powers and their Indian allies, testifies to the desire of Carolinians to create for themselves a New World
version of Old World polite society, and to the fountain of wealth that slave
plantation agriculture proved to be for white southerners. Balls, clubs, theater,
charitable groups, and intellectual organizations fed the insatiable desire for
reputation, pleasure, and power.

However, gentlemen and ladies achieved this way of life at a cost. The
personal friendliness and liberality that acquired for Garden and his friends
the social and economic alliances necessary to succeed also obliged them to
lend considerable sums of money for which, in the words of Thomas Dale,
they could not sue "without being convinced of any knavish inclinations."[16]
Colonists tended to view insistence of repayment of loans as akin to laboring
for wages; both essentially constituted grubbing for money. Too much attention
to their account books violated the norms of liberality that bound those who
claimed politeness, and it strained relationships.

While wealth did not guarantee entrance to genteel society, the connection
between wealth and politeness was important. Purchasing clothes custom-made
according to the styles popular among London aristocrats took money. To become conversant in French or Greek or Latin the polite person spent the time
that most people devoted to working for money; hence a polite person needed

at least to pretend as though he never had to stoop to the level of doing manual labor or even attending to the daily grind of bookkeeping and deal making. Building homes with dance floors and card tables made out of fine, imported wood cost money. In addition a truly polite gentleman or gentlewoman needed to demonstrate "liberality," the "quality that most nearly epitomized what was needed to make a gentleman."[17] Hosting a spectacular ball or throwing a lavish banquet or giving gifts not only impressed and gratified the recipients but also demonstrated that one lived free from and independent of the constraints of labor and time and moneygrubbing that so pressed the lower sorts. Liberality thus proved one's suitability for public office, for only the truly independent person could look after the needs of the community without resorting to bribery or other vices of the indentured, the enslaved, or wageworkers. All of this took wealth, and so virtually no authentically polite people were poor. Admiral Anson's young admirer likely misjudged his affluence even while she correctly linked fortune and politeness: "His Benevolence is Extensive, even to his own Detriment—what Pity, that his Fortune is not as extensive?"[18]

That said, wealth did not necessarily confer politeness, especially when it came to the newly rich or the almost rich. The rapidly expanding consumer culture of the eighteenth century made cheap imitations of goods often associated with gentility available to an increasing number and diversity of people. Even so, one still needed to be invited to upscale entertainments, and this privilege was carefully guarded by the wealthy and employed with devastating result against those who seemed to have fallen from social grace.[19] Bushman noted that "the invisible lines defining inclusion and exclusion could be the cause of great anguish in the higher reaches of society."[20] Politeness required social policing; one might be able to purchase a cheap imitation of the clothes of the gentleman but could not easily mimic the grace, cosmopolitanism, and affability of the truly polite. "The entertainment as performance . . . evoked critical reviews," wrote Bushman. "Diarists and letter writers reported on balls and evening diversions as if they were producing a theatrical review, evaluating the performance and the performers." He related the scorn heaped upon "an awkward country fellow" when entering "company better than himself." This man "knows not what to do with his hands or his hat . . . perhaps twirls his hat on his fingers, or fumbles with the button." When spoken to, he "answers with the utmost difficulty, and nearly stammers."[21] Minor details regarding personal comportment were thus amplified and judged according to a brutal rubric of acceptability. Anyone could dance, play cards, or eat at a banquet, but only the truly polite could do it with the element of grace and ease expected of the gentry, and only the polite could perform these activities in the lavish homes or other forums of the wealthy.

An article from the *South Carolina Gazette* illustrated the ways colonists claimed, contested, and certified politeness, as well as potential political consequences of imposture. In 1738 a writer in the *Gazette* attacked the lifestyle of a certain "Don Roberto Arenaso, or as tis Englishest, Robin Brazen-Nose," who, "as most of [the] intelligent Readers" understood, was a judge in Charles Town named Robert Younge. The conflict centered on suspected abuses of office and dissatisfaction with some of Younge's judgments, but the evidence for his misbehavior derived from the way he attempted to project the status of a gentleman. To "Phileleutheros," Younge was a fake: the "only Badges of Distinction which he knows, consist in Dress and a splendid Appearance; and therefore the Glare of a fine Coat, a broad laced Hat and Jacket pass with him for certain Marks of real Merit, because they give him a conspicuous Figure in the Eyes of those who proportion their Respect to every Man according to the Gaudiness of his Apparel."[22] Younge defended his pedigree as a gentleman by claiming that his "Family and Dress" were "much better known to many of the best People here" and that there was nothing unusual with his outward deportment.[23] What was at stake in this squabble was not merely the aesthetic acceptability of Younge's outward appearance but whether or not respectable and socially responsible Carolinians had let an imposter to politeness slip into an office of importance to the maintenance of law and social order.

The question of what constituted genuine gentility loomed in the foreground of many a conversation and confirmed the importance of politeness to social order. The wealth that sustained the display of politeness in the colony was secured by the labor of hundreds of thousands of slaves, many of them recently torn from their homes in Africa, and this tragic fact only added to the burden of politeness and made the question of polite authenticity an important one to answer correctly. Politeness in the Old World had never represented merely frivolous entertainment, personal vanity, and meaningless fashion; it most often served a social purpose by affirming political, social, and economic power. Hierarchy achieved peace and harmony by assigning ranks, roles, and rules to each stratum, overseen by the supervisory elites. Those norms of propriety were deeply engrained in the cosmological orientation of the Christian west. Europeans perceived a "Great Chain of Being" that joined the heavens and the earth in a hierarchy of moral value. Created by and descending from God, kings and priests ruled over lower governors, who oversaw local gentry, who ordered the lives of laborers. Slaves came next, just above animals, plants, and inanimate objects. Each of these strata could be further subdivided. Jewelers, for instance, outranked shoemakers. Everyone was needed, and consequently everyone needed to stay in his place. The order of the cosmos depended on it, and so did the social harmony on a daily basis.[24]

In the New World slavery only raised higher the stakes for the maintenance of power. In South Carolina the questions and consequences of politeness were fundamental to the social order that served the desires of white society. Politeness in a very real way was crucial to the ability of white society to persist in South Carolina; in the 1720s and 1730s, after the devastation of the Yamassee War and the massive influx of forced labor, survival was not guaranteed. Fear wracked southern minds long after the Yamassee War and for years after each slave rebellion. The emergence of polite society within such a hazardous context should therefore be seen not only as something of an accomplishment but also as a necessity. Regardless of the morality of imposed inequality, deriving any level of comfort and pleasure out of the crucible of the lowcountry for even a few people while providing the means of sustenance—rice—for hundreds of thousands of others seems remarkable. Production depended on social order, which was built on the maintenance of social hierarchy. There was nothing inevitable about this; there were other ways to make money besides slave plantation agriculture and other ways to organize society through cooperation that would have spread the demands for and benefits of labor more equitably throughout southern society. The question of whether or not South Carolinians could have produced such prodigious wealth without slave labor while exporting such great quantities of foodstuffs as they did is probably unanswerable. It is a great moral tragedy—sin, to use religious language—that they did not try.

Perhaps this judgment holds them to an unfair standard, considering the ubiquity of the institution of slavery throughout time. Garden's was the world before the American and French Revolutions, Thomas Jefferson, Frederick Douglass, Abraham Lincoln, and Martin Luther King Jr. It was a globe, east and west, north and south, that had for millennia made extensive use of bound labor, and Garden's generation would not be the one to change that. If one could somehow protest to them, "Why did you do that?" they might answer from the eighteenth century, "Why would we not do that?" Having seen the riches pouring from the slave plantations in Barbados and the rest of the West Indies, and despite the volatility inherent in building society on the basis of slavery, South Carolinians shifted most of their economic assets into African slavery after the Yamassee War and then busied themselves with reproducing, innovating, and expanding the genteel cultural controls that would enable them to keep such a society from spinning out of control.

The connection between white order and black disorder, real and imagined, and between levels of white hierarchy led by polite society was not lost on a white Carolinian who submitted an article to the *Gazette* complaining about the pretensions of those who "find themselves in Circumstances a little more easy." Immediately "an Ambition seizes many of them . . . to become Gentlefolks," and the consequences were unfortunate. "Without Experience of Men or

Knowledge of Books, or even common Wit, the vain Fool thrusts himself into Conversation with People of the best Sense and the most polite." In doing so, he becomes obnoxious to the better sort, who view him as if he were a "Monkey that climbs a Tree, the higher he goes, the more he shews his Arse." More potently, the man is like a "Molatto," who is "seldom well belov'd either by the Whites or the Blacks. . . . As they are next to Negroes, and put just above 'em, they are terribly afraid of being thought Negroes, and therefore avoid as much as possible their Company or Commerce: and Whitefolks are as little fond of the Company of Molattoes." Hence, when a Carolinian who found fortune in the colony presumed to join polite society without the social graces that flowed from a natural gentility, he blurred lines of class as much as Carolinians of mixed race blurred the lines of race. He became, in the words of the author, a "Molatto Gentleman" and made himself obnoxious to society. The writer was quick to point out to his readers, "I am an ordinary Mechanick, and I pray I may always have the Grace to know myself and my Station." If he truly were merely "an ordinary Mechanick"—a skilled worker rather than a great merchant or planter—his writing showed how notions of politeness and racism had permeated the lower ranks of white society already by the mid-1730s.[25] Such newspaper articles did the work of public humiliation of anyone who transgressed the social boundaries inherent in the great chain of being.

The rise of polite society as a means of imposing social order in an unruly slave society is perhaps best illustrated by looking at the place of the church in southern culture, and there is no better example of this than the experience of Alexander Garden as he made his way into gentility. Garden probably became familiar with politeness during his formative years in Scotland. During the early eighteenth century, Scottish thinkers and educators strove to cultivate politeness among the general population. Good sense, liberality, civil discourse, and other sorts of acceptable attitudes and manners made possible tolerance and social harmony and, it was believed, were attainable by virtually anyone of any background. In Scotland politeness was for everyone. In South Carolina the wealthy came to see it as the basis of their ascendancy, and they emphasized their exclusivity as a way to keep everyone else in submission.[26]

The importance of politeness helps illuminate the story of the Reverend John Winteley and his expulsion from Christ Church Parish. Indeed it was Garden who made a place for the Church of England in this southern polite culture, much to Winteley's loss. Winteley set about criticizing the wealthy members of Christ Church for their politeness and slaveholding habits. These members' responses to his censure demonstrate the ways that elite merchants and planters drew boundaries for their minister's pastoral care in such a way as to protect polite prerogatives. Garden's role in ensuring Winteley's ejection from his parish when he attempted to exceed those boundaries reveals how Garden attained polite status, and his subsequent participation in polite activities suggests practical purposes for why merchants and planters allowed him into their ranks.

The Reverend John Winteley arrived in South Carolina in March 1727 and settled in Christ Church Parish just outside Charles Town. He quickly took upon himself the task of correcting what he deemed to be the unseemly political and moral behavior of his polite parishioners, although the vestry claimed that he failed because he neglected to correct his own misconduct. Winteley stopped officiating in the church on January 21, 1728, and on October 1 the vestry discharged him, complaining in a letter to the SPG that Winteley "no sooner came amongst us than he begun to break out in Several Sorts of Wild and immoral behaviour; and this in so unreserved and open a manner that it quickly became known to all the Inhabitants of this Parish." His misbehavior included "Drunkenness and Lewdness towards Women" that caused scandal so damaging to the church that some parishioners left for the Presbyterian church that was "now about to Erect a Second large Meeting House."[27] However, it appears that it was Winteley's willingness to insert himself into colonial politics that got him into trouble with his vestry and with Garden, all of whose political adeptness proved superior to that of the missionary.

Winteley immediately defended himself to the SPG against the charges of immorality and drunkenness, and he attributed his dismissal to his outspokenness regarding political issues. "Immediately after my Arrival here," wrote the reverend, "there was a general unhappy Bandying into Parties and factions and Seditious Associations against the Government all over the Province, resolving to pay no Taxes, and in short to stand by one another in hindring the whole course of Law and Justice in which my Parishioners were none of the backwardest!" He considered it his "bounden Duty" in all of his "discourses both publick in the Pulpit and private" to "make them sensible of the Evil they were running into." Plunging into the political disputes of his new parishioners proved a fatal mistake. Some in his congregation took offense and, led by the vestryman Capt. Thomas Boone, who had "three brothers in law all of a Kidney, who are always in the Vestry, and therefore can always make a majority there," had him dismissed from the pulpit.[28]

According to Winteley, the vestry moved quickly, decisively, and collectively against their new minister. They informed him during a vestry meeting of their plans to dismiss him and "never more Draw for any Salary for me; (without which, being not elected I could receive none)." Winteley listened to their "venting a deal of malice, and Railing abundantly in general Terms" and left. The vestryman George Logan yelled after him, "Go your way for a whoremonger and a Drunkard as you are." Infuriated, Winteley confirmed Logan's wording with the church register, Robert Giles, and the two went to Charles Town and hired a lawyer to sue Logan. Giles, "whether Tamperd with by the Party, or obliged by his own Circumstances," left soon after for England, and the suit eventually was dropped because of lack of evidence, with the vestry "declaring they would swear that they did not hear Mr Logan say any such words."[29] According to the vestry, Logan "justifie[d] himself by charging Winteley with drunkenness and debauchery." Four women signed affidavits against Winteley for debauchery, with Winteley claiming that they were women of "low life and fame," and Thomas Boone, John Guerard (Alexander Garden's brother-in-law) and Alex Peronneau signed affidavits of his drunkenness.[30]

Winteley was slow to appreciate the lengths to which his opponents were willing to go. He attempted to carry out his ministerial duties, figuring that he could transfer parishes and be rid of the conflict. He preached at Christ Church the next Sunday after the clash with the vestry, "for the Vestry Men had for a long time absented themselves, some totally, and the rest generally." Having failed to intimidate Winteley, the vestry had "naild up barrd and fastend" the church doors and windows by that Sunday. Winteley moved the service to the vestry house. "By this time," Winteley wrote, "I found that this Malicious Combination to Distress and Ruin was more extensive and that more were concernd in it than I imagind." He "was credibly informed" that Alexander Garden had written a letter to the vestry approving their conduct. If they would continue their prosecution, Garden would secure a new missionary. Worse, there had been drawn up—Winteley had "reason to believe by Garden"—a "Representation," "which the Vestry Men . . . produced at a Rendezvous after a Horse Race . . . in a Public House, when most there were warm with Liquor, and some very drunk and in a most irregular and unfair manner persuaded and engagd all they could promiscuously, Dissenters, Youths under Age, all sorts of sizes, to sign it." When other parishioners signed their own "Petition or Remonstrance to the Governour and Church Commissioners" attesting to Winteley's "unblameable Life and Conversation" and the misconduct of the vestry, requesting intervention by the church commissioners, the governor refused, saying that "he believd they woud not meedle with this."

That Garden "was at the bottom of this combination" and "Spirited the Party in all their violent proceedings" was confirmed to Winteley on November 17. Upon arriving at the church, Winteley found the vestry and wardens already assembled. He remarked that he "was glad to see them again so near the Church, and hopd that we shoud now all go into it friends." Unsurprisingly they kept the doors locked. Soon thereafter Garden appeared with one of the vestrymen. Winteley expressed his appreciation for his mediation and reminded Garden of the blessings for peacemakers promised in the scriptures, to which Garden replied that he had not "come here to be taught any Duty by you." When Winteley produced his license from the bishop of London and from the SPG attesting to his authority over the parish—Garden had not yet been appointed commissary—Garden retorted, "'Hold your Prating, Ill not talk with you,' and so proceeded in the midst of Vestry Men and Church Wardens to the Church Door." While a vestryman held Winteley back, Garden took the minister's place in the assembly. After conducting the service, Garden and the vestry left and Winteley held his own service. An hour later they returned and commanded him to leave. When Winteley refused, Garden and the vestry retired to a "Dinner at one of the Vestry-men's house, where a great Feast was purposely prepard for the Occasion." Why "purposely"? By inviting Garden rather than their regular minister to the dinner, the vestry used a tool of politeness to elevate Garden above Winteley.

According to Winteley, Garden also used his political connections in Charles Town to enforce the will of the Christ Church vestry. Winteley met Garden in the public treasurer's office in town a few days after their tense meeting in Winteley's parish. They exchanged sharp words, with Garden threatening Winteley and Winteley accusing Garden of "Impudence and insolence," after which Garden "went away with Countenance falln, pale and trembling (as if possessd) with Rage, malice, and Revenge." While still in town, Winteley received a letter "signed by Two justices of Peace in the Town, Familiars of Mr Garden," informing him that Garden and some of the "chief Inhabitants of Christ Church Parish" had registered a complaint. Winteley needed to meet with the justices and the vestry and register his defense. Upon doing so he found himself confronted with a deposition alleging that on November 17 he had "disturbd the Congregation and Divine Service" at Christ Church. He asked the vestry if they would be willing to swear to the truth of the accusation, and after they said they would, he turned to the justices and exclaimed that "if those Gentlemen would Swear white was Black, and Black White," Winteley would have no business with them. He immediately appealed to the governor in Charles Town, who wrote a letter to the justices on his behalf, and Winteley "never heard more of the Affair."[31] Winteley's tenure, however, was over in Christ Church and in the colony.

Winteley's story rings true on several accounts and in ways that expose the political nature of the opposition to his tenure. He provided numerous names and other details and suggested to the SPG that they verify his story with the former church register, Robert Giles, "an Eye and Ear witness of most of the Matters of Fact," who had moved to England after being appointed a schoolmaster by the society.[32] The political upheaval against which he spoke in 1727 was no doubt the dispute over paper money that rocked the colony in the late 1720s. Parliament had withdrawn the bounty on naval stores in 1724, which not only made that trade less profitable but also resulted in a popular movement agitating for an increase in the supply of paper money. The inhabitants of Christ Church and northern parishes demanded legislative relief by obstructing the collection of taxes and personal debts. The new governor of the colony, Arthur

Middleton, already tainted by charges of simony, had his main political opponent arrested and was then reduced to calling out the militia to quell the ensuing riot. The militia promptly allied with the mob. The issue was soon eclipsed by rumors of an Indian war that required a concerted response.[33] In light of this episode, the unpopularity of Winteley's reproof of his parishioners' political disobedience can be better understood. Already locked in combat that required popular action against the governor, the vestry would brook no challenge to its authority, especially from their own minister. Thomas Boone, the leader of the anti-Winteley campaign, who though not a vestryman signed letters from the vestry to the bishop of London, too helped lead the political campaign in favor of paper currency.[34] This explains why the governor would intercede on Winteley's behalf after the parish had already discarded their minister. The governor did represent ultimate authority in the colony, and in light of the other controversies, he knew that the vestry would feel no need to pick another fight over a clergyman who had already been dismissed.

What of Alexander Garden? According to Winteley, Garden did not like Winteley. His willingness to confront his parishioners' politics was merely one manifestation of an attitude of independence that also irritated Garden. "I have indeed sometimes at our meetings refusd to join with him in his rash, peevish, and arbitrary Measures of condemning without Hearing, and hanging without Trial," Winteley wrote to the SPG, "and because I am not merely his Creature, he has resolvd to ruin me, at least, to drive me out of the Country."[35] Curiously, Garden also berated Winteley for "Vanity of Carriage" and "prodigality."[36] Was Winteley not only insubordinate but also exhibiting pretensions incommensurate with his social station?

Garden's opposition appears to have been motivated by personal animosity and the commissary's attachment to colonial vestries, not by any immoral conduct on Winteley's part. Revealingly, Garden took extreme action against Winteley within Christ Church Parish and in the presence of the vestry. In town, however, Garden seems to have held his fire, frustrated but hesitant to take action in public. At the close of his career as commissary, Garden would remember taking legal action against four clergymen, including Winteley, who he said chose to resign rather than stand trial, but no record of this exists, and one would think that Winteley would have mentioned this in his letters.[37] Likely Garden did not take legal action against him in Charles Town. In fact, in a letter to the bishop dated November 1729, written on the heels of the hottest confrontation with Winteley, Garden reported to the SPG that "Mr. Winteley is now referred to officials in the Parish of St. Bartholomew, a Parish on the outmost Confines of the Settlement, and which was utterly demolished in the Indian War," but he was being resettled "by a few stragling Families of Church People."[38]

Having just been made commissary that year, Garden would have had the authority to suspend Winteley altogether but chose not to do so. Earlier Garden had accused Winteley of "gross immoralities," of appearing often "in Taverns, and sometimes in the open Streets, much disguised in Liquor," of lewd behavior toward women, and "obscenity in Conversation," behavior that one would think merited more than a censure and reassignment.[39] If Garden's goal were to banish the unruly minister, as it appears, perhaps this was because the governor and the country mobs who opposed Winteley demanded, among other things, the printing of paper money, a policy unpopular with nearly all of Charles Town's merchants.[40] This would explain Garden's simultaneous country explosion and urban reticence. Sending Winteley to a frontier parish would allow Garden to gratify all of his allies, urban and rural, by satisfying the Christ Church vestry without alienating his merchant friends in St. Philips who might have perceived Winteley to be a martyr.[41]

Winteley's successor at Christ Church hardly fared better. John Fulton arrived there in 1730, and the vestry quickly sent to the SPG a letter of approval and gratitude for their having sent him. Later that year Fulton spoke excitedly of his new mission, claiming that his ministry was acceptable even to some of the dissenters in the parish.[42] However, the beginnings of another conflict between minister and vestry were evident by April 1733. Like Winteley before him, Fulton had much to say about issues that the vestry and Garden considered none of Fulton's business, particularly with regard to the way southern elites, including Garden, wielded their power over subordinates. Consequently, Fulton faced the same charges of immorality that were used against his predecessor.

Garden and the vestry accused Fulton of drunkenness, but it appears that he may have demonstrated a similar attitude of independence that had annoyed the vestry in their dealings with Winteley. In a letter to the SPG describing a meeting of the Carolina clergy, Garden reported that Fulton had been warned twice about his drinking habits and that Fulton, "therefore apprehending a publick Admonition before all his Brethren, (as indeed I intended)," refused to come to the meeting.[43] A year later the vestry informed the SPG that Garden had suspended Fulton for two years. Not wanting the SPG to think that the parish was full of "captious People," they assured the society that they simply could not abide "so bad a man."[44] Fulton appealed to the SPG and to the bishop of London. He first justified his drinking by claiming that his doctor had told him his "days would be shortened if [he] did not drink somewhat stronger Licquor in this hot climate."[45] He then began a lengthy description of his treatment at the hands of the vestry. An older couple lived with Fulton and did his cooking. Thomas Boone, a wealthy parishioner who had helped expel Winteley, persuaded this couple to move in with him, leaving Fulton without a cook. Boone also had failed to deliver cows purchased by Fulton from Boone's mother before she died. A Mr. Fowler had "not used me well" regarding the sale of a horse, complained Fulton, and the minister got into a tangle with Thomas Barton, who had served in the past as a vestryman, sheriff, and assemblyman, over the sale of a horse. In addition the treasurer's wife berated Fulton for finding fault with her daughter's cooking.[46]

Do these minor incidents depict a missionary whose personality simply did not mesh with those of the vestry? Perhaps these were merely symptoms of a character that few could have tolerated. Other behaviors, however, cannot be so easily dismissed, for it appears that Fulton challenged some of the habits of his polite parishioners and his commissary. He described how Fowler was upset because Fulton "refused his wife for a surety for a child that I baptized tho she never received the Sacrament," a sign that the minister fulfilled his spiritual duties with seriousness and scrupulosity. The vestry criticized Fulton for making his slaves attend church and "for spending so much time in instructing them at home." George Haddrel, brother-in-law of Thomas Boone, blamed Fulton when he lost a seat in the assembly. In addition Fulton apparently had taken too seriously his pastoral duty to improve piety among his parishioners by refusing to wink at their ill behavior: "I was wearied out with taking notice of their horrible cursing and swearing drinking and gaming for the Barbarous usage of their Negroes, some for whipping them to Death Some for Branding in Sundry places with hot irons for cutting off their ears and scarifying their faces." Getting help from Garden was impossible, for Fulton had already made him upset. Fulton was in attendance when Garden publicly chided Winteley for reading responses to prayers too loudly during a church service. "When some of the Congregation took notice of [Garden's public reprimand] to [Fulton, he] said that it had been more proper when divine service was over." When Garden found out about Fulton's questioning of his conduct, he told Fulton that he "would remember me, and that my continuance should not be long here."[47] By challenging the trademark behaviors of southern gentility, Fulton, like Winteley before him, had broken the two cardinal rules for successful pastoring in South Carolina: accommodate the behaviors and preferences of the vestry; and yield to the leadership of Alexander Garden. By meddling in affairs outside the realm of his duties, he incurred their wrath and doomed his tenure.

The final blow to Fulton's ministry illustrated the cooperation between commissary and vestry as they punished his disobedience of South Carolina's informal social laws. According to Fulton, Boone swore that Fulton would last no longer in the parish than had Winteley and Benjamin Pownall, a predecessor in the pulpit who appears to have been ejected from the parish for equally dubious reasons—he lasted less than a year. Boone persuaded Thomas Barton and several other men to pay Fulton a visit after "a cockfight at 10 at night."[48] When Fulton answered the door, the men entered his residence and "sat up all night, broke 2 flask bottles and hauling those that were not able to ride into my best Beds, which they abused shamefully." They then "strove after the most malicious manner to irritate and provoke Mr Commissary against" Fulton. The commissary, already looking for a chance to punish Fulton's insubordination, complied. When Garden failed to convince people to swear that they saw Fulton drink, he convened a "Court of Summons," convicted him, and made him "pay 70 pounds upon pain of Excommunication."[49]

According to Garden's description, this "court" took place in Christ Church. Garden hoped that "so many Admonitions from myself, his other Bretheren, his own Vestry and Parishioners" would procure a confession from Fulton. The official record kept by Garden of the trial read as follows: "You, the said John Fulton, did resort to & frequent divers Taverns and punch Houses several hours together, and at very unseasonable times. And that you, the said John Fulton, during the said months was much addicted and given to excessive and hard drinking, and have been very much fuddled and drunk within the Town or Village of Charles Town and the Parish of Christ Church . . . and at the Time of your performing divine Service in the said Parish Church; and thereof, there was and is a publick Voice, Fame, and Report in the said Town and Parish." According to Garden, Fulton refused to confess and grew "more open and harden'd in it," so that he deserved a suspension that should "justify the Parish to" the bishop of London and the society "for refusing ever to employ him any more." When the court met again at Garden's St. Philip's Church in Charles Town to impose the sentence against Fulton, he did not appear, and "Contumacy" was added to his crimes. Apparently this convinced Fulton to appear and plead guilty. He was sentenced to suspension for two years, "publicly denounced on the front of the church," and charged ten pounds "under pain of excommunication."[50] It was not Fulton's drinking that was the problem; it was his willingness to challenge the vestry and Garden. Like Winteley, Fulton left no record of having owned any property.

Fulton's successor in the pulpit, Lawrence O'Neill, lasted less than a year, having "made a Party among the small number who adhered to the Church, and who were for having him for their minister or none, tho a man of very little Worth as has appeared since by his Behavior at Charles Town." At least so said John Fullerton, who succeeded O'Neill and was well received by the church before succumbing to that other nemesis of missionaries: disease.[51] Christ Church would not have another successful minister until 1740, when Levi Durand took over and learned how to accommodate the wishes of his congregation.

Other clergymen as well failed to secure permanent tenure because of their unwillingness to adapt to the demands of their vestry and commissary. From the beginning of Brian Hunt's tenure, Hunt exhibited religious zeal and optimism regarding the spiritual state of St. John's Berkeley Parish, which he described as "eminently a Sober and Religious Parish." He assured the SPG that he would gladly comply with their "orders for instructing my Negroes in Christianity."[52] He requested three hundred pamphlets "against Schism" and other tracts. However, within a couple of years financial concerns crept into his letters. He worried about a debt he owed a "print seller."[53] His benefice as a missionary included three slaves, but they were "useless," and he resisted being "as cruel as some are here to slaves, from whose wounds they extract their estates." He began requesting more monetary support from London, at one point hoping that although the secretary of the society had chosen celibacy, he still could empathize with "those of your weak brethren who by marrying too young and too precipitously have cast themselves at the feet of the wiser and more happy part of men and that tho you are not a father, or husband, you have tender regards for every state of humanity that's honorable tho poor of necessity."[54] All of this suggests that marrying the Cawood/Wright couple, ironically "too young and too precipitously," was merely the final blow to his unhappy relationship with South Carolina's elites, who thought of him as a sanctimonious thorn in their carnal sides.

Thomas Thompson, frustrated after ten years of putting up with the parsimonious vestry of St. Bartholomew's Parish, the frontier parish recently reconstituted after the Yamassee War and that refused to elect him "lest he should grow to sawcy and negligent," asked to be removed to another parish. He was quick to point out that he was not seeking riches but rather a parish that would respond to his teaching. In St. Bartholomew's the people were afflicted with an "excessive love and eager pursuit of the things of this world, as makes men . . . indifferent about all the means of religious Instruction." He was well aware that a clergyman ran great risk "when he throws himself out of business and parts with the means of subsistence," but he was growing so desperate that "death itself . . . is more eligible than a dishonourable useless and most uneasy life."[55] By 1744 he had transferred to the vacant pulpit in St. George's. He had already, however, met with "unfriendly treatment and angrey distant behavior" from Garden. The commissary had been upset with a sermon that Thompson preached at St. Philip's, understanding it to have been directed against Garden's authority to discipline clergy. When Thompson offered to make up for the misunderstanding by reading prayers at St. Philip's, Garden "answered [him] in a passion" that Thompson would never preach again in his church. Garden then accused him of delusional visions and fornication. Garden worked against Thompson's transfer to St. George's Dorchester Parish by telling "Coll Blake the leading man of the Parish that though he would not advise the people what to do, yet he thought they might refuse to accept me." Later, Garden seemed to get into a "beter humour," and Thompson moved to St. George's Dorchester.[56]

Thompson's predecessor had lasted fewer years at St. Bartholomew's. The Reverend Charles Boschi arrived in the parish in 1745 after spending most of his money on lodging in Charles Town while waiting—upon Garden's advice—for the vestry to retrieve him. His parishioners persuaded him to purchase a family of slaves, he "not knowing full well the ways and management of country affair," which put him in severe debt that he estimated would take two to three years to repay.[57] Soon he came into conflict for teaching and baptizing slaves and for "exclaim[ing] too much against the Prophaness and iniquities that reign in the Parish."[58] When he attempted to procure an election, he was told that the vestry preferred to withhold the permanent salary from their clergyman so that "he will be very cautious to not guide them in so rigorous a manner as he is bound in duty to exclaim against iniquity."[59] He did make at least one friend in the gentry, a Colonel Hyrne, who according to Boschi said that the minister had brought the congregation "to a better modesty and regulation in the time of divine service. It seems the best people used there to go throng and fro' continually out of the chapel, and made punch in time of sermon or Prayer, and they used to bring water in the chapel to give drink to the people in the time of worship; upon this I exclaimed against this great Indecency and the most part of the congregation was displeased about it." Virtually every couple who approached him seeking marriage was already expecting a child. Sometimes in hot weather he needed to provide a chair for a pregnant bride so that she would not faint. When he wondered to "some of the Parishioners if this was the fashion of this country to lye with the woman before they are married, some made a jest, and some other made no answer and was displeased at my Interogation."[60] With his family impoverished, with no other means of making a living, and with a determination to hold to his religious principles or leave, Boschi made plans to leave the colony for Honduras, but he died before he could take ship.

All of these ministers—John Winteley, John Fulton, Brian Hunt, Thomas Thompson, and Charles Boschi—and likely other ministers failed because their commitments to Christian ethics with regard to personal morality, social responsibility, and the humane treatment of slaves ran against the grain of South Carolina's polite society. Rather than support his colleagues, Garden abandoned them to the wiles of their vestries and chose instead to ingratiate himself with the polite laity. By doing so he proved himself a reliable ally of the vestries and the slave system they managed. His social adeptness not only ensured his own survival as a lowcountry minister but also aligned the Church of England in South Carolina to the reigning social orthodoxies in that colony.

In his effort to protect himself and the Church of England in South Carolina, Garden did more than merely intervene on behalf of vestries as they drove contentious clergy out of the pulpit. Garden joined the ranks of the wealthy elite. The practicality of his union with Martha Guerard and her substantial dowry and social connections has been noted. Garden also became financially enmeshed in the Carolinian economy as a property owner and as a creditor and debtor, two key indicators of the attainment of wealth and social trust. Shortly before he married Martha, Alexander purchased a lot in Dorchester, which they owned until his death.[61] In 1731 the Gardens sold the 842 acres of land in Colleton County that Martha had brought to their marriage.[62] In the early 1740s they purchased a barony, 12,000 acres, in Granville County near Georgia.[63] In St. James Goose Creek Parish, extant evidence suggests that only 41 percent of landowners owned more than 1,000 acres and only 14 percent owned more than 3,000 acres. These figures excluded, by definition, slaves and white laborers.[64] Garden owned more land than did a large majority of his fellow colonists.

Garden also gained the trust of his wealthy peers. When Thomas Osborne, "bookseller in London," needed to collect money from two merchants in South Carolina, he granted power of attorney to Garden. Thomas Rose and Nicholas Burnham borrowed £2,155 from Garden.[65] In 1746 Daniel Laroche borrowed £600 from the Gardens, and in 1747 Daniel Laroche, Andrew Delavillette, and David Montaigut, "merchants of Georgetown," borrowed £1,500.[66] There were at least four instances when power of attorney was granted to Garden; eight instances of loans involving Garden, most of the money owed to Garden; and transactions involving the purchase or sale of eight different pieces of urban or rural property.[67]

Garden's estate as described in his will testified to his material success. When he died, he left his two daughters and two sons personal possessions that were appraised at over £2,500, which included "Negroes, four namely Tom, Lucy and her two children"; 300 pounds cash; "bonds and Notes for Value 3,035" pounds; two town lots; and his barony. Excluding his real property, Garden's estate placed in the top one-third of wealthy South Carolina estates in the period 1756–65, a phenomenal statistic for a man who needed to spend considerable time pastoring his own large congregation and overseeing a host of congregations that grew from eleven in 1725 to fifteen in 1749.[68]

The lives of other successful ministers confirm this link between wealth, politeness, and long-term maintenance of a pulpit, as well as the necessity of getting along with Garden. Because they stayed out of the illumination of recorded scandals, less can be told of their tenures. Enough remains, however, to demonstrate their ability to adapt to colonial exigencies.

William Guy served St. Helena's Parish from 1713 to 1717 and then moved to St. Andrew's Parish adjacent to Charles Town. He survived by accommodating himself to South Carolina's society and economy and allying with, or acquiescing to, Commissary Garden. Not long after arriving in St. Andrew's he described his new parishioners' "Sentiment in matters of Religion [as] very unsettled, and generally Latitudinarian." Apparently this did not bother him too much, for he stayed until 1751 without controversy or scandal.[69] By 1740 he described his parishioners as "a mighty well behavd People, constant in their attendance on the Publick Worship of God and very kind and affectionate to me their minister."[70] He maintained a positive working relationship with Alexander Garden, as evidenced by their cooperation in several projects. In the 1730s he and Garden assumed power of attorney for the disposition of the large estate of the Reverend Richard Ludlam of St. James Goose Creek Parish, as well as other legal business on behalf of the society.[71] Brian Hunt complained that Guy and Garden both "stirr'd up" the controversy surrounding the Cawood marriage and, together with Francis Vernod, "especially insulted [Hunt] cruelly publickly and inhumanly."[72] In a revealing observation, Hunt noted that Guy manifested a "weakness in being overruled by Mr Garden," and one suspects the same of Vernod.[73] The three ministers served as commissioners of the Free School in Charles Town.[74] Guy and fellow minister Thomas Hasell assisted Garden in a venture into slave education in the 1740s.[75] Guy's property in the province was considerable. His land grants and purchases included one thousand acres in Granville County, fifteen hundred acres in Berkeley County, and four pieces of town property, including his house.[76]

Francis Vernod and Thomas Hasell, Guy's and Garden's associates, also enjoyed long tenures in the province. Vernod occupied the pulpit of St. George's Dorchester Parish from 1723 to 1736. His property included 1,231.5 acres of land.[77] Thomas Hasell served as rector of St. Thomas and St. Denis Parish from 1709 to 1744. His will distributed the plantations Pompion Hill, Mount Pleasant, and Bury; three other tracts of land; and two town lots, in addition to land owned, apparently, by his wife.[78] He married Elizabeth Ashby, daughter of John Ashby Jr., the brother-in-law of Hunt's antagonist Thomas Brough-ton and the father-in-law of the "wealthiest merchant and private banker" of South Carolina, the famous vestryman, local official, and assemblyman Gabriel Manigault.[79] Mary Hasell, the daughter of Thomas and Elizabeth, married the notable Christopher Gadsden, longtime assemblyman and later patriot hero of the American Revolution.[80] Mary's sister Elizabeth married William Gibbes, a prominent vestryman and politician who would lend South Carolina £250,000 for the revolutionary cause.[81] Two other Hasell daughters married assembly-men.[82]

Brian Hunt's successor, Daniel Dwight, served the parish from 1729 until his death in 1748.[83] Although he "Labourd by all the means" he knew to "persuade the People to a more generall and more frequent attendance upon the Sacrament of the Lords Supper," indicating that he pursued some religious goals, the Carolinian economy clearly occupied a considerable portion of his time. His land interests included 100 acres in Berkeley County and 2,472 acres in Craven County.[84] He was, it should be recalled, the one who sold a barony to Alexander Garden. "Furthermore," explained the historian Annette Laing, "it could not have hurt that he formed an alliance with the most powerful layman in his parish, when, in 1731, he married Christiana Broughton, the daughter of Hunt's nemesis Thomas Broughton, who was by then the colony's governor."[85]

Meanwhile in 1742 Levi Durand secured in Christ Church Parish what John Winteley and John Fulton had failed to obtain before him: election—unanimously, no less—as rector. In fact the parish had not hired a permanent minister since they booted Fulton in 1734. Like Winteley and Fulton before him, Durand did not appreciate all of the behaviors of his parishioners, but by marrying well in terms of social respectability and by learning to choose his words carefully, he lasted in a parish where others had met disappointment. In 1741 he praised the piety of his female parishioners but noted that "the leading men have depraved notions of the Christian Religion occasiond by their Reading Books written by Modern Infidels imported by the Merchants of this place."[86] In a 1747 letter to the society he vented his frustration in a scathing denunciation of his parishioners' behavior:

> A contented mind is the greatest Blessing a man can enjoy in this world, but this I shall never possess, while I live in this Province, Where Infidelity, Prophaness, heresy, Blasphemy, and the most Offensive Breaches of Common Morality have scarce ever appeared with more Insolence, and tho for these things the Lord does yearly visit, sending Pestilential Diseases amongst Men and Beast, which yearly Sweep away Numbers of Both, yet some Regard these things but as tho nothing were the Matter, Sad Omen! We eat, We Drink, we Play and shall continue to do so till everlasting Flames surprise us; I may well say with the Royal Psalmist woe is me that I'm constrained to dwell with sech[?] and shall endeavour to content myself with that Province God has allotted me in one of the dark corners of the World, even tho amidst a perverse and crooked Generation.[87]

That Durand resigned himself to "contentment" with his allegedly perverse and crooked neighbors suggests why he survived in Christ Church, where Winteley and Fulton failed.

Durand expressed disgust at the behavior in his parish, as had the other two ministers, and yet he survived until 1751, most likely because he learned to keep his opinions to himself and adapt to the realities of Carolinian life. In 1744 Durand mentioned in a letter to the SPG that he had preached "against the Presbyterians," of whom he had several in his audience. When "two of the principal members amongst them" got up and left, Durand took the cue. He would "intend for the future to explain only the fundamental principles of Christianity and inculcate moral Duties as resulting from those principles, and let the Fanaticks alone, for they are numerous Body in this Province."[88] Until 1751, therefore, Durand preached on more acceptable lessons. That he married Susannah Boone also indicates another moderating influence. Susannah's father was the wealthy Thomas Boone, the longtime vestryman and local official who led the charge against Winteley and Fulton. In 1752, two years after his father-in-law died, Durand had had enough. After a blowup with his vestry, Durand pleaded for a transfer to a more pious parish. This was not approved until 1760, when he took up the parish of St. John's Berkeley Parish, Brian Hunt's old parish, where he served for five years until his death in 1765.

In the meantime Durand left the Christ Church Parish and presumably tended to his more earthly interests. His will mentioned two lots with houses in Charles Town that would have been investments, since Durand lived in the glebe houses of Christ Church Parish and St. John's Berkeley Parish, and a financial investment in London.[89] Records also indicated several land deals involving properties that his wife likely brought to their marriage. While the exact nature of his estate remains unclear, certainly it was sufficient to furnish him material comfort.

These ministers avoided breaking the two inviolable rules for success as a Carolina clergyman. First, there is strong evidence that at least some were close friends and associates of Alexander Garden, and there are no indications that those who left no record of their relationship with the commissary did anything to upset him. Second, most left no record of dissatisfaction with the polite—and impolite—behaviors of their parishioners, and the one who did, Levi Durand, learned to keep his opinions to himself.

Furthermore all of the successful ministers maintained substantial interests in the Carolina economy. This would seem to violate the principle expressed by numerous wealthy Carolinians that a clergyman's financial independence tended to make him too bold in the pulpit. Simply put, they were wrong. When ministers engaged in land speculation and the business of personal credit and married into wealthy Carolinian families, their parishioners became business partners and family members. Had they any qualms about polite society—and their engagement in the material pursuits of the colony indicates that they did not, Durand notwithstanding—to speak out against it would be to attack the social world into which they had become ingrained. Anglican ministers had little ecclesiastical power to discipline their parishioners, so any verbal carping would serve only to challenge the social authority of the vestry without accomplishing real change. In short, the only avenue to any sort of social power for an Anglican minister lay in joining polite society. Those who refused either became increasingly impoverished, as did Thomas Thompson, or were eliminated altogether, as Winteley, Fulton, Hunt, Thompson, and Boschi experienced.

Garden and his friends had figured out the sole avenue to success in Charles Town and beyond: ally oneself with the vestrymen and wardens, marry into their ranks, join their commercial pursuits, and wink at the dubious behaviors and ethical codes frowned upon by the church. One might wonder, however, why vestrymen and wardens cared. What real difference did it make to them if their ministers scolded them for their immorality? Unlike the Puritans and Pilgrims in New England or the Quakers and sectarians in Pennsylvania or even the Catholics in Maryland, all of whom founded their colonies in large part for the sake of religious piety and purity, South Carolina had been founded by and for planters and their merchant associates. Given their success in attaining earthly luxuries, historians have often assumed that church life meant little to southerners. In that case it may seem odd that these money-minded men cared if their ministers objected to pregnant brides. Given the exorbitant wealth gained through exploiting black labor—the system was working for the vestrymen quite nicely—why would they bother even to notice a minister who complained to a distant bishop about their abuse of people they considered mere chattel? Why would they welcome into their ranks a frail, relatively older Scottish divine with a rather infamous temper?

The realities of South Carolina in the eighteenth century suggest some answers. At that time church was not merely a place for consuming the spirituality offered up by the ministers and staff but also something to be done or enacted, as much a verb as a noun. In addition there were few other options for Sundays. Throughout the eighteenth century Charles Town, even with a population of six thousand in 1740, was the only town of note from North Carolina to the border of Florida.[90] Everywhere else white people congregated in the courthouses, the homes of the large planters, and the churches, and for most people, church was the only meeting place they regularly visited. The courthouse concerned legal and other official business, although monthly court days could involve convivial interactions as well. To gather at a planter's house required an invitation, except when people resorted to a large planter in order to hire labor from among his servants and slaves.

For white Carolinians, therefore, church buildings represented vital locations of large social gatherings in the rural South, which is to say throughout the South. If cultural historians and other theorists are to be believed when they say that social discourse produces and reproduces culture, that social conventions and perceptions emerge out of the daily and often mundane and largely unnoticed interactions of people in communication, then southern colonists did most of their culture making during the few hours before, during, and after church services on Sundays. Certainly the social interactions of neighbors or of a small farmer making a deal with a large planter modified and perpetuated cultural norms as well, but something special happened in the weekly moments when the many people who were dispersed across the countryside came together for church.[91]

When people gathered for services each Sunday, they re-created the social order and reinforced social norms. Pews in colonial America were rented out, and unlike in churches today, the favored and thus most expensive seats were located in the front and the public seats for those without fortune in the back. Slaves allowed to attend church stood in the back, sat in the balconies, or looked and listened through the open windows. The church filled from the rear, with the poorer people taking their places first, followed by the families of more means. Last, the wealthiest planters and their families, dressed in their latest English fashions, paraded their way to the front, with their boots thudding against the floor and the beautiful dresses of the women brushing across the pews. They would take their seats just before the minister began or perhaps a few minutes after if they wanted to display their independence more emphatically. After church the planters would leave first and the church would empty from the front. Outside, as the people milled about, exchanging news and gossip—the differences often being hard to distinguish—and perhaps making business deals and other arrangements, a planter might circulate within the crowd, bestowing upon families of his choosing invitations to a grand Sunday evening meal, perhaps accompanied by a dance.[92]

The idea here was that social hierarchy was performed every Sunday. Economic stratification took seats along with the parishioners. A bench left empty by an absentee planter only amplified social difference, especially in a crowded church; those down the social chain had to look over the empty benches, perhaps shifting weight from one foot to another if there were no public seats in the rear. Planters owned pews like they owned social power—they paid cash, and the deeds were recorded in official records kept by themselves, now as vestrymen and wardens, to ensure that not only did parishioners pay up but also that they did not violate the very public private property or the social prerogatives of the better sorts.

In the midst of all of this cultural discourse of action and invitation, one man stood above the crowd in a perch in the middle of the church and directly in front of the wealthy planters. His role privileged him with the right to command everyone's attention for one or two or three hours at a time. There he could preach about matters heavenly and earthly, eternal and temporal. On the pages of his favorite book lay lessons to be told about the wages of sin and the promises of righteousness, about how to love one's neighbor and punish the evildoer, about honest business dealing and family making. There were even a few things to be said about slaveholding. On the only day of the week when the far-flung community gathered as community, the minister held court on the topic of his choosing.

His influence and that of the church extended throughout the week in ways that Americans today forget. The minimal formal, organized schooling that took place often involved the church, in part because the teacher often was a missionary sent by the SPG. Daily and less urgent needs, such as road maintenance, legal suits, taxes, and other civil matters, might be managed by separate, secular offices, but in moments of deepest crisis, vulnerability, or joy, people turned to the church. Most practically, relief from the frequent bouts of disease and harsh weather was dispensed by church vestry and wardens. A family left homeless by a hurricane or a woman widowed or children orphaned by epidemic disease would appeal to the church for financial support. On the occasion of a particularly devastating calamity, when the colonial legislature consented to extraordinary expenditures, money usually flowed through these ecclesiastical conduits into the homes of the suffering. Meanwhile ministers performed marriages—and the stories of William Wye, Brian Hunt, and Alexander Garden demonstrated the social and economic ramifications of such unions and how they could be moments of particular contention—and funerals.

This explains why rural vestries cared so much about the messages delivered by their ministers on Sundays. The concerns that governed their interest in churches and ministers were amplified in an urban setting. Garden held the only Anglican town pulpit in the South, and this urban setting could have diminished the influence of his pulpit. As a site of public discourse, St. Philip's Church had to compete with the courthouse and the seats of colonial government. Additionally workers often congregated on the wharves and filled taverns. Crowds mingled on the streets and haggled in the marketplaces. The theater attracted audiences of some means, and various fraternal organizations advanced this or that policy or pleasure. These sites could have diluted the cultural saliency of St. Philip's Church and its minister.

Under the capable leadership of Alexander Garden, St. Philip's Church emerged from the 1730s with increased cultural power rather than less. The church wardens and vestrymen oversaw the poorhouse where the destitute lived and worked to pay off debts. When Charles Town merchants and country planters funded a school for slaves in the 1740s, the only such school in the South, it was organized and supervised by Alexander Garden and the vestry and wardens of St. Philip's Church.[93] By using his commissary's office to bolster rural vestry disciplinary action against contentious ministers, Garden had moved country parishes into alignment with polite order. By following the rules of politeness in town and working himself into polite society, he turned St. Philip's into a center of power comparable to the slave auction, the house of assembly, or the governor's chambers.

Garden also lent his church to forms of polite display and reenactments of social hierarchy. In December 1738 members of the town's Solomon's Lodge of Free Masons gathered to celebrate the Festival of St. John the Evangelist. They met at the home of one of the colony's most esteemed gentlemen and a church warden of St. Philip's Church, the "Hon. James Crockatt, Esq.," from whence they paraded "properly cloathed with the Ensigns of their Order, and Musick before them, to the House of the Provincial Grand Master James Graeme, Esq." From there they marched "in Procession to Church to attend divine Service" before moving on to "the House of Mr. Ch: Shepheard, where in the Court Room to a numerous Assembly of Ladies and Gentlemen the new elected Provincial Grand Master made a very eloquent Speech of the Usefulness of Societies, and the Benefit arising therefrom to Mankind." Notice the stated concern for the social utility of their society, a concern without which a claim to polite society was simply selfish ambition and presumption. They had "usher'd in" the day by "firing Guns at Sun-rise from several Ships in the Harbour, with all their Colours flying," and after the grand master's speech and "an elegant Dinner," they again relocated their claim to social authority, this time to the harbor, the port without which many of them could scarcely have prospered, by removing to Capt. Thomas White's ship, the *Hope*. Here "several loyal Healths were drunk, and at their coming on board and return on Shore, they were saluted by the Discharge of 39 guns, being the same Number observ'd in each of the different Salutes of this Day, so that in all there were about 250 guns fired. The Evening was concluded with a Ball and Entertainment for the Ladies, and the whole was performed with much Grandeur and Decorum."[94]

The massive gun firings, the parades of colors, the "Grandeur and Decorum," and the marching in procession speak of a public ritual meant to impress on social inferiors the power and sophistication of the elites. Those poor whom James Crockatt and the other church warden and vestrymen had "ordered . . . remouv'd from their/several/Lodgings to the Work House" likely saw those same men marching through the streets in all of their regalia and hierarchy.[95] But this was not simply entertainment; the church service was part and parcel of their ability to demonstrate and maintain their authority in the face of social instability and implied God's blessings on their earthly endeavors. Importantly, the elites incorporated the sacralizing power of the Church of England by, in their constructed hierarchy, marching through town, entering the church, and taking their rented seats—the best in the house.

There were other ways that St. Philip's Church, along with its country counterparts, reproduced and represented cultural power throughout South

Carolina. As the official church of the colony, St. Philip's received government money for salaries and physical maintenance. Anglican ministers prayed in the colonial legislatures, and Garden would have been most available. One of his prayers survives. It is nothing particularly remarkable: it asks in the name of Jesus that God would enable the governor and his council to exercise properly their authority, which meant to do things "to the terror of Evildoers, and to the praise of them that do well."[96] Evidently he approached this task with as much judicious reflection as he did his sermons, for nothing there prompted any protest among Anglicans or dissenters.

More important, his own pews were filled with the richest and most powerful men and women in the colony. His parishioners represented the key white culture makers of the colony. In a colony made rich by the production of crops, landowners stood to gain economic and social ascendancy. Unfortunately no study yet purports to correlate landownership with religious preference. However, merchants, though constituting a much smaller proportion of the population, also vied for power and wealth, and their relative wealth can be inferred by their duties paid on cargo. Identifying the religious adherence of slave traders can shed light on the wealth among various denominations, since slavery and the slave trade were arguably the most crucial components of the southern economy.[97] Charles Town was by far the most important slave port in North America, particularly before Georgia legalized slavery and the slave trade in 1750. By the time South Carolina turned to African slavery as the primary form of labor after the Yamassee War, Virginia's slave population had achieved a positive rate of natural increase. South Carolina's achieved a slight natural increase in the 1720s, but it experienced negative growth in the 1730s until at least the 1750s. South Carolina therefore began its rise to wealth at the exact moment that its slave population threatened to die out, and therefore the colony relied heavily on slave importation.[98]

Not just anyone could become an importer of slaves. Colonists needed money and connections across the Atlantic to make money in the slave trade. To break into the trade one needed immense amounts of cash to pay for cargoes of slaves and the backing of established, reputable traders who would vouch for the health of the slaves. Planters would travel up to one hundred miles to purchase slaves, and they did not want to be disappointed by slaves who were sick or otherwise unsatisfactory. Neither did the slave importer want unsatisfied buyers, for slaves who were difficult to sell still needed to be provided for and perhaps moved to another port for another attempt at sale. For those reasons slave traders most likely had become wealthy by other means and then invested that wealth in the extremely lucrative slave trade.[99] A study of slave traders therefore can provide a useful index by which to measure the relative economic standing of religious groups.

Anglicans clearly dominated the slave trade. W. Robert Higgins compiled a list of slave traders during the period 1735–75 that included the particular years in which traders participated in the trade, the number of cargoes they imported, and the duties they paid.[100] The probable religious preference of over half of the traders who were active during the period 1735–50 can be discerned by comparing Higgins's list to church records.[101] Nine of the fourteen colonists who paid the top ten duties—four were paid by partnerships—during the period 1735–50 could be identified as certainly or probably Anglican. One of the remaining was unidentifiable, and four were probably Congregationalists. Of the top twenty duties paid, 53 percent (sixteen of thirty) were most likely Anglican, 27 percent (eight) were unidentifiable, and 20 percent were Congregationalists. Of the entire number of colonists who paid duties during this period, 43 percent (forty-one of ninety-five) were likely Anglican, 48 percent were unidentifiable, and only 9 percent (nine) were Congregationalists. Because three of the Congregationalists appeared in the records as both individuals and as members of a partnership, a total of six different colonists, rather than nine, made up the Congregationalist presence in the slave importing business, and those were mostly toward the top of the list. In other words, aside from three very wealthy traders, Congregationalists did not participate heavily in the trade. No doubt some of the unidentifiable were Presbyterians for whom most church records no longer exist, but certainly some traders were from Anglican families but either did not go to church, did not register baptisms in the surviving Anglican records, or were not wealthy enough to crack the rank of vestry and thus did not appear in the vestry records.[102] However, because most of the unidentifiable traders appeared below the top twenty duties paid, the fact that some may have been dissenters does little damage to the argument that Anglicans outright dominated the colonial slave trade. If the ability to deal in slaves was any measure of colonists' wealth, Anglicans had the most.

Identifying religious preferences of slave owners is even more difficult, but some clues appeared in a letter from the minister of St. George's Dorchester Parish, Francis Vernod, to his superiors in London in 1725. Again, Anglicans figured prominently. Vernod listed for his superiors how many slaves were owned by each dissenting and Anglican family within his parish. As in the slave trade, Anglicans held an advantage in slave wealth. The fifty-two dissenter families owned 363 slaves, an average slaveholding of almost 7 slaves per family. The fifty-seven Anglican families owned 944 slaves, for an average of over 16 slaves per family. Eight of the ten largest slaveholders were Anglican, and the three largest Anglican slaveholders, with 94, 91, and 77 slaves respectively, owned more slaves than the two largest dissenting slaveholders, who, with 61 slaves each, owned 30 percent fewer slaves than did the top Anglican slaveholders.[103]

The immense profits that accompanied this economic leadership secured Anglican membership and leadership in polite society. Wealth, however, did not necessarily translate directly into politeness. In the old country in particular, gentility and politeness derived as much from inherited status and personal comportment as from the size of one's personal estate. But in a new society that lacked a hereditary aristocracy, outward appearance, land and slaves, generosity, and other personal behaviors and personalities were the only ways to elevate oneself socially, and wealth was essential to the securing of these attributes. While wealth did not guarantee entrance to polite society, it was a prerequisite, and Anglicans appear to have held the upper hand when it came to acquiring it. Alexander Garden affirmed and reinforced this link between religious affiliation and social and economic power by embodying both. The presence of a man who represented ecclesiastical power, economic wealth, and polite leadership enhanced the reputation, social standing, and social importance of the Church of England. His office had been given to him by a bishop at a moment of weakness in the church after about a decade of turmoil in St. Philip's Church and scandal, real or imagined, in its pulpit and those of several other parishes in the colony. The bishop's confidence proved well placed. Alexander Garden had made the most of the office in terms of social standing.

This achievement of cultural influence, amplified in the urban setting of St. Philip's, came at a cost. To attain this sort of stature Garden had to acquiesce to the whims and wants of his parishioners. Had he chosen a more prophetic path for his ministry and tried to enforce an emphasis on godliness rather than on great gain among his colleagues in the country, calling his listeners to account for their brutal exploitation of slave labor, their headlong pursuit of profit, or their neglect of the common good, he and the Church of England may have lost everything. Instead he aligned the Church of England, rural and urban, with the social order prescribed by polite society. The relationship between the church and polite society was symbiotic and dialectic, reinforcing and clarifying each other interdependently. It worked. Garden and his friends prospered, and everyone else in his racial minority got along in the presence of a discontent and unruly majority.

By the end of the 1730s Garden had become a friend, even a business partner of sorts, with his culture. Having become acquainted with its workings in the 1720s, by the end of that decade he had launched his own enterprise of personal ambition. By the end of the 1730s he and his cohort of polite ministers had molded what he could of this society, the church, into a shape that fit his ambitions and those of his fellow polite friends, now one and the same. Together they had created a social hierarchy with themselves nicely ensconced on top. This hierarchy still looked rather shaky at this point, but Garden and his friends were working hard to shore it up with all the tools of polite society they could muster, and as the colony prospered, more tools became available. Certainly this arrangement worked out to their financial and social benefit, but Garden's less polite ministerial associates paid a horrible cost.

It takes little imagination to suspect that John Winteley, John Fulton, Brian Hunt, and other unsuccessful ministers viewed Alexander Garden with bitterness. They made clear in their letters to the SPG and the bishop of London that they thought their commissary ruled like a despot. Rather than pursue what was good for his ministers and defend their right to speak out against the behaviors of their parishioners that ran against the grain of the moral teachings of the church, he chose instead to side with the vestrymen and other wealthy merchants and planters. If their testimonies are to be believed, he preferred to humiliate his ministerial colleagues in public displays of solidarity with his polite friends.

However, there is more to be noted than hurt feelings. Losing access to the only job for which they had been trained, in a small colony devoted to agricultural production and little else, meant for many of them financial calamity and material impoverishment. Garden reported to the society in 1735 that Fulton had "turn'd his hand to Rice planting" and given up hope of ministry, and then Fulton disappeared from the historical record. Starting a rice plantation required immense financial capital for the purchase of land and slaves. Likely Fulton got hired on as some sort of laborer, and a particularly humiliating form of it, given the close association between rice work and African slavery in the minds of his white friends. Meanwhile, Boschi, with his family impoverished, with no other means of making a living, and with a determination to hold to his religious principles or leave, made plans to leave the colony for Honduras, although he died before he could take ship. Winteley was unable to secure any other parish pulpit or other employment. In 1730 Fulton described Winteley as being "in great strait and necessities," and in 1734 he reported that Winteley was "now in eternity."[104]

Garden thus represented much more than a failed commissary or a traitor to his profession. To these men and their wives and children, Garden was poverty personified: he was morally deficient, and they were materially bankrupt because of his failure to defend their interests. Perhaps his polite friends appreciated his manipulation of his mission and his ministry on their behalf. Perhaps he accurately perceived the necessity to use the church to buttress social order in the face of its collapse. Perhaps he did white society a favor by working hard to prevent calamity at the hands of rebellious slaves or even discontent whites. Perhaps the pursuit of gain into which he threw himself was too universal to hold much to account. Or perhaps he failed to grasp opportunities to support his ministerial colleagues who approached their ministry with a critical eye. In this case, he not only failed them; he also failed a society that would plod on through the next century firm in its resolve to exploit African slave labor for the wealth that undergirded elites' polite privileges.

*Chapter 4*

# DALLIANCE

Beginning in 1739 Alexander Garden encountered something startlingly unique to his experience: a wave of evangelical revivals that broke across the British Isles and the North American eastern coast. Historians call it the Great Awakening and credit its transatlantic scope to the youthful energy of the Anglican minister George Whitefield, the "Grand Itinerant." Born in 1714, raised and educated in England, and ordained by the Church of England, Whitefield maintained a fondness for the British North American colonies and visited them seven times between 1738 and his death in 1770. During his first two visits, in 1738 and 1739–41, he met with rapturous approval from many Congregationalists, Presbyterians, Baptists, Moravians, Anglicans, and others. Crowds of ten thousand or more people gathered to hear him preach in some of the larger cities, an astounding number at a time when few of America's cities numbered over ten thousand in total population. Although a member of the Church of England all his life, he was ecumenical and egalitarian, willing to preach the same evangelical message in any church building—or in an open field, which was scandalous at the time—and to women, slaves, and Indians. The Great Awakening was an immensely important event in the history of the British Atlantic, and historians have been crediting and blaming it for fostering the American Revolution, imbuing evangelicalism in America with cultural power, instigating a paternalistic form of slavery, fracturing churches and denominations, and causing other social upheavals.[1]

Alexander Garden initially blessed Whitefield's ministry, but in time he came to label it "the fascinating Gibberish of the Young George Fox, alias Whitefield," Fox being the seventeenth-century founder of Quakerism, which Anglicans despised as rebellious and delusional heresy.[2] Garden became Whitefield's most ardent opponent and published critiques in Charles Town and Boston, but not because he found the revivals radically different theologically. The Great Awakening appeared unique to Garden because of its power, not because of its evangelical nature. Garden, like most others who would come to reject the Great Awakening, shared much with evangelicalism and initially viewed the revivals with some interest. Plenty of his neighbors maintained sympathies with evangelicalism, and he had seen religious excitement before in numerous forms,

South Carolina having been a fertile field for religious diversity and intensity since its founding. He saw nothing in essential evangelical doctrine that needed to be rejected, at least not actively: not the preaching of heart religion; not the active use of scripture as the recorded word of God; not the centrality of the doctrine of justification by faith in the crucified and resurrected Jesus Christ; not the expectation that Christians live pious and useful lives; and not the need to be converted away from pandering to the lusts of the flesh and toward life according to the spirit of God.

The latter, the conversion of a soul to the ways of God, can easily be misunderstood as strictly an evangelical sort of life event. Almost all Protestants believed in the need for transformation from worldliness to godliness, from a mind-set focused on the pursuit of carnal pleasures to one intent on the attainment of spiritual truth and eternal life. There has never been a lasting consensus, though, on exactly what that transformation should look like. A crucial difference between an evangelical "New Birth," today termed being "born again," and a nonevangelical conversion process inhered in those very terms: for evangelicals, salvation from spiritual deadness and eternal damnation occurred in a particular moment that the believer would remember for the rest of his or her life, as datable and memorable as one's physical birthday. For nonevangelicals, conversion and salvation emerged through a lifelong process stretching from the moment of baptism as a child all the way through to one's final breath. Evangelicals were saved in a moment and then spent their lifetimes growing in the ways of Christ, while nonevangelicals spent their lifetimes growing in the ways of Christ as the means for their ultimate salvation. Evangelical ministers preached the New Birth persistently and with great hope, sermon after sermon, in hopes that persons would respond and be saved, and indeed small numbers of individuals announced their own born-again experiences right along. Likewise nonevangelical ministers taught the ways of God week by week, eagerly awaiting converts to the ways of God while nurturing their flocks in moral living, and individuals were added to their numbers right along as well. However, it seemed to evangelicals that at times God opened wide the doors of grace and salvation and many souls were born again all at once—that was called a revival or awakening—and for that nonevangelicals had no real corollary. To everyone, though, conversion was something to be pursued and cherished.[3]

Both Protestant camps associated conversion with justification. The term "justification" identifies the moment when God's merciful grace bridges the gap between the righteous demands of a perfect and holy God and the decidedly unrighteous situation of the sinner. In Garden's words, justification is at its core "Forgiveness or Remission of Sins."[4] To be justified is to have the moral record of one's soul brought into alignment with God's just requirements of perfection. To a Christian, a truly just and wholly good God could not abide evil in his presence, and so the chasm between his perfection and human imperfection damns humans to eternal separation from God. God, in his perfect mercy and love, bridged this gap in the form of his son Jesus, who died on the cross in place of the rest of humanity, taking human sin and death upon his shoulders so that humans could live. He did so out of sacrificial love toward his creation, and so justification, the removal of guilt from and attribution of Jesus's goodness to the individual soul so as to bring the soul up to God's standards of perfection, occurs as an unmerited, undeserved gift from God to humanity. The theological historian Gregg R. Allison defined "justification" as the "right legal standing before God." The term "legal" in his definition is important because according to Protestant understanding, "justification is a legal act of God who, as Judge, declares sinners not guilty but righteous instead," because of Jesus's atoning sacrifice.[5] This is the Gospel—literally, the "good news"—of Jesus Christ, and Christians have been teaching it in some form or other for centuries, and they taught it with vigor in the American colonies. Alexander Garden preached it, George Whitefield preached it, and virtually every other Christian minister, regardless of his feelings toward the Great Awakening, preached it.

The dividing line between the Great Awakening's proponents and opponents was thin, probably more so than historians have typically allowed. Garden held to the gradual transformation model of conversion, and in that he was not as evangelical as his Great Awakening counterparts. However, he did not consider those sorts of doctrinal distinctions significant enough to divide over and was content to let them pass between mutually respectful Christians. Garden and Whitefieldian evangelicalism easily could have been compatible, and not because historians in retrospect can find common ground that contemporaries unfortunately missed; Garden and evangelicalism could have coexisted peacefully not because historians say so but because Garden insisted so. Garden usually avoided theological disputes, but when prodded by evangelicals, he insisted that any difference between his and evangelicals' theologies was insignificant and usually a matter of semantics. At first Garden personally encouraged Whitefield and invited him to preach in St. Philip's. Southerners liked the dynamism of evangelicalism, and Whitefield initially found great success in Charles Town. Garden could have cast his lot with George Whitefield and moved South Carolina in an evangelical direction, and for a short time he did.

Historians have long underestimated the liveliness of evangelicalism, and of Protestant devotion to Christianity generally, in the South before the nineteenth century, when the Second Great Awakening reshaped its religious landscape into the Bible Belt of today. Recent scholarship has illuminated evangelicalism's deep roots in the lowcountry. Many of the earliest dissenters in South Carolina could trace their family lineage and spiritual heritage to Puritan New England.

Such fellowships as the Congregational Church, under the leadership of Harvard-educated Josiah Smith; the Ashley Baptist Church; and other Baptist and Reformed assemblies sustained evangelical dispositions toward experiential religion. Although they were too small in number to provoke much opposition, Baptists' remarkable willingness to proselytize among slaves and incorporate them into their congregational life as equal Christian brothers and sisters demonstrated the limited but nonetheless important capacity of lowcountry religion to accommodate evangelical zeal. Pietism's inner subjectivity and search for unity with God through sacrificial repentance and deep, mystical reading of the scriptures found their way into the colony as well, partly through the libraries of some Anglican missionaries and laypersons. As one historian has concluded, the Great Awakening "was as much an evolution from South Carolina's background and circumstances as an exogenous development produced by religious activity outside the colony."[6] Garden never vigorously opposed these evangelical trends, choosing instead to follow the lead of the parish vestries in maintaining social conformity while allowing spiritual diversity. So when his fellow Anglicans welcomed the Great Awakening into their midst, he followed along.

By any historian's account from the last twenty years, the leader of the Great Awakening was the Anglican Reverend George Whitefield of England, whose seven tours of the British American colonies gave the series of local revivals, otherwise seemingly too diverse and sporadic to be called a singular event, a unity and coherence. Whitefield's preaching and counseling ministry did much of the work, but he also relied heavily on masterful and surprisingly modern public relations and marketing campaigns involving a network of supporters who published his itinerary before his travels and his journals afterward in cities anywhere within his reach. Overtaken in American history textbooks by Jonathan Edwards from Massachusetts, who as a homegrown evangelical usually gets credit for the Great Awakening among American students, Whitefield, the English tourist, actually was responsible for most of the Great Awakening's accomplishments. Whitefield's fame can be compared favorably to that of Billy Graham, the internationally renowned evangelical revivalist of the twentieth century. In terms of percentage of the population that turned out to hear him speak, his crowds probably outnumbered Graham's. If one focuses on the tendency of the Graham crusades in its later years to rely on cooperation with local churches, the likeness would be even stronger. Whitefield's voice captivated and his Gospel message resonated; seldom has one person so thoroughly held the attention of an entire population.

Whitefield has never, then or now, been recognized as a great theological mind, at least not on the level of the great Jonathan Edwards of Northampton, Massachusetts, or Charles Chauncy of Boston. He did preach, however, a coherent evangelical message commonly summarized as conversionism—the

New Birth, or being born again; biblicism, stressing the supreme authority and divine inspiration of the Bible; activism, whereby converts are expected to be doers of the commandments of God and not merely hearers; and crucicentrism, a focus on Christ as the author and finisher of the believer's faith. Beyond this, evangelicalism was a big tent housing varieties of Anglicanism (including Puritanism), Presbyterianism, Baptist and Anabaptist congregations, pietism, and Lutheranism, among others. Indeed evangelicalism was a hierarchy of spiritual priorities and experiences that could be adapted to virtually any formal Christian organization.[7]

Garden claimed to subscribe to just this sort of theology and went to great lengths to agree with evangelicals. Garden preached the necessity of conversion, quoted the Bible as the authoritative word of God, taught holy living as foundational to a Christian life, and believed that all of this rested firmly on the sacrifice of Jesus on the cross, the act of God that relieved the sentence of death from the soul and brought it back to a warm relationship with God. At one point in the contest over the Great Awakening, Garden read directly from Whitefield's sermon titled "What Think Ye of Christ" to explain his own theology of conversion and piety: "The Faith we preach," Garden quoted, "is not a dead speculative Faith, an Assenting to Things credible as credible, as it is commonly defined; it is not a Faith of the Head only, but a Faith of the Heart. It is a living Principle wrought in the Soul, by the Spirit of the everlasting God, convincing the Sinner of his lost and undone Condition by Nature, and continually exciting them to shew forth that Faith, by abounding in every good Word and Work." Garden agreed and protested when Methodists—as Garden called Whitefield, the Wesley brothers, and their fellow revivalists—drew the limits of orthodox Christian conversionism to exclude his own: "Now Sir, this being the Doctrine of Justification as taught and explained by the Clergy," meaning Garden and his non-Anglican colleagues, "and by you Methodists; how comes it to be a false Doctrine in the Mouths of the one, and not of the other?" When Whitefield famously spurned Archbishop of Canterbury John Tillotson as being ignorant of true experiential Christianity and claimed that Tillotson preached salvation through intellectual assent to "bare Historical Faith," meaning traditional church teaching, Garden responded by comparing passages from sermons by Tillotson and George Whitefield to demonstrate that Tillotson believed like Whitefield in salvation through a lively faith born of God's love and resulting in holiness and good works.[8]

As Garden understood it, the key distinction between Garden's theology and Whitefield's lay in their conceptions of Christian conversion, namely, whether it took place instantaneously as a recognizably distinct and datable act of God's spirit upon the soul, as Whitefield claimed, or if God, upon seeing a repentant heart ready to confess to sin and helplessness, initiated a gradual conversion over the course of one's lifetime in cooperation with the active willingness of the convert, as Garden preached. In a sermon initially titled simply "Regeneration," Garden summarized George Whitefield's evangelical doctrine of the New Birth as "an immediate, instantaneous Work of the Holy Spirit, wrought inwardly on the Hearts or Souls of Men, critically at some certain Time, in some certain Place, and on some certain Occasion; and by which the whole Interiour is at once, in a Moment, illuminated and reformed; the Understanding open'd, the Will over-ruled, and all the Inclinations, Appetites and Passions, quite alter'd and turn'd from Evil to Good, from being corrupt and vicious, to being pure, virtuous and holy."[9] Remove the modifiers "immediate," "instantaneous," and "in a Moment," along with the limitations of a certain time, place, and occasion, and Garden could affirm such a formulation.

Garden explained his own understanding of conversion in remarkably similar terms, with the exception that conversion in his view carried out over the lifetime of the convert. The transformation of a person from a "miserable Pagan, to the blessed Gospel state," Garden wrote, does indeed involve a wholesale change of "heart," "mind," "Understanding," "Will," "Affections, and Inclinations" so complete, in fact, that God, seeking terms by which mortal humans could apprehend the process, chose in scripture to liken it to a New Birth. In choosing those terms, though, Garden claimed, God did not mean to imply that people should mark a spiritual New Birth temporally the way they do the comparatively swift separation of a baby from the mother. God meant only to emphasize how complete and life changing spiritual rebirth was to be. In using such language God was not limiting the onset of salvation to the moment when the new personhood was recognized. "Thus, my Brethren," Garden counseled his parishioners, "the Work of Regeneration is not the Work of a Moment, a sudden instantaneous Work, like the miraculous Conversion of St. Paul or the Thief on the Cross," which he took to be normative only in that they demonstrate the graciousness of God in forgiving the most desperate sinners.[10] Rather, regeneration was "but a gradual and co-operative Work of the Holy Spirit, joining in with our Understanding, and leading us on by Reason and Persuasion, from one Degree to another, of Faith, good Dispositions, Acts, and Habits of Piety." This work commenced upon the exercise of faith in the new believer and would be perfected only upon the resurrection to new life in the eternal heavens.[11]

In the meantime the Holy Spirit used prayer, the reading of the Bible, the sacraments, attendance at church service, and other means of sanctification in the life of the believer to bring about an internal love for God and for humankind that resulted in good works toward others. God's spirit was essential for all of this. Like evangelicals, Garden claimed that all of this was made possible only by the intervening love and enabling grace of God's spirit, for "without him we can do nothing."[12] He felt that people should perceive salvation as an undeserved gift from God bestowed upon the willing soul over a lifetime of faithful Christian practice.

Garden and Whitefield divided most sharply on this question of the New Birth as instantaneous or lifelong, but only in his "Regeneration" sermon did Garden draw this distinction as an important difference between the two ministers. According to the introduction to the printed sermon, he did so merely to defend himself against evangelical attacks on clergy who could not claim the instantaneous rebirth experience. Tellingly, Garden also chose not to emphasize the distinction between his own Arminianism, which allowed for human free will in choosing to accept or reject God's offer of salvation, and Whitefield's Calvinism, which stressed God's sovereignty in choosing for himself which individuals to save. Garden often identified his opponents as Calvinist and implied that he preferred Arminianism, but he let pass many of the more traditional distinctions between Calvinist and Arminian soteriology.

Fairly early in his public ministry, Whitefield declared his preference for Calvinism. One of George Whitefield's converts and preaching protégés summarized his doctrines in a sermon preached shortly after Whitefield's death in 1770. Whitefield "taught and insisted on" five core tenets: "(1) Original sin; (2) The new Birth; (3) Justification by faith in Christ; (4) The final perseverance of the saints," which holds that truly converted persons will never fall from the saving grace of God; and "(5) Eternal and unconditional election," whereby God elected, or chose, some to salvation before the world began and according to his own inscrutable counsel and completely independent of the behavior, will, or spiritual state of individuals.[13] Those chosen by God for salvation were classified as the elect. John Calvin of the mid-1500s Reformation period emphasized perseverance (Whitefield's number 4) and unconditional election (Whitefield's number 5); they are perhaps what most distinguish Calvinists from other Christians, who generally hold to what has come to be termed Arminianism, after Jacob Arminius of the early 1600s. Whereas Calvin believed that a person's status as elect or nonelect depended solely on God's active will, Arminius agreed that God elected individuals to salvation before the world began but maintained that God based his choices on his foreknowledge of which individuals would ultimately respond positively to the offer of salvation through Jesus. Calvin asserted that salvation, because it is so wholly dependent on God's overriding will, is irresistible and inalienable to the elect, and that therefore God ensures that every Christian persists in faith until the end of his or her earthly life. Arminius broached the possibility that an individual, having once chosen to exercise faith in Jesus Christ and gain salvation, could come to reject that faith and forfeit salvation. These issues have vexed certain parts of the Christian community for centuries; indeed they are the Christian version of the ubiquitous problem of free will versus determinism. The largely Calvinist revivalists of the eighteenth century used them to draw lines of distinction between themselves and their opponents during the Great Awakening.[14]

Garden never directly addressed his understanding of election in the sermons he chose to publish, although at one point he noted irenically that such concepts were rooted in "less intelligible Texts of Scripture," and so Anglican leaders "wisely, and with the Modesty becoming a reformed Church, left a Latitude as to these."[15] He referenced perseverance only in passing. As a quasi-evangelical, Garden believed in original sin but said that he did not want to argue over the particulars about it. At least he would not recommend emphasizing it to the point of dehumanizing fallen humanity: "I receive no Man to doubtful Disputations on the Point of Original Sin; (a Point fully debated, but not agreed, amongst the most learned Christians) yet cannot recommend it to such Men as carry this Point so high, as to insist on all of Adam's Posterity being born half Brutes, half Devils."[16] He also held to the New Birth, with the caveat described above, and to justification by faith in Christ.

In all of his responses to his evangelical critics, Garden aimed most of his rhetoric toward demonstrating the compatibility of his own teachings to those of his detractors. To do this, he highlighted what he held to be confusion and contradiction in Methodist preaching and suggested that, in the end, perhaps the differences between the two camps were minor and tolerable after all. In 1741 he published a sixty-six-page response to a forty-eight-page public letter written to him by the New England minister Andrew Croswell. The controversy in this case revolved around whether Garden believed in justification by faith alone, the hallmark doctrine of the Protestant Reformation, or justification by works, what Croswell alleged was the Roman Catholic doctrine of salvation. Protestants complained that Catholic doctrine detracted from the sufficiency of Jesus's sacrifice on the cross in securing salvation for humanity by positing the possibility that good works can help close the gap between God's perfection and human sin. To Protestants, Catholics sullied the glory of the cross by teaching that Christians could contribute to their own salvation by enacting the practices of the Church of Rome, whether partaking of mass, venerating the saints, honoring relics, purchasing indulgences, or praying prescribed prayers. This was salvation by works, not grace offered through faith in the cross.

Calvinist evangelicals of the eighteenth century parsed the terms of salvation even more closely than merely distinguishing between faith and works in the process of salvation. To Calvinists, faith—not just salvation—had to be a gift of God. For a person to say that he had gained salvation by freely choosing to exercise faith in Jesus Christ was robbing Jesus of his rightful glory. Every human being, elect or not, remained helplessly corrupted by sin, such that nobody could ever choose to exercise faith. Rather, God bestowed faith on a person by regenerating the hearts of the elect, freeing them from the corruption of sin, and moving them to choose salvation. From beginning to end, salvation was thoroughly God's work among a spiritually passive humanity. For Arminians to say that the Holy Spirit freed every individual from sin enough to choose to exercise faith—or not—was to make faith into a work that redounded to the credit of the individual. To a Calvinist, faith must be a gift or it is a work, and if it is a work, then an Arminian is no better than a Catholic trying to merit salvation through good deeds. In this way, while both Calvinists and Arminians laid claim to the core Protestant doctrine of "salvation by faith and not works," Calvinists accused Arminians of turning faith into a work and making salvation something earned, rather than something merely received by the unworthy sinner. This was the nub of Croswell's rub against Garden's theology.

Garden claimed that all of this was mere semantics, but this was no small controversy, and the fact that Garden wrote such a lengthy response reveals how seriously he took the criticism. One way to condense the dispute is to narrow it down to two closely related questions that the two ministers struggled to answer: Can faith be a means of salvation without meriting salvation? Can faith be a condition of salvation without causing salvation? For Garden, faith—and repentance and obedience—could be a means of salvation without thereby meriting salvation, and it could be required of God as a condition for salvation without it becoming a cause of salvation. In his letter Garden asked the reader to imagine a scenario where a king catches a traitor in rebellion. The traitor is rightly condemned to die, and he has "neither Friends, nor Money, nor any Means in his Power wherewith to attone for his Crime, or on which to ground the least Hopes of Mercy." Fortunately, before the sentence is executed, the king's son, "of a tender and compassionate Nature," offers to suffer "Banishment, Disgrace, Penury, and Want, in a foreign Country, for a certain Time" in place of the traitor, provided that the traitor repents of his evil deeds and demonstrates allegiance to the king. "Now in this whole Affair, where can the least Idea of Merit enter, but in the Part of this compassionate Son? The Rebel subject is reprieved for a Time from Execution, through the Intercession and Merits of this Son, and conditionally on his sincere Repentence and renewed Obedience for that Time, is finally pardoned and received into his Prince's Favour: And what Idea of Merit can arise from these Conditions complied with or performed? What Grounds has this Subject for boasting on such Performance?" That repentance and loyalty were conditions was only reasonable, for "this dutiful and obedient Son could never intercede with his Father to take an open and professed Traitor into his Bosom while he continued such, and still went on to oppose his Government and Laws."[17] In like fashion, God could not be expected to forgive a sinner of his rebellion without that sinner exercising faith, repenting of his sin, and embracing loyal obedience to God, but that did not mean that the man could thereby make himself deserving of forgiveness. Pardon for sin was still a free gift bestowed on unworthy humankind solely through the merits of Jesus's sacrifice on the cross. The point Garden was making here was that he, like evangelicals, held to salvation by faith and not by works.

Garden also distinguished between duty and merit, claiming that obedience to God's commands ranked as mere duty, the doing of what was rightly expected, whereas the merit, the going beyond the expected in an act of altruistic mercy in a way that credited goodness to the sinner's account, belonged solely to Jesus. The exercising of faith in responding to the Gospel by repenting of and confessing one's sins and by allowing the Holy Spirit to melt one's heart to receive God's forgiveness were one's duty, a "sine quibus non" that did not make one deserving of mercy, but without which God could not grant mercy. Therefore, "neither Faith itself as our Act, Virtue, or good Work, hath any Hand in Justifying; much less any other Acts, Vertues, or Good Works of ours whatsoever." Faith and its associated works were means and conditions of salvation and duties of a grateful humankind toward God, but they did not cause salvation or make the sinner deserving of salvation and therefore were without merit.[18]

Throughout this explication Garden associated saving faith, the condition upon which God granted his mercy, with particular works, primarily repentance and confession. For this, Croswell, again, accused him of preaching salvation by works. To Croswell, the notion that works of repentance must precede justification implied salvation by works, not faith. Here Garden asserted the difference between means and merits, and he enlisted revivalists' words in his defense. He quoted the Reverend William Cooper, George Whitefield's friend in Boston, and highlighted what Garden believed to be a contradiction in Calvinist thinking about election: he said, quoting Cooper, "'God's Decree [in electing some for salvation] does not at all take off the Use [of] our Endeavors; for in the Use of Means the very Decree itself is to receive its Accomplishments.' Thus that learned Gentleman asserts, that good Works are Means of Salvation, and so necessary means, that they are a Part of the very Decree of Election; (which is either asserting the Decree to be conditional with the Arminians; or asserting decreed Conditions of an unconditional Decree, which is Nonsense)."[19] In fact, Garden pointed out, Cooper was not the only revivalist to call for a "lively faith" that included the works of holy living and gracious deeds. Garden explained that Croswell's letter argued that "Followers of Calvin . . . do indeed more than any Men press the necessity of an universal Obedience to the Laws of God, testifying . . . that Faith without Works is dead." Garden retorted, "You should set your Contradictions a little more asunder."[20] When Croswell asserted that "The Man who Repents and Believes" is instantly justified by God without the man doing any good work, Garden declared, "how a Man can Repent and

Believe to the Salvation of his Soul, without having done one good work, will require a Consultation of Suarez, Scotus, Aquinas, &c. to resolve."[21] In other words, only the sophistry of medieval Catholic scholastics could explain how a person needed to do the work of repentance to be saved and yet could be saved without work.

In a similar vein, Garden wondered at the utility of Calvinists preaching repentance to great crowds when under their doctrine of unconditional election God had already selected those he determined to save without any movement at all on their part, leaving all others to damnation. Would it not make as much sense for Calvinist preachers "to imploy their Time and Talents, in vehement Addresses to so many dead Corpses?" Anticipating the common Calvinist response that preaching was merely a means that God employed to save his elect, Garden continued, "If you say, that Preaching is a Means of God's Appointment for bringing poor Sinners to Christ I shall readily admit it is," but in that case, "I must insist on Hearing the Word preached, being a Means of his Appointment for the same also; for except People will hear, Preaching can signify nothing. And if Hearing the Word Preached be a Means of God's Appointment for bringing Sinners to Christ, then must one good Work at least . . . go before Justification as a Means of it, which you know is rank Arminianism."[22] If Croswell argued that God decreed that preaching would be the means of saving souls, Alexander Garden would not disagree, but then Croswell should admit, with Garden, that God used human works to bring about salvation. In all of this Garden attempted not to convert Croswell to Arminianism but to point out that they were not so far apart after all.

Garden tangled with Whitefield on such matters and again downplayed the significance of any difference in language between the two Anglican ministers. Like Croswell, Whitefield often attacked Arminian Anglican clergy such as Garden for their supposedly works-based soteriology. As with Croswell, Garden responded by denying such a caricature of Arminianism. In one of his letters to George Whitefield, Garden argued for faith as a nonmeritorious means to justification, and there he marshaled the Calvinist revivalist Jonathan Edwards in support. Quoting Edwards's "Discussion of Justification," Garden wrote, "In one Sense Christ alone, performs the Condition of our Justification and Salvation; in another Sense, Faith is the Condition of Justification; in another Sense, other Qualifications and Acts, are Conditions of Salvation and Justification too." Thus, protested Garden, Whitefield slandered Garden when he drew a distinction between Garden's conjoining of faith, works, and salvation and that of the evangelical revivalists.[23] If Edwards, whose Christian credentials nobody seriously questioned, could so indiscriminately throw together such terms as "condition," "justification," "salvation," "faith," "acts," and "qualifications" without drawing reproach upon himself, why could not Garden?

In all of these writings, Garden returned again and again to the theme of common theological ground to end the dispute. In defending Archbishop Tillotson, Garden pointed out key places where Tillotson and Whitefield described the relationship between holiness and regeneration in similar terms.[24] Garden noted that George Whitefield and his friends could not actively seek to disprove the notion of faith as a nonmeritorious condition for justification because their own doctrines were too similar. They knew "that such Proof must equally conclude against yourself and Brethren Methodists" in their preaching of salvation.[25] To the Methodist insistence that faith and justification were granted by God coterminously—recall that Calvinists held that God granted faith as part of salvation, rather than perceiving that a person exercised faith and subsequently received salvation—Garden referred again to Jonathan Edwards, pointing out that he had described faith going before, occurring at the same time, and coming after justification, all in the space of just one of his writings.

Repeatedly, Garden blamed evangelical argumentativeness as the source of contention and wished that his opponents would be quiet. Garden insisted that he would have been satisfied to allow his opponents to "remain undisturbed, if they would not disturb, insult and abuse their Neighbors, for differing from them in Judgment."[26] Similarly, when evangelicals questioned the authenticity of faith in a person who could not claim the mystical New Birth experience, Garden sniffed, "would they be content quietly to enjoy their own Feelings, no one would disturb them in the Enjoyment; but if they will be running about the World with their Feelings, and telling us, that, tho' they cannot explain or make us conceive them, we must yet have the same Feelings in ourselves, or we cannot be saved; . . . this I conceive to be not only amusing but Insulting of Mankind, instead of Teaching them."[27] Over and over Garden tried to demonstrate that good Christians could legitimately disagree about finer points of theology, that their disagreements were usually minor and tolerable, and that only Methodist contentiousness motivated him to take up his pen. If they would mind their own business, he would mind his.

As the leader of the dominant church in South Carolina and the possessor of its most influential pulpit, Garden had little reason to mind the revivalists' theology, especially since he perceived little important difference between their doctrinal understandings. He had rubbed shoulders with plenty of evangelicals before the outburst of revivals, and he had never felt a need to oppose them publicly. South Carolina's climate of religious toleration and diversity did not threaten his social standing or the colony's social tranquillity, and so for years Garden remained content at the helm of its most prominent church. He did not immediately perceive any threat from the revivalists, and during the public controversy that erupted by mid-1740, he sought only to make the ruckus disappear.

For these reasons Alexander Garden initially responded to George Whitefield in Charles Town quite amiably. Whitefield visited Charles Town briefly on
his first tour of British North America in 1738. He preached three sermons in
short order. He reached the town late on a Monday night but preached twice the
next day in Garden's pulpit in St. Philip's, which he described in his journal as
"very beautiful." Garden and his parishioners must have taken to his preaching,
for "there was a general and earnest expectation of my [Whitefield's] preaching
on Sunday." Commissary Garden and George Whitefield got along well. "The
Bishop of London's commissary, the Rev. Mr. Garden, a good soldier of Jesus
Christ, received me in a most Christian manner," Whitefield wrote.[28] According
to an early Whitefield biographer, Garden even "thanked him most cordially"
for his sermons and assured him that if anyone dared try to silence the young
evangelist, Garden "would defend him with his life and fortune."[29] Whitefield
appreciated that Garden "and several others," no doubt some of the liberal
gentlemen and women of St. Philip's, "offered me a lodging, and they were more
than civil to me. How does God raise me up friends wherever I go! Who is so
good a God as our God?"[30]

These journal passages are well known today and have frequently been
quoted by historians before they moved on to the more delectable details of
their eventual conflict. The passages should not be passed over so quickly, for
they are indicative of Garden's compatibility with theological evangelicalism. Garden was not ignorant of the itinerant minister and his preaching, for
Whitefield had become wildly popular in England before he ever set foot in
the Americas. Crowds in the thousands attended his sermons, smaller crowds
mobbed his carriage as he passed through the streets, artists depicted Whitefield
preaching, and the press in England and in British North America printed any
news they could find about this dazzling orator. Multitudes snatched up his first
printed sermon, *The Nature and Necessity of Our Regeneration or New Birth
in Christ Jesus.* His evangelical message was old hat, but his theatrical style
of preaching thrilled his audiences, a point emphasized in news accounts. He
moved around in the pulpit, cried, raised and lowered his voice, and gesticulated
animatedly.[31] All of this excitement made its way across the Atlantic before
Whitefield stepped foot inside St. Philip's; that he preached twice on a Tuesday
to huge crowds strongly indicates that they were thrilled to hear finally the one
who had by then become something of a pop star and that Garden shared their
anticipation.[32] The fact that Garden personally witnessed three sermons by the
young evangelist and still offered to host him as his personal guest demonstrates
the commissary's approval of Whitefield's evangelical ministry. Perhaps Garden
too was mesmerized by Whitefield's theatrics. Perhaps Garden's loss of his
daughter and his wife in the previous few years sensitized his heart to affective
spirituality probing this life and the next. Regardless, opposition to the Great

Awakening in the South was never inevitable. Neither Alexander Garden nor his polite friends in St. Philip's pews were inimical to evangelicalism or even to religious revivalism. In the early stages of the Great Awakening, in late 1739 and early 1740, their response to George Whitefield's preaching matched that of supportive crowds in England, New England, and the Middle Atlantic colonies.

Garden figured out that George Whitefield's animated preaching style played an important role in attracting large audiences. At the conclusion of his sermon *Regeneration,* he proposed that Whitefield's only attraction was his style: "How intoxicating, how fascinating Things are an agreeable Voice and Manner of speaking? The only Excellencies of this Preacher." In Garden's estimation these were the only unique attributes Whitefield could claim, for the content of his messages was unremarkable. "Put his Discourses into the Mouth of an ordinary Speaker, I dare say, no one would step out of his Way to hear them," Garden claimed.[33] Whitefield entertained his audience; he did not enlighten them to true church doctrine. Emotion and theatrics, not theological substance, accounted for Whitefield's success. This was not the only time Garden injected such observations into the discussion; such comments fit Garden's larger concern with reason and emotion, as discussed in the next chapter. Garden's comments reveal ironically as much about his own capacities as a minister as they do Whitefield's. Garden apparently saw himself as an ordinary preacher who could not compete with the captivating style of his opponent. His congregation probably saw him the same way.

The historical record contains no direct comments about Garden's preaching. People noted his strong leadership, his piety, and his faithfulness to his ministerial duties, but they did not remark on his ability to hold an audience's attention. In a sermon he titled *Take Heed How Ye Hear,* Garden noted how often the mundane facts of daily life distracted people from attending services: "Something or other is always the Matter they cannot come; or marrying of Wives, or Farms, or Merchandize; or still much lower, the Church begins too soon or too late, they have not a proper Seat, or proper Cloaths to appear in; 'tis either too hot or too cold, too dusty or too dirty Weather: Some or other of these, or such like Reasons of Absence, is always at hand." When a minister preached like "a sounding Brass or a tinkling Cymbal," though, the otherwise apathetic responded with glee.[34] Some of his words came from scripture—Jesus spoke of marrying and the marketplace as potential distractions from spiritual practice—but others, particularly the "lower" excuses, must have come from Garden's own experience dealing with reluctant parishioners who were not enamored with their rector's preaching style.

It was not that Garden was a poor speaker—nobody said that either—but that he was an unremarkable but solid preacher worthy of his parishioners' attention when they felt like showing up. While Garden put Whitefield's affective style in another and less admirable class than his own, he did claim to be known for emotive speaking on some level: "'Tis also true, and known to all that know me, that when I talk on any serious and important matter, I naturally do it with some Enthusiasm and Earnestness."[35] He probably had a loud voice that filled the spacious St. Philip's sanctuary, for when he retired and his assistant resigned in 1753, the vestry in their letter to the bishop requesting their replacements asked that the new candidates be "good Audible preachers, As our parish Church is large & in general a great Auditory."[36] Garden complained about a guest speaker who spoke so softly that he could not understand him from his seat close to the pulpit. The minister, Charles Boschi, successfully preached in his home parish for four years, so Garden's complaint should probably be taken as an indication of what kind of voice was required to fill St. Philip's cavernous interior.[37]

Most likely Garden was a talented preacher who hewed close to the homiletic norms of his era, which put him at a disadvantage relative to Whitefield. His sermon *Take Heed How Ye Hear* was the only full sermon he preached and published without significant redaction—he merged two sermons for his *Regeneration, and the Testimony of the Spirit, Being the Substance of Two Sermons,* clearly edited to fit the Whitefield controversy—and thus only it represents something close to a Garden-variety sermon. If so, it indicates that Garden generally followed the structure common among Anglican colonial ministers in writing sermons. He began by reading a short passage from the Bible, laid out the key points to be noticed, provided careful exegeses for them, and then drew out lessons from the text to be applied to the lives of his hearers. The lengthy sentences, carefully constructed and elegantly decorated with strong verbs and titillating adjectives, depended heavily on assortments of colons and semicolons. Such sermons were intended to awe the audience by virtue of their erudition, and the minister gained influence among his parishioners when he could demonstrate his superior education and intellect in the pulpit. None of this was intended to be entertainment. That would have to wait for the Baptist and Methodist revivals of the early 1800s, when preachers drawn directly from the laity spoke in the vernacular and chose themes relevant to the social situations immediately at hand. Many of those ministers followed the lead of more dynamic slave preachers, whose African influence generated sermons with strong voice inflections and close attention to audience response. When such a preacher sensed that a word or phrase or topic resonated particularly well with his audience, he moved his sermon in that direction, departing from his notes to capitalize extemporaneously on the evident needs and delights of the audience. The use of melisma, syncopation, call-and-response, and exaggerated multitonality drew hearers into the message. No wonder even many wealthy white people chose to listen to slave preachers rather than their own, more conventional speech makers. That kind of preaching set off the Second Great Awakening, another tidal wave of evangelical revivals.[38]

A prototype of that kind of preaching set off the First Great Awakening of Garden's time. George Whitefield published many of his sermons, and they do not differ much from those of his colleagues in form and purpose, but his published work was not what made him famous; his preaching did. Whitefield's theatrical style from pulpits or from a traveling, collapsible pulpit that he often used in open fields anticipated the innovations of the next century. His dramatic movements, his crying out in tears of joy or anguish, his pleading with his audience for signs of repentance, his spontaneous changing of topic to meet the perceived needs of his audience, and his frequent recording of his audiences' reactions in his wildly popular journals all produced an interactive experience that far exceeded the boundaries of propriety and reverence adopted by his peers. His listeners loved it.

In that light, in seeking to understand how Alexander Garden's congregants viewed him as a preacher, it is probably best to discuss such views as being before the Great Awakening or after the Great Awakening. Before the Great Awakening, Garden likely seemed sufficiently authoritative, arrayed in his robes and perched above them in the pulpit reading from his carefully arranged script. Although he was small of stature, his steady confidence and firm voice likely commanded a hushed respect as he read off liturgies and worked his way methodically through homilies. The quietness of the preindustrialized town, the heat of the Carolina summers, the stultifying formality of the polite audiences, and the academic nature of the messages probably conspired at times to turn the hush into slumber. One could easily imagine such an audience being thrilled by the dramaturgical performances of George Whitefield. Even Garden had to see for himself what all the excitement was about. One wonders if he felt a twinge of envy at the crowds' responses or if he felt at all threatened by his young colleague's ability to capture the attention of Garden's own parishioners. After the Great Awakening, his parishioners probably felt some disappointment with their minister's relatively sober style. Yet Alexander Garden's fascination with the newcomer, Whitefield, melted, and he returned to the business of polite society. He maintained a thriving congregation who seemed satisfied with his more staid style of preaching. Most important, his commanding presence in the pulpit never diminished, even if it seemed a bit less entertaining than before.

*Chapter 5*

# ENGAGEMENT

Garden's dalliance with evangelical revivalism proved brief. Within a few months after hearing and approving of Whitefield's preaching, Garden turned against the young minister and became his most outspoken enemy south of New England. Virtually any biography of Whitefield or historical account of the Great Awakening has mentioned Garden's opposition. The question, then, is why did Garden turn against Whitefield? According to Garden, theology was not the problem; he took up his pen to defend his theology only briefly and sporadically in the early years of the Great Awakening, and his only sustained theological response occurred several years after the Great Awakening's peak, in 1744. Whenever he did respond theologically, it was to emphasize his compatibility to evangelicalism and silence his critics on the matter. So what was the problem? Whitefield asked the same question. At the start of their conflict, on his second visit to Charles Town when Garden was in town, Whitefield wondered at Garden's change from hospitable friend to angry foe. "You did not behave thus, when I was with you last," he noted. Garden's answer was, "but you did not speak against the clergy then."[1] Garden rejected evangelicalism only when evangelicals rejected him, and when he did respond, theology remained secondary to social concerns.

Whitefield's first visit to Charles Town, in September 1738, lasted about one week, and during that time he recorded in his journal no tension between him and Alexander Garden. At the end of the week he returned to the British Isles. There he preached to large crowds and enjoyed a favorable audience with the bishop of London. The *South Carolina Gazette* periodically posted news items announcing his whereabouts, his crowds, and his message in a way that served Whitefield's ministry by stirring the imaginations and expectations of Carolinians. In July 1739 the lowcountry learned of how "wonderfully laborious and successful" Whitefield was in preaching to the imprisoned and the poor in Newgate and Kingswood and to an audience of five to six thousand laborers in Hannum, near where he later enjoyed a crowd "computed at Twenty Thousand People." In August the *Gazette* announced that he had preached to "10,000 People at Kennington–Common." In September the *Gazette* printed the most sensational news yet: "Yesterday morning at Seven O'clock the Rev. Mr.

Whitefield preach'd to about 20,000 People in Moorfields; and in the Evening at Six O'Clock to about 50,000 on Kennington Common, where were about Eighty Coaches, &c., among whom were many Gentlemen and Persons of Distinction." Then came the clincher: "He is daily preparing for his Voyage to Georgia."[2] Additionally Whitefield's journals and printed sermons performed the work he could not do in his absence, finding their way into the homes and thoughts of Garden's friends. Sometime in mid-1739 Catherine Bryan, wife of the immensely important lowcountry planter Hugh Bryan, experienced a Methodist-style conversion after reading Whitefield's materials. She was "born again of God" in a moment.[3]

In the fall of 1739 Whitefield sailed back to the American colonies, arriving in Pennsylvania on November 2, 1739. From there he made his way over land to Charles Town, arriving on January 5, 1740. When Whitefield arrived back in Charles Town, his local followers received him as if he were a prophet. His journal described his reception in words carefully calibrated to convey the excitement he felt among Carolinians. "Several gentlemen" sought him out and "expressed great willingness to hear me preach." In fact, "most of the town" was "eager to hear me." When "many of the inhabitants, with full hearts, entreated" him to "give them one more sermon," he graciously agreed to delay his departure for Georgia. It took only "about half an hour" to collect "a large congregation" for this last sermon; clearly his readers were to understand that people were so anxious to see him that they dropped everything to run to church. Some people, eager to prove how attentively and excitedly they followed his exploits, showed him news accounts of his successes in New York.[4]

Garden was out of town at the time, and he left no record of what he thought of the itinerant preacher at this point. The church commissioner refused to let Whitefield preach in St. Philip's on account of Garden's absence. The rector had to consent to allowing a visitor into his pulpit, although it seems strange that someone as well known as Whitefield, whom Garden had already received into his pulpit three times in the fairly recent past, would be denied access. Perhaps Garden had already indicated some reservations about the young evangelist.[5]

Whitefield spent most of 1740 in South Carolina and Georgia. He visited Charles Town in January, March, July (twice), August, and December, for a total of about thirty-four days there, and then spent another three weeks there the next January before setting sail for England. While in Charles Town, he sought for his hearers not only eternal salvation through the evangelical New Birth experience but also a visible "alteration," as he would call it, in the public display of luxury among Charles Town's polite inhabitants and their enjoyment of genteel entertainments that he considered unbecoming of heavenly minded saints.[6] He also wondered aloud why Anglican clergy failed to admonish southerners for such behaviors. Their negligence proved, for him, the hollowness of clerical moral leadership in South Carolina. Not only could they not claim the New Birth experience, but in addition their moral laxity proved their spiritual dullness. Whitefield pointed to recent calamities in the lowcountry as proof that God shared his critique and would do something about southern corruption if the clergy did not repent and fulfill their calling as exhorters and admonishers.

Garden took all these criticisms personally, especially when Whitefield aimed them at him explicitly. It had to smart when the upstart preacher declaimed against Garden's best friends and family. It had to hurt more when Whitefield reprimanded Garden and the rest of the clergy for not calling out the perceived faults of southern gentlemen and gentlewomen. Garden was thirty years older than Whitefield and had many more accomplishments to his credit. Personal slights probably meant little to him at this point. Whitefield's attack on southern society was an entirely different matter. When Whitefield criticized the clergy for neglecting the prophetic nature of their pastorship, he loosened the genteel binding that kept southern society together. In Garden's mind, and he was probably not too far off, to attack politeness and the clergy's own polite leadership was to hold a knife to the throat of white southern society. His leadership and that of his Anglican friends, and their ability to hold at bay the social collapse that would open the floodgates of rebellion and war, depended on his successful defense of the clergy and of the polite society to which they belonged. The Great Awakening broke out in the midst of two particularly vulnerable years for the colony, and those conditions inflamed Garden's sense of urgency but also proved helpful to Garden in making his case. His campaign against Whitefield would be quick, decisive, and comprehensive.

George Whitefield's social critique crushed whatever attraction Garden felt toward the revivals and superseded Garden's eagerness to prove the inconsequentiality of their theological disagreements. Alexander Garden and South Carolina's polite society rejected George Whitefield and the Great Awakening because George Whitefield and the Great Awakening rejected Alexander Garden and South Carolina's polite society. By challenging southern politeness, Whitefield threatened the close friendship between Garden and South Carolinian society. Garden faced a choice not unlike that of a person smitten with the advances of a new amour. Garden could turn on polite society by adopting the evangelical critique of southern politeness, a critique that better fit the mission of the SPG, or he could spurn evangelical advances and strengthen his ties to his surrounding culture. He chose the latter. He carefully defended polite society as religiously neutral and socially reasonable and derided George Whitefield's theatrical preaching as the product of an overheated imagination that would beguile southern colonists and lead them down the path of vice and destruction.

He purposed to defeat the Great Awakening in order to spare southern society and preserve his own social status, and he succeeded.

Whitefield's criticisms plowed deep into South Carolinian culture. To the list of the most obvious sins warned against in the Bible, such as adultery, drunkenness, and murder, Whitefield and his evangelical friends added other behaviors that they believed were inconsistent with a holy life and were a distraction from a single-minded purpose of spreading the Gospel. Whitefield warned a wealthy friend against seemingly innocent pleasures that were an affront to God and a hindrance to true spirituality: "we entangle ourselves with the world, we indulge ourselves in sensual pleasures, we trifle away our time in what the world calls innocent diversions, and thereby we grieve the spirit of God, and lose the comforts we should otherwise enjoy, from a close walk and communion with God." Whitefield pulled no punches when describing those supposed sins. He labeled actors "evil doers" and "sturdy beggars" and called theaters "nurseries of debauchery" and the "pest of our nation . . . and bane of true Christianity." He described a crowd of "drummers, trumpeters, merry andrews, masters of puppet shows, exhibiters of wild beasts, players, &c.&c." as the "enemy's agents" ready to gather in "Beelzebub's harvest."[7] What could be done about such behavior? "I see no other way" to halt such entertainments, he wrote in his journal, "but by going boldly, and calling people from such lying vanities in the Name of Jesus Christ."[8] Before a young woman could fall "in love with the blessed Jesus," Whitefield counseled a friend regarding his daughters, "all pertness, and lightness of spirit, must be taken away, and they must not only leave off dancing, but be made new creatures." In a letter to a friend he used even more dramatic language: "I am now about to attack satan in one of his strongholds. Tonight I preach, God-willing, where an horse-race is to be."[9]

What he was describing with disapproval was, of course, politeness as most people then would have recognized and coveted. Against this Whitefield posed what he believed to be the simplicity and authenticity of the converted Christian, who worried not of what others thought of him or her but only of what would please God. Compared to this, said Whitefield, English—and Carolinian—politeness was merely "false politeness." Certainly Whitefield had nothing against friendly behavior, but he maintained that this could be genuinely achieved only through the love of God. He yearned in a letter that a friend could be "entirely freed from the world, and inflamed with the love of God. . . . Throw off a false politeness, study the simplicity of Jesus Christ, and be despised for something." He worried that it was a "fear of contempt" that "render[ed] religion unfashionable." When he warned "some ladies concerning the vanity of their false politeness," he was getting at the difference he perceived between a politeness born of an inordinate desire for approval of one's peers and a godly sociability generated by the working of the grace of God from within one's soul. In Whitefield's mind, only the latter could avoid the contrivance and meaninglessness that for him seemed to characterize English gentility. Yet even as a Christian, Whitefield worried that he would succumb to the seduction of vanity. Only God would be "able and willing to deliver me also out of the fiery furnace of popularity and applause," he wrote to a "Sister in Christ."[10] In sum, the path of salvation led directly away from the entertainments of the world and straight toward simplicity, quietness, and otherworldliness.

Salvation demanded piety of all Christians, but especially of spiritual leaders. "Reverend Sir," Whitefield wrote to a fellow minister, "does your going weekly to a club, where the company play at cards, and sit up late at night, does this, dear Sir, agree with your holy vocation, either as a Christian or a minister?" After wondering at the hostility of a fellow Anglican minister who refused to share a boat with him, Whitefield pointed out that he had seen his colleague "shaking his elbows over a gaming table." Such behavior by clergy would prove to be only "a stumblingblock to thousands." He wondered, "What diversion ought a Christian or a clergyman to know or speak of, but that of doing good?" Even Archbishop Tillotson came under Whitefield's censure for not preaching against parents who let their children play cards and men who played dice.[11]

Such a condemnation proved too much for Garden. When Whitefield asked Garden why Garden was so upset at him, and Garden answered that it was because previously Whitefield had not come out against the clergy, the dispute continued for a few more moments. Whitefield explained,

> I then said to him, "If you will make an application to yourself, be pleased to let me ask you one question, 'Have you delivered your soul by exclaiming against the assemblies and balls here?'" "What," said he, "must you come to catechize me? No, I have not exclaimed against them; I think there is no harm in them." "Then," I replied, "I shall think it my duty to exclaim against you." "Then, Sir," he said in a very great rage, "Get you out of my house." I and my friends then took our leave pitying the Commissary, who I really thought was more noble than to give such treatment. After this, we went to public prayers, dined at a friend's house, drank tea with the Independent minister, and preached at four in the afternoon to a large auditory in his meeting-house.[12]

So what ended the conversation was Whitefield's denunciation of Garden for not preaching against what Garden perceived to be instrumental forms of polite entertainment. In Whitefield's account, Garden came off as a vengeful, perhaps guilt-ridden host who could not abide brotherly admonition. Note that Whitefield and his friends went to prayers—they were not too disturbed to go to St. Philip's for prayer—and then enjoyed fellowship with another minister in town before, once again, the evangelist preached to a welcoming crowd in the Independent, or Congregational, church. Whitefield constructed this journal entry to draw sharp distinctions between his own godliness, courage, and long-suffering in the face of persecution and Garden's obstinate defense of his friendliness with an ungodly world.

This evangelical onslaught occurred at a particularly vulnerable time for southerners. The interim year between Whitefield's first two visits, between the end of 1738 and the beginning of 1740, holds the key to understanding why Alexander Garden and his genteel friends responded so vigorously against the evangelical censure of southern society. It was one of the most momentous years in South Carolina history. On December 30, 1738, the Indian presence—and threat—was felt in Charles Town when the officers and soldiers of the "Charles Town Regiment" escorted the chiefs and warriors of the Choctaw and Chickasaw through the town to meet with the colonial council, smoke a pipe together, and then retire to the house of James Crockett Esq. for "an elegant Dinner."[13] Then on May 3, 1739, the *South Carolina Gazette* reprinted news from London regarding "a very numerous and splendid Appearance of Nobility and Gentry at the Masquerade in the Hay-Market." One of the gentlemen dressed up as a Spaniard with "an Ear very curiously painted" and surrounded by the word "JENKINS" displayed on his chest. Gentlemen who were dressed as English sailors, some with the words "No Search or No Trade" inscribed on their hats, paid mocking tribute to this "Knight of the Ear." This satire of the mounting tension between the empires of Britain and Spain—infamously incarnated in the ear allegedly cut off by Spanish officers illegally searching British ships in the Caribbean and displayed in London by its rightful owner, British captain Robert Jenkins—may have been good fun in London, but in South Carolina, just a few hundred dangerous miles from Spanish Florida, imperial warfare was no laughing matter. This War of Jenkins' Ear would evolve by 1744 into colonial participation in the Atlantic conflict known as King George's War. Carolinian battles in these wars were few and, owing mostly to ineptitude on all sides, did little lasting damage, but the disruption to colonial trade would cause what the historian Robert M. Weir has called "an economic disaster for the colony."[14] People would not have known this in 1739, but they certainly would have recognized the impending danger.

During Whitefield's absence Carolinians also felt the ravages of epidemic disease. In 1739 another fierce bout of yellow fever swept through the population just as it was recovering from a smallpox outbreak of the previous year and, according to the Reverend Andrew Leslie, "carried off an abundance of its Male Inhabitants."[15] The disease killed so many people, about 7 percent of the population, and "there were so many funerals every day that the tolling of bells was prohibited."[16] Although this bout was estimated by some scholars to have been less deadly than the yellow fever epidemics of 1728 and 1732, the memory of those earlier scourges must have raged along with fever in the minds of Carolinians. At any rate, it afflicted the Timothy family, printers of the *Gazette,* enough that they shut down the newspaper for a month, and it sent members of the assembly home at least twice.[17]

Slaves often chose these times of instability among the white community to strike for their freedom, and the threat of war and the disorder of disease in the years 1738 and 1739 appeared to many slaves to be an opportune time for taking advantage of the Spanish offer of freedom for British slaves who could make it to Spanish Florida. In November 1738 dozens of slaves made their escape. In February 1739 rumors spread of a conspiracy of slaves "to rise and forcibly make their Way out of the Province."[18] In April four bondsmen escaped, killing one white and wounding another in the process, and a few days later several other slaves were caught attempting to flee and were punished. Meanwhile it could not have comforted Carolinians to read of a battle with maroons on the island of Jamaica, who, "being very troublesome to the Inhabitants all over the Island," were hunted down by a militia of 250 "shotsmen," armed slaves, and soldiers. The contest ended in truce, which, considering the more usual climax of annihilation, was something of a victory for the Africans.[19] Fearful, the Carolina governor, council, and assembly moved to "make some further Provision for securing the Inhabitants of this Province against the Insurrections and other wicked Attempts of Negroes and other slaves" by requiring all white males eligible for the militia and "possessed of Ten Slaves" to carry their firearms to church meetings.[20]

On Sunday, September 9, 1739, nearly two dozen slaves broke into a store in St. Paul's Parish near the Stono River, killed the storekeepers, and seized guns and powder. They set out for the freedom of Florida, killing white men, women, and children along the way. Their shouting and beating of drums attracted several dozen more slaves, and they might have succeeded in their escape had they not decided to stop in the afternoon to augment and organize their growing force and had they not come upon Lt. Gov. William Bull. Barely eluding capture himself, Bull fled toward Charles Town and raised a militia. It took a week to kill, capture, or disperse the slave army, and for months afterward the felt presence, real and imagined, of surviving rebels lurking in the countryside reverberated across the colony, even inspiring Gen. James Oglethorpe to warn his Georgia constituents to "have a watchful Eye upon any Negroes."[21] Fear of rebellion rose again in December, causing the council to conclude that "many of our [white] Inhabitants are determined to remove themselves and their Effects, out of the Province." Robert Pringle, a Charles Town merchant and St. Philip's vestryman, wrote days after Christmas that people had "been fatigued for this

Week past keeping Guard in the Town, on acco[un]t of a Conspiracy" detected among slaves.[22] As late as January 1741 St. Paul's Rev. Andrew Leslie wrote to the society, "Several of my principal Parishioners being apprehensive of Danger from the Rebels Still outstanding have carried their Families to Town for Safety and if the Humour of People moving continues a little longer I shall have but a Small congregation at Church."[23]

In all, the Stono Rebellion cost the lives of approximately sixty slaves and twenty white persons.[24] The repercussions would be felt by slaves and white southerners for years. Spurred by the rebellion, the Carolina government raised the duty on slave importation so high that the external trade dropped precipitously for most of the 1740s. The government also completed a slave code that had been languishing for years in committee. "An Act for the Better Ordering and Governing Negroes and other Slaves in this Province" represented a curious mix of attempts to subvert conspiracy by making slaves' lives both more bearable—by, for instance, prohibiting the use of excessive punishment when disciplining slaves—and more restricted—for example, requiring slaves to procure passes when traveling off their plantations and prohibiting the teaching of slaves to write. The law also included a provision rendering colonists immune from prosecution for any illegal act committed during the suppression of the rebellion, including the killing of slaves, "as fully and amply as if such rebellious Negroes had undergone a formal trial and condemnation."[25] No wonder whites feared impending doom and worked assiduously to prevent it, particularly during what the historian Peter H. Wood has called the "time of particular unrest," the late 1730s.[26] The slave trade would boom again in the 1750s and wax and wane over the years, but clearly the threat of slave rebellion lingered palpably in the air through the early 1740s, exactly the time when Whitefield most actively pursued ministry in the colony.

Not every event during Whitefield's absence was calamitous. In spite of the violence and disorder—or more likely because of it—polite activity continued with renewed vigor. In December 1739 the would-be aristocrats performed their parade, harbor gun demonstrations, and dinner mentioned in the last chapter. On March 29 of that year, "Henry Campbell, Master" announced in the *Gazette,* "A BALL, at the Play House." He held another ball in December.[27] Also that month the "Philosophical Lectures" resumed, having been discontinued because of the yellow fever epidemic. Meanwhile merchants continued their importation of European goods, advertising the sale of such luxury items as "English Brussels and Flanders Lace, Gold and Silver Watches." Catherine Kay posted an ad inviting women to have their "Brussels and Mecklin Laces washed in the best manner and dressed the English fashion." Jane Voyer invited to lessons "any young Ladies that have a mind to learn Embroidery, lace-work, Tapistry or any other sort of Needle-work" and offered to sew any patterns "after the Newest

Fashion and in the best manner." A landlord advertised a house to rent with a billiard table. Those critics of the romantic pretensions of the imposters of gentility would have taken notice of a newspaper account of a supposed gentleman who, having succeeded in wooing a young woman of "great fortune, Merit, and Beauty," took her on a country ride. Upon being accosted by a robber, the man "leaped out of the Chaise, and shew'd a light pair of heels," leaving the woman to be robbed of everything but her underclothes. "It is to be hoped this may serve as a necessary Caution to the Fair Sex, not to trust themselves abroad with any but those whose Courage they have experienced."[28] On December 1 the paper published another ad by Jane Voyer, this one announcing that she was reconvening her school "since the sickness" and that to make the various courses of instruction more accessible to her students, she would now accommodate at her facility "Dancing and Musick Masters." That same day Henry Campbell advertised for a ball that would be held on December 20. Then on January 5, 1740, the *Gazette* announced, "This day arrived here, the Reverend Mr. George Whitefield, who came by Land from Philadelphia."

Whitefield lost no time in taking on South Carolina's genteel society. When he described in his journal his first sermon on January 6, he omitted anything about the scriptural text or the spiritual message. Instead he focused on the appearance of the audience and his consequent judgment: "The auditory was large, but very polite. I question whether the court-end of London could exceed them in affected finery, gaiety of dress, and a deportment ill-becoming persons who have had such Divine judgments lately sent amongst them. I reminded them of this in my sermon; but I seemed to them as one that mocked." So, wrote Whitefield, he decided to double down on his anti–false politeness the next time. He did, and he liked the results: "Many were melted into tears. One of the town, most remarkably gay, was observed to weep." He noticed their gravity as they left the meetinghouse.[29]

Whitefield's friend Josiah Smith of the Congregational Church immediately published a review. He credited Whitefield's animation and the "modulations of his voice" and his "Zeal, Pathos, and Fire" to "his divine Warmth and Zeal." Whitefield seemed to preach as though his tongue had been "touch'd with a Coal from the Altar," a reference to the biblical prophet Isaiah; and when Whitefield spoke of the judgment of God against sinners, "the Pulpit seem'd almost to be the Tribunal, and the Preacher himself, if the Comparison may be pardon'd, the Great Judge, cloathed in Flame and adjudging a guilty World to penal Fire." Smith "couldn't conclude, without wishing Success to Mr. WHITE-FIELD's publick and repeated Censures upon our BALLS and MID-NIGHT ASSEMBLIES" especially during such a time of suffering. With Whitefield, he wondered how "any Minister of Christ who desires to be found faithful, dare to Shew any Indifference to it; nor . . . that Religion and Virtue can thrive under the Shadow of a Theatre."[30] He probably meant this literally as well as metaphorically, since the theater was southwest of and close enough to St. Philip's Church to cast a shadow on the church building in the winter months.

More friends joined in print to praise Whitefield and turn his unconventional preaching style and criticisms of Carolinian society into virtues, often using pseudonyms and abbreviations, as was common for the time. Those who scolded Whitefield for his animated delivery, S—claimed, preferred "a cold Religion," and "the colder, the more rational."[31] Was not Whitefield to be admired for following in the footsteps of Christ in holding a "generous Disdain of the World" and by waxing "zealous and warm against the Errors and triumphant Vices of the Age," another asked.[32] A poet heralded Whitefield as a steady, heavenly guide illuminating the path of life: "Serene as Light is Whitefield's soul / And active as the sun, yet steady as the Pole."[33] "Zealot II" defended evangelical women's choice of relatively moderate clothing by focusing attention on the polite ostentation of a published critic: "I fear our Author's own Merit lies chiefly in the Glare of his Dress, and this leads him to asperse the Daughters of Zion, who have been taught not to place Religion in tinkling Ornam'nts, [illegible], Bracelets, Ear rings, and any changeable Suits of Apparel."[34]

The contest had begun. Over the next few years, it was fought over the pulpit and in print. No doubt it became a common topic over meals, on street corners, and in the churchyards and market alleys. One wonders if opponents bumped into each other passing in and out of the printer's shop. Rationality; gender norms; cosmology; poetry; name-dropping of famous authors, thinkers, and theologians; Catholicism; personal character; politics—it was all there on the front pages of the town newspaper, pored over by men and women who could read and recited to those who could not. The commotion pulled many onto the field of battle. Unfortunately editorials were often signed pseudonymously or with abbreviations, so it was and is difficult to ascertain identities. Some historians have assumed that Garden wrote as "Arminius," though without strong evidence.[35] Garden published materials under his given name, both in newspaper articles and in special printings of his sermons, including articles attacking Whitefield; his opposition to Whitefield was intentionally obvious and known up and down the coast; and his Arminianism was not a major point of contention for him, so it is not evident why he would publish using that moniker.[36] Because of these factors, this chapter focuses more on what was indisputably written by Garden, although some articles in his support are simply too intellectually delectable to ignore.[37]

Alexander Garden published four responses to Whitefield and his supporters: six letters to George Whitefield published together as a set, likely in the first half of 1740; his sermon *Take Heed How Ye Hear,* delivered from the pulpit in 1740 but not published, with an introduction, until 1742; two sermons preached separately but printed together as *Regeneration, and the Testimony of the Spirit* in 1740; and a lengthy reply to the New England minister Andrew Croswell's critique of his six letters to Whitefield, published in 1742. Little escaped Garden's pen; he referenced writers of various eras and persuasions, Catholicism, Islam, persecution, deism, Native Americans, gender norms, dancing, theater and other entertainments, pleasure as part of human experience, philanthropy, biblical study, antinomianism, homiletics, predestination and God's sovereignty, Adam and Eve, Noah, the Lady of Loretto, and "the Bones of Thomas à Becket," among other things. Against his opponents' arguments he threw such epithets as "shuffle and contradiction," "a poor Jingle of Words," "silly Subterfuges of Scrupling," "confused and contradictory Gibberish," "Crotchets" in "your own Brains," "slander and abuse," "error and mistakes," and "a Medley of Truth and Falshood, Sense and Nonsense, served up with Pride and Virulence, and other like sawcy Ingredients."[38]

Much could be said about this wide-ranging conflict, but one generalization is most important to understanding Garden's religious beliefs and response to evangelical revivalism. Garden's objective throughout his dispute with George Whitefield was to buttress the social order against the onslaught of Whitefield's rhetoric. While he sought to demonstrate that his own theology differed from evangelical "Methodism" only in the particulars he perceived as relatively unimportant, he did respond vigorously to the social ramifications of evangelical attacks on polite society. Therefore he worked hard to steer every debate back to the potential hazards of rebellion and anarchy. Against evangelical emotionalism he posed latitudinarian moderation and reason. Against homiletic innovation he thrust church tradition and authority. Ultimately he chose to try Whitefield in an ecclesiastical court for what amounted to sedition against the Church of England. To Garden, theological difference was something to be tolerated, but social annihilation was not.

Repeatedly Garden tried to prove that George Whitefield's preaching style and message were nothing more than what eighteenth-century religious thinkers labeled "enthusiasm," a pejorative term. "Forsaking the ordinary Ways and Means of attaining the knowledge of our Religious Duty, viz. Natural Reason and the Written Word of God," Garden explained, "and substituting in their Place our own Conceits of immediate Revelations, by certain Impulses, Motions, or Impressions of the Holy Spirit on our Minds, without any rational objective Evidence, or clear and sufficient Proof;—this the proper and direct Enthusiasm, in the bad Sense of the Word to which it is now commonly restricted."[39] Today an audience might compliment an orator by calling his or her delivery enthusiastic; two hundred years ago that term was derogatory, and according to Alexander Garden, for good reason. He argued that enthusiasm could lead otherwise sensible and good-hearted people down paths of destruction they never expected. The intense excitement and emotionalism that attended enthusiastic preaching enticed right-thinking people, albeit usually the weaker-minded ones, he would say, to abandon reason and accept the words of the preacher at face value rather than weighing them against truths long accepted by dispassionate and proven thinkers. Garden sought to expose Whitefield as an enthusiastic charlatan and guard his parishioners from engaging in behavior destructive to him, them, and southern society.

Garden believed that Whitefield's success could be explained wholly by his enthusiastic teaching methods. The preface to his sermon *Regeneration* exhibited a pastoral concern to warn "the Inhabitants of the Parish of St. Philip" away from the enticement of Whitefield's preaching by explaining their attraction to him. The "Sound of that Gentleman's Voice in your Ears;—that enchanting Sound!" was the "natural" cause—as opposed to a supernatural, or divine source—of "all the Passion and Prejudice, that prevailed 'mong some (the weaker some indeed) of you, in his Favour, against them and every thing else that opposed him." It was "not the Matter but the Manner, not the Doctrines he delivered, but the Agreeableness of the Delivery" that "had all the Effect upon you." Alter his delivery he warned, "no more Multitude after the Preacher!" From the pulpit Garden struggled to be heard because Whitefield, "That Seraphim! The wondrous WHITEFIELD!" drowned out Garden's more sensible words. "You heard the Contents of the following Pages from the Pulpit, 'midst that inchanting Sound in your Ears, exciting your Passions, and foreclosing your Understanding against them." This, Garden explained, prompted him to set his sermon in print so that in quieter moments the people could coolly evaluate Garden's teaching. "Patience, my Brethren;—a little While, and your Passions subsiding," Garden's reasonable words, now committed in print to "the Flock lawfully committed to my Charge" and for whom he felt "jealous over . . . with a Godly Jealousie," would gain a proper hearing and illuminate the deceptiveness of Whitefield's doctrines. It was only because Garden, their faithful shepherd, had seen "the Wolf a coming" that he felt compelled to "rise up" and defend his people.[40]

Garden more fully explained his fear of the damaging effects of enthusiasm in his sermon *Take Heed How Ye Hear.* With George Whitefield sitting in the audience, Garden led his congregation through Jesus's parable of the sower and the seed in Luke 8. In this parable Jesus used an agrarian metaphor to convey the need for his audience to prepare their hearts, the soil, to receive the word of God, the seed, from Jesus, the sower. Some soil, and some hearts, came unprepared to his sermons, and consequently they experienced no good effects from his teachings. Some came with their hearts like "good soil," ready to let the seed take deep root. The text proved useful for Garden's purpose of managing his audience's reception of Whitefield's ministry. Garden could define for them exactly what he believed were the impediments to the proper hearing of a sermon and thereby inoculate them against what he claimed was the dangerous but enticing preaching of the Grand Itinerant. Most important, Garden warned against the irrationalism of evangelical enthusiasm, the uncritical "hearing" of which could lead only to every form of social injustice and moral transgression.

In the first half of the sermon, Garden spoke of various impediments to proper hearing. A "stony" heart, weighed down by "corrupt Habits, Lusts, and Passions," terms that in his sermon remained vague as to their application, could not properly receive the word of God. Neither could a heart choked by the thorns of "Things, the Cares and Amusements of the World." He referred not to theaters and balls but to a preoccupation with anything pleasurable, especially when perverted through overuse, including "Honours or Preferments, immoderate Gains or Losses, Wives, Children, Weddings, Births, Funerals" or anything else that could be enjoyed to an extreme but, it seemed, were nonetheless universal occasions of the human experience. Sin occurred not in the mere participation in business, family, or recreation but in the invisible depths of the heart where such elements of life may be idolized. Garden attempted to refocus attention to the sinfulness of pleasure away from Whitefield's censoring of polite entertainment and toward a more benign rendering of sin as a private failure of the individual, as something concealed within the heart and, coincidentally, out of reach of evangelical judgment.[41]

The first impediment to proper hearing mentioned in the biblical text, that of the "wayside," Garden saved for last, he said, in order "more fully to observe" its truths, and no doubt because it played into Garden's critique of Whitefield's enthusiasm. For Garden, the wayside represented "the Field or Ground sowed in open and unfenced, so as to have Roads or Path-ways made thro' it." What did one do to keep "all Comers and Goers" from treading down the soil, making it too hard for proper hearing? One should build "the Fence of Zeal according to Knowledge," for without this fence, "what Pathways also will Enthusiasm make in our Hearts? And how will its wild and frantick Notions devour up the Seed of the Word sown there?" Enthusiasm would make the hearer vulnerable to any "fine Preacher, the man whose Tone and Air they are best pleased with, whose Voice is unto them as a very lovely song." Their itching ears would cause them to want to "hear new Things, strange or mysterious Doctrines, new Lights, or Revelations, tho' only to amuse their Heads, and perplex their Understanding," and "God only knows where they will stop, whether in Bedlam, or Rome, or no Christianity, or no Religion at all."[42]

What galled Garden more than anything else was evangelical enthusiasm's seeming imperviousness to reason. He complained bitterly that whenever he asked Methodists what the basis was for their assurance of a New Birth, they replied that they felt it in their souls. To Garden, this meant that the proof of evangelical truth lay inscrutably within the believer's heart, inaccessible to examination by a rational and objective mind. Garden repeatedly challenged Whitefield and his colleagues to substantiate their claims against him and his fellow clergy: "where are the Proofs of your Accusation? What Evidence have you . . . brought to support your Charge?" There were none, in his view. When Whitefield refused to answer more than the first of his six letters, and that one only briefly, Garden called his refusal to engage in intellectual debate a "Jesuit," or Catholic, tactic to "never regard the Arguments or Objections of an Adversary; but to neglect them, and always return to their own Assertion, as if nothing had been offered against it."[43] Garden believed that atheists, Catholics, deists, pagans, Jews, and Muslims could all be reasoned with, but when people "come to place strong Conceit or Imagination in the Chair of Reason, and to subject the standing Oracles of God, to the fancied immediate Revelations of his Holy Spirit to them; they straight assume the Airs of Infallibility upon you," and rational conversation would be lost.[44]

Against this Garden proposed what he believed was a more scriptural and reasonable method of understanding truth. He perceived that in attempting to stress the sufficiency of God's grace in salvation in opposition to the efficacy of human good works, evangelicals construed humans as "wholly and absolutely passive, as a Clock or Watch is under the Hands of the Artificer." Thus one's only recourse for understanding whether or not one had been saved was some mysterious impression of the mind and heart, not the reasoning of the intellect or even the rational sensation of one's conscience. This simply did not accord with the Gospel's revelation of God as a provider of "Fatherly Counsels or Admonitions, by the Mouth of the meek and humble Jesus,—rather advising than commanding us such Things as we cannot but see and approve as agreeable to our rational Nature, and necessary towards our own Well-being and Happiness." Against evangelical passivity Garden asserted humans as "moral agents" able to assent to and cooperate with the reasonable guidance of the gentle Holy Spirit, who worked in tandem with the precepts laid out in scripture. People could choose to comply with the Spirit's commands or not, but if they did, God's Spirit would guide them and enable them to walk in obedience to the clear teachings of scripture regarding the love of God and the love of their neighbors. Then the Spirit would testify with their spirits, upon cool reflection upon the fruits of their obedience, that their lives measured up to the reasonable teachings of scripture. The testimony of a life well lived before God and society, therefore, was the proof of one's birth into the family of God and the truth of one's beliefs. All of this was testable against the scripture, open to examination by them and others. "And as this is the most perfect, sure and certain Testimony of the Spirit, so there is no Dispute, but every one must be CONSCIOUS, whether, or how far he has, or has not this Testimony."[45]

Garden also asserted the weight of ancient and contemporary thinkers against what he believed were evangelical innovations. Repeatedly in all of his works he dropped the names and quoted the words of such esteemed church fathers and thinkers as "Clemens, Origen, Cyprian, Basil, Chrysostom," and Augustine.[46] He warned that evangelicals "departed from the ancient Testimony" and deviated from doctrines "ever taught by the Catholick Church of Christ in any Age," "Catholick" here referring to the universal family of believers, not the denomination of the same name today.[47] He wrote an entire letter to Whitefield defending Archbishop Tillotson.[48] Many times he called Whitefield back to the accepted teachings of the Church of England, quoting at length entire passages of the articles and of writings by bishops in order to convince Whitefield of his unfaithfulness to his ministerial vows.[49] Whitefield routinely claimed that he was faithful to the articles of the Church of England because the articles were Calvinist. Garden disagreed and for support summoned the complaints of the "old-Calvinists" of the 1600s who had sought reform of the articles because the articles taught "universal Redemption" and "falling from Grace," two Arminian doctrines. "How differently our modern Calvinists judge of them," Garden wrote.[50] In laying claim to the Anglican past, Garden sought to demonstrate how reasonable and reliable his own teachings were in contrast to Whitefield's dangerous radicalism.

Garden's interest in all of this was social, not theological. For him, the importance of a theological position lay in its practical consequences. Though he worked either to minimize or eliminate the more philosophical differences between evangelicalism and his own perceptions of justification by faith and the work of Jesus on the cross, the social effect of evangelical teaching was another matter. The potential hazards of the evangelical critique of southern society, and evangelical ineptitude in negotiating those hazards, worried Garden immensely. The undermining of politeness particularly disquieted the minister. Entertainments that evangelicals denounced as empty or immoral pleasure seeking were perceived by Garden as the social ligaments that bound together the basic structures of colonial life and made survival possible.

An anonymous contributor to the *Gazette* nicely outlined a perception of pleasure compatible with Garden's views. There were "some so rigid, who profess a Distaste of all Pleasure" and thus reject any notion of pleasure as immoral. However, to the author, pleasure properly understood played an essential role for the individual and for society because "it is essential to human Nature to be delighted." One simply could not endure and sustain life without a measure of "relaxation." Likewise a proper understanding accrued to the benefit of society. Pleasure correctly enjoyed was "not to confine our delights to the gratification of sensual Passions, but to make it an enjoyment to perform Acts of Humanity, generosity and virtue."[51] A well-balanced person did not reject earthly pleasures completely but rather used them for both individual health and the good of society. Entertainment in Charles Town, in Garden's mind, reflected just this sort of understanding.

That Garden theologically undergirded cultural aspects of elite culture can be teased from his sermon *Regeneration*. In dismissing the evangelical construction of the New Birth experience as the work of God upon and within the individual, not situated and not contingent upon the social environment, Garden wrote, "we may carefully attend the outward Ordinances, of publick Worship, Preaching, and Sacraments, nor ever neglect our Closest and Family Devotions;—we may fast, and pray, and give Alms, both in publick and private; behave ourselves blameless; and yet alas all to no Purpose." Such a righteous man would yet be damned forever without the emotional experience of an instantaneous spiritual rebirth.[52] This list of works, almost entirely social in nature, corresponded nicely with the public behavior of Garden and his merchant friends—church attendance and ritual, family community leadership, and upright social behavior. To Garden's understanding, this behavior counted for naught in the evangelical world but meant nearly everything in Garden's, not only because it brought him social acclaim but also because, in his view, it would be unlike a benevolent God not to reward such righteousness.

In fact Garden's theology of Christian justification required these public works. To be sure, the individual's heart needed first to be renewed and regenerated, as explained in a sermon that expanded on the list of evil works described in the biblical text of Matthew 15:18–19. "For as out of the evil Treasure or Dispositions of the Heart proceed evil Things, Murders, Adulteries, Fornication, Thefts, false Witness, Blasphemies, &c.," wrote Garden, "so out of the good Treasure of or Dispositions of it proceed good things, Blessing our Enemies, Feeding the Hungry, Cloathing the Naked, and all sorts of charitable, virtuous, and good Things, whether Words or Actions."[53] Note that while the list of evil actions that flowed from an evil heart corresponded with the biblical text, those of the good heart did not; they represented public acts of charity, piety, and virtue that exalted the social graces and capabilities of Garden's wealthy audiences. They refused the gap between the social and the religious implied by Whitefield's individualistic construction of the New Birth.

In addition the process of regenerating the heart differed in detail from Whitefield's in requiring community. Rather than an instantaneous work of the Spirit, this work, "in the ordinary and established Method, consists of these two branches": first, hearing the word of God; and second, "God's blessed Aids and Influences" of baptism and abiding in God's word. As a whole, regeneration consisted of "a gradual and Co-operative Work of the Holy Spirit, joining in with our Understandings, and leading us by Reason and Persuasion, from one Degree to another of Faith and good Dispositions, Acts, and Habits of Piety."

God's Spirit worked on the soul not as "a Mechanick upon dead Materials, but as on living and free Agents."[54] By actively carrying out their proscribed social duties and rituals, Garden's parishioners furthered the work of salvation both personally in terms of their eternal destination and socially as they worked to uplift their community.

In this way Garden's theology took issue with the Calvinist and evangelical means of regeneration in a way that placed a cornerstone of the Christian faith—the work of regeneration—within the southern social context. The acts of charity, the political work that ostensibly furthered the welfare of the community, the distribution of public funds to relieve the poor and suffering, and the founding and administration of the workhouse and the public school, all of whose oversight lay with Garden and his vestry and church warden associates; the church sacraments and services; and even the running of honest and upright businesses that provided the material sustenance for the colony—all of these social behaviors conducted in a public manner not only reflected but also carried forth the work of regeneration. In other words, unlike Whitefield's highly individualistic moment of justification by personal faith, Garden's regeneration not only took place within the community but also *required* the community.[55]

Garden dismissed the notion that somehow polite entertainments were immoral. He claimed that balls were held when young dancing students performed recitations for their families or on some celebration of the king's "Accession or Birth Day," events that numbered no more than six and sometimes zero during a typical year. "And as to Assemblies," he claimed that small groups of men and women gathered occasionally to "pass two or three Hours in Conversation, or any other innocent Diversion or Amusement" that never involved "the least Excess either of Drinking or Gaming, or with the least Suspicion of any sort of Vice or Immorality whatsoever." Clearly working up steam, Garden fumed, "And I very freely declare, that had there appeared to me but half the Danger to Religion, or the Peace and Happiness of Society, from such Balls and Assemblies, which has but too plainly appeared from [Whitefield's] Mobb-Preachings; and the Assemblies of his Institution of Men and Women, Boys and Girls, building up one another in the Conceit of their being righteous and not only despising but damning all others round about them, I should have preach'd against them with all my Might."[56]

This is not the place to make a full assessment of what might be called the "Great Anti-Awakening" in Charles Town, but it is useful to note that many in Garden's community joined him in opposing Whitefield, echoing each of Garden's concerns. "Arminius" compared Whitefield's "Weakness, Ignorance, and Rashness" to the three great Christian virtues of faith, hope, and love. Whitefield's doctrine of original sin perverted scriptures and lay "below Reason." In addition he reminded his readers that "not only the censured but the Censurers must all appear before the Judgment Seat of Christ; where they who judge without Mercy will receive Judgment without Mercy."[57] "T—" submitted a poem written by a friend, "C—," that began by calling Whitefield a "Pig" with

> a pretty num'rous Litter
> Who squeak at cards, and Scream and tremble
> To see our Beaux and Belles assemble
> And if a Sob or sad Grimace
> You can't admit as proof of Grace . . .
> You're a Polite, a Devil, a Scoffer.

"C—" protested that no one "could bear to pass the Wicket, Who has not their peculiar Ticket." He then invoked Protestants' fear of Catholicism, a lively topic in a colony not many miles from Spanish Florida, by accusing Whitefield of wanting to impose "Penance, Convents, and Confessions" while he "infuse[d] Spirits into Nuns and "refresh[ed] . . . pretty, vagrant, Sisters."[58] An author who signed his contribution with only a "—" threw his support behind Garden's leadership by concluding that he could not "countenance and encourage a Person, by attending his irregular Motions, who is under the Censure of our very learned, judicious, and vigilant Diocesan [Alexander Garden] for a strong Ticture of Enthusiasm." However, he expressed confidence that the "steady members of that Church upon sound Reasons, and Christian Principles" and of "right and Steady Judgment" would resist Whitefield. He invited his readers to think of Whitefield as a "wandring comet" that for a brief time distracted attention from the stars and did "disturb and inflame the Order of Nature and interrupt the regular Influences of the heavenly bodies." Such things inevitably are "consumed" by swerving too close to the sun, while the "much reproached regular Stars and Planets will continue to shine and move on" in their regular courses.[59] These defenses echoed Garden's themes of rationalism versus enthusiasm and social order versus disarray.

Another anonymous author published a fictional story that tied together all of the concerns of the antirevivalists, from perceived evangelical antinomianism and social destructiveness to Catholic alleged servility and irrationalism. The article took the form of a "Conference Twixt a famous Roman Casuist and an Emissary" in which the casuist instructed the emissary in "The Propagating of our holy Religion among Hereticks." The emissary was to "make bold pretences to Illumination"; persuade the heretics "not to trust their own Judgment or Examination"; "proclaim their Teachers carnal Men, Enemies to God"; "bring them to renounce Reason, and depend on their Spiritual Guides"; and distrust "an orderly Call to the Ministry." If successful, the end would be the subjugation of the society to the "holy Catholick Faith," though the final elimination of dissent could come only through violence: "when men are once brought to look on their Neighbors as HEIRS OF HELL, and INCARNATE DEVILS . . . they will soon think no Treatment too bad for such; and so by an insensible Gradation, Fines, Imprisonments, Loss of civil Rights, nay Fire and Faggots, and the most wholesome Severities, will be introduced to curb the Insolence of" those with whom they disagree.[60]

To illustrate the seriousness and likelihood of these dire warnings, Garden recounted in his sermon *Take Heed How Ye Hear* an incident in South Carolina from the 1720s involving a French family, the Dutartres. The story, at least as he told it, provided a poignant illustration of all the social ills Garden wanted to warn his audience against and that would be the result of their uncritical hearing of Whitefield's preaching. The Dutartres were carried away by the same type of enthusiastic notions of spiritual revelation that Garden detected in evangelical experiential Christianity and that failed to yield to the superior judgment of Anglican wisdom, with deplorable result.

In Garden's depiction, the Dutartres' simplicity led to their gullibility and delusion. Poor but honest, they "for many Years behaved themselves regularly and blameless, in all outward Instances of religious and moral Duty." However, in the late 1720s an "enthusiast named Christian George, or some such Name" itched their ears with "many wild and fantastic Notions." As a result, the family "withdrew from publick Worship, and all outward Ordinances of God in his Church, and from all Conversation with the World." Here they committed their first transgression: social and religious withdrawal. Without the oversight of the proper religious authorities and wandering from the constraints of governed society, the Dutartres exposed themselves to further delusion. This boded ill not only for the family but also for society.[61]

According to Garden, moral corruption soon followed social delinquency. One of the Dutartres' sons-in-law, Peter Rombert, persuaded the others that God had raised him up as a prophet equipped with an apocalyptic message for the world. God revealed to him that "The wickedness of Men was now again become as great upon Earth as in the Days of Noaeh." God "therefore purposed to destroy mankind a second Time from off the Face of Earth, as he did in those Days, all but that one Family, whom he would preserve as he did Noaeh's, for raising up a godly Seed again upon it." Peter knew this because he "felt it." To raise this seed, God commanded Peter to reject his wife and take her younger sister as his new bride. This did not sit well with the father, who demanded a supernatural sign that would confirm the truth of Peter's alleged revelation. If Peter had heard from God, then "on their going to the next Plantation, the first living Creature they should see there, should be such a one, a Horse, suppose, or a Hog." The prophecy came to pass, and the father consented. In this way further transgressions, "Adultery and Incest," followed from the father's meeting one of the hogs or horses that would have been difficult to avoid in the Carolina countryside.[62]

The worst was yet to come, for the family soon sank to the depths of rebellion and murder. "So far possessed were these poor Wretches with a Conceit of their own Holiness, and of their Impurity and Wickedness of others, that they would give no Obedience to the civil Magistrate, nor any the Laws or Ordinances of Man; and accordingly refus'd to comply either with the Militia Law . . . or the Law for reparing the High-Ways." The authorities were patient, but in the cause of order warrants needed to be served and penalties paid. That Peter's "Revelation Wife" gave birth to a child born out of lawful wedlock posed another problem. The constable and several neighbors of the Dutartres attempted to serve the warrants, with tragic result. Believing that God would protect them and that "no Weapon formed against them should prosper," the family "forthwith arm[ed] themselves, fire[d] upon the Constable and those Persons with him, and d[rove] them out of their Ground. This was not to be suffered; and therefore the Justice taking with him ten or a Dozen Men of the Militia, went straight to protect the Constable in the Execution of his Office." Unfortunately, the constable and one other person were killed in the ensuing gun battle. The militia did arrest the family, several of whom were promptly "arraigned and tried for Murder, found guilty, and condemned."[63]

Garden broke his narrative there to insert a few words of commentary meant to contrast the Dutartres' enthusiasm with his own clear-headed leadership: "Alas, poor miserable Creatures! How amazing a Delusion prevailed over them! They had the Spirit of God (especially the Prophet) leading them into all Truth. . . . The holy Spirit of God commanded them to commit Adultery, Incest, Rebellion, and Murder." Garden had in fact carried out his duty of counseling "these unhappy Creatures with more than ordinary Pains and Diligence." Three of the leaders, including "the Prophet," Peter Rombert, refused his counsel. When Garden approached them to "reason" with them, they "treated [him] with great Disdain" and went to their execution determined to suffer martyrdom. When they failed to resurrect from the dead, the other three under trial recanted of their delusion and were set free, although one boy suffered a relapse and committed another murder. "And thus ended this tragical Scene of Enthusiasm; in which no less than seven Persons lost their Lives; one killed, two murdered, and four executed for those Murders. A remarkable Instance to what Heights of Extravagance, Folly, and Wickedness, this Turn of Head or Imagination will hurry the poor Sons of Men!"[64]

Nobody in Garden's audience could have missed the analogy to Whitefield and his fellow evangelicals. From his perspective, evangelicals had followed the siren call of Whitefield, in the place of Peter Rombert, and had placed themselves in opposition to the larger culture, claiming revelations of God substantiated only by their internal feelings and the spurious spectacle of his wondrous ministry. In fact Whitefield recorded his thoughts about Garden's sermon in his journal, noting the obvious correlations Garden was making between Rombert and Whitefield: "The Commissary seemed to ransack church history for instances of enthusiasm and abused grace. He drew a parallel between me and all the Oliverians, Ranters, Quakers, and French Prophets," sects often blamed within the Church of England for many of the religious upheavals and conflicts of the seventeenth century, "till he came down to a family of the Dutarts, who lived, not many years ago, in South Carolina and were guilty of the most notorious incests and murders."[65] Garden seized on Whitefield's words, noting that he had never mentioned Whitefield or his evangelical friends by name when preaching the sermon. "I must take Leave to let Mr. Whitefield know," he wrote in the preface to the published sermon, that if Whitefield detected any parallels between Rombert and himself "with Respect either to Principles or Practice, he is very welcome to either or both of them, for I mean not to make him any the least Apology."[66]

Garden defended southern society with vigor and considerable deliberation in preaching and writing against these evangelical threats to southern society, but the question remained what practical steps he could use to put an end to Whitefield's ministry. He had two answers, beginning with a tongue-in-cheek suggestion that they follow the Roman Catholic example as explained by the noted English author Joseph Addison, who wondered why Catholic lands were not plagued by enthusiasts. Addison concluded that it was because Catholic leaders put them all together in convents and monasteries where they could be happy without bothering anyone. Such religious orders "serve as Receptacles for all those fiery Zealots who would set the Church in a Flame, were not they got together in these Houses of Devotion. All Men of dark Tempers, according to their Degree of Melancholy or Enthusiasm may find Convents fitted to their Humours, and meet with Companions as gloomy as themselves."[67] Garden no doubt used Addison in jest, but the suggestion did reinforce the fact that his main goal was to preserve social peace, not coerce Whitefield to conform to Garden's theological commitments.

Garden's second answer was to suspend Whitefield through legal action sanctioned by the Church of England. He charged Whitefield with violating the canons and articles of the Church of England by not following the Book of Common Prayer, which laid out the order and content, or liturgy, of an Anglican service. Garden also reprimanded Whitefield for breaking the vows he took at ordination by preaching in dissenting churches. Garden and four clergymen friends, William Guy, Timothy Millechamp, William Orr, and Stephen Roe, sat as judge and jury, a situation that Whitefield rightly protested, being that

Garden had already come out against him. Whitefield also pointed out that the bishop had commissioned Garden as commissary for the Carolinas and the Bahamas, not Georgia, the Grand Itinerant's official home parish. In the end the court found him guilty anyway. Whitefield promised to appeal to the Lords Commissioners of the Church in London within twelve months, and the case was put on hold. In the meantime the "tryal" was described briefly in the *Gazette,* which claimed that "many attended" to see what would happen.[68]

Both Garden and Whitefield would write about this ecclesiastical trial, Garden in his preface to *Take Heed How Ye Hear* and in response to Whitefield's account in his journals, which Garden derided as "so full of Errors and Mistakes (notwithstanding he had a Copy of the Proceedings in his Hands)" that he could not expend the time and ink to counter all of them. He focused on two. Garden pointed out that Whitefield had vowed to respond to Garden's allegations and abide by the findings of the court if the court would grant him a day to consult legal experts and discover whether or not Garden had the authority to bring the suit. Garden granted him this favor, and the authorities confirmed Garden's jurisdiction, but Whitefield broke his vow anyway, said Garden. He also failed to follow through with his promise to lodge an appeal with the bishop within a year from the date of the trial. This description of Whitefield's broken vows accomplished Garden's goal of demonstrating the willingness of Whitefield to disobey the established orders of the Church of England.

The trial did not slow down Whitefield's ministry, but it did continue to serve Garden's rhetorical purposes for several years. On February 13, 1742, Garden announced in the *Gazette* that, having not received word that Whitefield had successfully appealed to the church in London, Garden had suspended Whitefield from the ministry. The situation continued to fester for several more years. On May 5, 1746, Garden published in the *Gazette* affidavits dated May 25, 1744, attesting to Whitefield's attempt to lodge an appeal with the church and claiming that the Lords Commissioners of the church in London had failed to meet to resolve the conflict. Whitefield claimed that this was the commissioners' fault. Garden pointed out that the affidavits did not prove that Whitefield had tried to appeal within twelve months after the trial in Charles Town, as Whitefield had promised. Therefore, said Garden, the affidavits did not acquit his opponent. Garden made the affidavits public and wrote in his introduction to them that they would "assist in undeceiving a Number of People" who still followed Whitefield.

It would be too easy to follow other historians and assume that this legal effort accomplished nothing, or even that it backfired against the commissary by making him look ineffectual. One historian has even proposed that the trial and suspension played into Whitefield's efforts to play the part of the martyr, claiming that Whitefield's journal "account of his 'trial' before Garden's 'court' read like Stephen before an unconverted Paul and the Jewish Sanhedrin."[69] Perhaps, but it may also have played into Garden's efforts to reveal Whitefield as a disorderly and arrogant upstart minister who could not be trusted. Garden gave his rebuttal to Whitefield's account of the trial in the preface to *Take Heed How Ye Hear.* A few pages after showing his readers that Whitefield had broken his vows and refused to reason together with proper authorities, he told the Dutartres' story, in which Rombert the enthusiast disdained and ignored the counsel of wiser authorities. Readers were to remember how that played out. Garden's cultural authority in Charles Town did not diminish because of his antirevivalism, and there is reason to believe that the suit and Whitefield's casual dismissal of it became an effective tool. Other ministers fighting their own battles against George Whitefield referred to Garden's trial to disparage the young itinerant. Rev. Nathanael Henchman of Lynn End, Massachusetts, claimed that Garden had cast Whitefield "under the Frowns of the Church of England."[70] Perhaps church sanctions seem beneath notice in today's cultural setting, but they mattered to people in the 1700s. In a time when churches loomed large in people's minds and daily experiences, refusing church authority could easily be construed as just a few steps down from treason against the Crown, especially since the king was the head of the Church of England and represented its highest authority. At any rate, Garden persisted in believing that the trial helped his cause, as evidenced by his publishing the affidavits as late as 1746.

When Whitefield tried to portray Garden's opposition as persecution against the true ministers of the word of God, Garden invoked South Carolina's tradition of religious toleration. Whitefield would often portray himself as a martyr for the Gospel. After hearing Garden preach against him, he recorded in his journals that he "immediately retired to my lodgings, rejoicing that I was accounted worthy to suffer this further degree of contempt for my dear Lord's sake."[71] This struck Garden, who had endured much of Whitefield's encomium, as ridiculous. "Ours is no persecuting Country for Religion," he countered in one of his open letters to Whitefield, for "every Man may enjoy his own Way in Peace and Safety." Whitefield was the one persecuting Garden and his neighbors of all spiritual stripes who had been content to live side by side in peace until Whitefield had come to town, casting "Slander" against those with whom he disagreed.[72]

The aggressive nature of Garden's attempts to counter the social threats represented by Whitefield's critiques stand out all the more when compared to the actions of other antirevivalists elsewhere in the colonies. In Philadelphia, where Whitefield enjoyed enormous and long-lasting acclaim, efforts to combat his "enthusiasm" arose entirely because of the religiously competitive nature of Pennsylvania society. There the lack of a religious establishment produced a marketplace of religious options, and ministers fought hard to gain and retain membership. Religious controversies stayed within denominational boundaries, and clergy worried that theological disputes would repel potential members. The Anglican ministers Archibald Cummings and Richard Peters used the event to settle long-standing political scores, and the Presbyterian minister Jedidiah Andrews worked to bridge differences and spoke as if he just wished the whole conflict would go away. Nobody tried to prevent Whitefield's crowds, which rarely caused much disruption anyway. The threat of social upheaval never occurred to antirevivalists there as it did to Alexander Garden in South Carolina.[73]

Neither did Whitefield's greatest opponent in Boston, the famous Rev. Charles Chauncy, worry about the social consequences of Whitefield's ministry. Like Garden, Chauncy preferred to view the New Birth as a gradual, not instantaneous or momentary, process of eliminating carnal behavior and learning piety. He too warned against extrapolating the metaphor of birth beyond what Jesus intended. Like Garden, to ascertain whether or not one had begun this process of New Birth, Chauncy turned to a rational assessment of the degree to which one's life matched with the reasonable commands of scriptures.[74] When Garden warned against zeal "not fenced with knowledge," Chauncy cautioned his hearers about the dangers of "zeal not governed by knowledge, or not temper'd with prudence, or not accompanied with charity."[75] Like Garden, Chauncy preached an entire sermon on enthusiasm, and in it Chauncy defined "enthusiasm" in terms almost identical to those of Garden, highlighting the self-referencing and allegedly arrogant tendencies of the evangelical. "The word is more commonly used in a bad sense," Chauncy wrote to the evangelical James Davenport, "as intending an imaginary, not a real inspiration: according to which sense, the Enthusiast is one, who has a conceit of himself as a person favoured with the extraordinary presence of the Deity. He mistakes the working of his own passions for divine communications, and fancies himself immediately inspired by the Spirit of God when all the while, he is under no other influence than that of an over-heated imagination." Most discouraging was the fact that "they are not therefore capable of being argued with; you had as good reason with the wind."[76] There are many other examples, but this should suffice to demonstrate the similarity between these two venerable opponents of George Whitefield.

The only significant difference, and it is a striking difference, between Garden's and Chauncy's antirevivalism during the Great Awakening, at least according to the historical record, is that Chauncy's rhetoric never exceeded the bounds of theology, personal piety, and salvation. He did worry about disorder, but only in that vulnerable minds could be led into theological confusion. He fretted that the ecstatic behavior exhibited during evangelical worship would interrupt "a just decorum in speaking in the house of God." When he warned against the "damage [enthusiasm] has done in the world," and here he did briefly mention the practice of holding all things in common, "wives as well as goods," he focused on the disdain for the sacraments and the Bible. In all of the confusion, people would be led astray and the ungodly dissuaded from true and necessary repentance. Whereas Garden spoke of enthusiasm leading to all sorts of public evils, Chauncy noted the much more internal and individualistic danger of enthusiasm's seeming tendency to breed unbelief and deception. He would have had reason to give more attention to the social disruptions caused by the revivals because his sermon on enthusiasm was directed chiefly toward James Davenport, not Whitefield; Davenport's excesses in calling out unconverted ministers went further than virtually anyone else's and ended sadly in what appears to have been a mental breakdown. Chauncy, however, saw no serious threat to the well-established social order in his community, and so he chose to maintain his theological focus.

Because of this, Chauncy's sermon ended in a place much different from Garden's. Chauncy proposed something that Garden would never have countenanced; he suggested that the people should sit quietly and look for good to come out of the revivals: "Greater advantage may, in the end, accrue to true religion, by the utterance of an enthusiastic Spirit, and the prevalence of it, at certain times, than we may be capable of discerning at present." What advantage? The Great Awakening represented an opportune circumstance for searching one's own soul and mind for evidence of genuine piety and for rooting the church more firmly in doctrinal truths. In other words, evangelical delusion provided a splendid foil to true religion. His sermon thus ended on a more positive note, calling his flock to "look with comfort for the appearing of our Saviour Jesus Christ."[77]

What accounted for this difference between the antirevivalism of Garden and his polite fellows and that of Philadelphia and Boston ministers? These three cities plus New York City were America's largest. Their populations all stratified within a social hierarchy. They all served the same king and to a similar degree received the same ethnicities among non-African immigrants. They all faced problems dealing with Native Americans; they all engaged in overseas trade; and they all operated with the same imperial tensions that pervaded the New World empires. However, one difference stands out in such relief that it is a wonder historians have not emphasized this as the key to understanding the course of the Great Awakening in South Carolina: slavery. Each of the cities used slave labor, but only in Charles Town and its environs did African slaves outnumber whites; the populations of the other cities did not even come close to such a ratio. Of the other three, New York City had the most slaves as a percentage of population, about 20 percent, and Boston the smallest, approximately 8.5 percent.[78] Hence, although each city lived with potential hazards common to all New World settlements, only Charles Town faced the ever-present and enormous threat of annihilation at the hands of rebelling slaves. Boston and Philadelphia ministers did not discuss the threats to social stability inherent in the evangelical message because social stability was not such an abiding concern within their populations.

Garden capitalized on this difference in crafting his most potent argument against evangelicals: following their message would lead inexorably to the success of slave rebellion and the death of white society. In recommending that evangelical clergy be dismissed to monasteries, Garden meant to scorn and humiliate his opponents and caution potential converts to evangelicalism. His legal action officially branded Whitefield as a religious rebel, which could prove useful in any Atlantic context. Garden's action mounted a campaign against Whitefield that worked in South Carolina and helped to slow down Whitefield's Atlantic ministry, at least for a time. Whitefield simply took his preaching elsewhere.

Even though Whitefield's views of Garden changed over the course of the first months of 1740, it took him longer to give up completely on his ecclesiastical superior. Whitefield described Garden as a "good soldier of Jesus Christ" and a "friend" after his first visit to Charles Town in 1738. When Garden confronted him the next time he saw Whitefield, in March 1740, Whitefield engaged him on the topic of "justification by faith alone" and "found he was as ignorant as the rest." When the exasperated commissary told him to leave his house, Whitefield claimed that he and his friends left "pitying the Commissary, who I really thought was more noble than to give such treatment." He described one of Garden's antievangelical sermons as "virulent, unorthodox, and inconsistent," born of a "heart" that "seemed full of choler and resentment." He concluded, "I could not help thinking the preacher was of the same spirit as Bishop Gardiner in Queen Mary's days," drawing comparisons between Garden's temperament and that of the scourge of radical Protestantism of the seventeenth century.[79] That was about the strongest language Whitefield would use against his colleague. Remarkably, Whitefield continued to worship in St. Philip's even after Garden publically preached against him from the pulpit; the sermon *Take Heed How Ye Hear* was only one of several sermons directed against evangelicals. These observations may suggest some sort of calculation on the part of Whitefield, such as an attempt to demonstrate his orderliness and faithfulness in the face of persecution, like a true martyr. Maybe he attended Garden's sermons to collect evidence of Garden's supposed misunderstanding of scripture and right doctrine. Or maybe he took seriously the biblical principle of resisting the urge to misunderstand spiritual battle as a battle against "flesh and blood," and so he was reluctant to cut short his church attendance and abandon hope of personal reconciliation with his elder.

There are reasons to believe each of these conclusions, and likely all three are true to some degree. Whitefield often spoke of persecution, at times almost yearning for it as evidence that he stood in a long line of faithful, and prominent, saints of the church. After hearing Garden preach a sermon "full of many bitter words against the Methodists . . . and me in particular," Whitefield wrote in his journal that he "immediately retired to my lodgings, rejoicing that I was accounted worthy to suffer this further degree of contempt for my dear Lord's sake." Then, echoing the words of Jesus on the cross and those of the first Christian martyr, Stephen, in the book of Acts, Whitefield broke into prayer for his adversary: "Blessed Jesus, lay it not to the Commissary's charge!" That Whitefield attended sermons in order to accumulate evidence of Garden's false doctrine is less convincing, since he mentioned the sermons without spending much time describing them or using them in some sort of analytical comparison of the two doctrinal camps. More persuasive is the idea that Whitefield refused to see persons as enemies, choosing instead to cast this conflict as a contest of ideas.

After Garden preached his first sermon against Whitefield with the itinerant in the audience, Garden pressed the legal suit. Whitefield reported in his journal that the following Saturday night they "conversed . . . amicably," so that the young minister had hopes that Garden would take a more irenic stance the next day in the pulpit. Instead, Garden preached the sermon *Take Heed How Ye Hear.* Disappointed, Whitefield "advised the people, since the Gospel was not preached in the church"—note the passive voice that avoided naming Garden— "to go and hear it in the meeting houses," meaning dissenting churches. If by this he intended for them to quit attending St. Philip's altogether, he led by example, explaining that his conscience forbade him from attending where the Gospel was not preached. According to his account, his preaching during this time effected noticeable change, inside and out, as polite folks came confessing that they "spent more on their polite entertainments than the amount raised by their rates for the poor," while "jewellers and dancing-masters beg[a]n to cry out that their craft [was] in danger," women hid their jewels in embarrassment or disavowed them altogether, and masters promised to teach their slaves Christianity. Internally, claimed Whitefield, many were "awakened to seek after Jesus Christ." In all of this excitement for Whitefield's ministry, he "sometimes feared they would be too hot against the Commissary; but I endeavored to stop their resentment as much as possible, and recommended peace and moderation to them, in most of my discourses."[80] Whitefield barely mentioned Garden from this point on.

Indeed, Whitefield seemed to discount Garden's importance, judging that the commissary's power failed to extend beyond the confines of Charles Town.

When Garden wrote his first letter to Whitefield, a sincere and measured request for Whitefield to explain some apparent contradictions in his theology, or to "untie this Knot," as Garden worded it, Whitefield replied with a brief letter that refused the challenge, saying that "it would be endless to enter into such a private Debate, as you, Rev. Sir, seem desirous of." Just read his published sermons and let the people decide, he advised. Whitefield could not waste time in personal correspondence with the commissary.[81] Whitefield did show up at Garden's trial against him and seemed to take it seriously while in town. Instead of relating his version of the trial in the appropriate date in his journal, he noted instead, "Here would follow a particular account of my trial, but it is judged proper not to publish it, whilst the cause is depending." Apparently he had secured friendly counsel to advance his cause during the trial. Nonetheless, once he left town he continued his ministry as usual. He may have pursued a hearing with various authorities in London, but when nobody took up the case, it faded away and Whitefield never looked back.[82] When in 1746 his good friend Josiah Smith, minister at the Congregational Church in Charles Town, wrote to Whitefield of Garden's publishing of the affidavits in the *Gazette,* Whitefield scoffed, "I am not at all disposed to take any notice of Mr. G[arde]ns performances, only to pity and pray for him."[83]

In short, Whitefield seemed to view Garden as a decent man who was ignorant of true evangelical doctrine. He never commented on Garden's style of preaching or other spiritual demeanor, although he might have agreed with one of his friends who defended evangelicalism in a way that backhandedly commented on the relative formality of the Anglican rector: "If a Man in prayer rises a degree above the Pathos of a Parrot . . . tis Enthusiasm, beneath man's Reason, and Powers of Intelligence."[84] It is likely that as Whitefield sat listening to Garden preach, he saw not the powerful leader of the most important church in South Carolina but rather a small and frail older man whose demonstrations against the revivals proved more pathetic than problematic, or perhaps even amusing. Rather than sensing in him a formidable opponent whose ministry needed to be destroyed, he moved past the commissary and took his preaching to more promising audiences. His ministry extended across the Atlantic, while Garden's reached only to the surrounding parishes. In this view, Garden appeared more as an annoyance at most, a pitiable theological child who could whine to the few people listening. Let Garden have his hundreds; Whitefield had his tens of thousands.

If this telling accurately describes Whitefield's early confidence, events would prove his casual dismissal of antirevivalism in Charles Town to be a mistake. Under Garden's guidance, an antirevivalist tide had begun to sweep evangelical revivalism and its social critique out of the lowcountry. By early 1741 the

Great Awakening in South Carolina had burned out. Garden's sermons proved effective after all. His friends' journalism had struck more powerful chords than Whitefield's criticisms of polite society had. Most important, Garden had capitalized on the biggest blunder Whitefield made in his ministry in South Carolina.

*Chapter 6*

# MARRIAGE

The evangelical threat of social disintegration perceived by Garden took its most lively form, and a form unique to southern American culture, in the context of colonial slavery. One can scarcely suppose that any major event in South Carolina could take place without some reference to the institution that saturated its laws, traditions, habits, beliefs, and prejudices. To ignore the fact that nearly two-thirds of the Carolinian population suffered as slaves and thus represented the most potent source of colonial discord is to misunderstand the course of the Great Awakening in the South. Unlike Whitefield, Garden was acutely aware of the need to control the slave population tightly by any means if white colonists hoped to survive in such a volatile environment, especially after the disastrous Stono slave rebellion of 1739. He correctly perceived that the egalitarian strain in Whitefield's evangelical ministry could be exploited as a potent example of the dire lengths to which Whitefield would go to overturn polite society. Garden devised a masterful strategy to use the institution of slavery to prove the legitimacy of his own Anglican, polite social leadership while demonstrating the social dangers inherent in evangelical enthusiasm. His strategy worked. Garden's ministry emerged from the Great Awakening stronger than ever, with cultural consequences that would last for centuries. Meanwhile, Whitefield was forced to moderate his social critique and look elsewhere for evidence of the work of God's saving grace according to evangelical revivalist terms.

Ironically, George Whitefield gave Alexander Garden a perfect opening to use slavery as a bludgeon against the Great Awakening. In late 1739 and early 1740, en route to his home in Georgia from a trip through the mid-Atlantic colonies, Whitefield crossed through Maryland, Virginia, and the Carolinas. After he reached Savannah, he wrote his infamous letter against Archbishop Tillotson. He also penned a letter directed toward southern slaveholders. In that letter he castigated southerners for their inhumane treatment of slaves. Virtually every line was quote worthy, filled with remarkably colorful and startlingly vituperative language. Benjamin Franklin published the Tillotson and slave letters as a set sometime after March 1740. Garden appears to have obtained a copy of the letters in July, probably from friends or maybe from Whitefield himself. Interestingly, the letter to slave owners was never printed in South Carolina. The local printer and editor of the *South Carolina Gazette,* Peter Timothy, printed many of Whitefield's other works, including his letters against Tillotson, so why not this one? The answer was, because of its potential for inciting slave insurrection. Garden knew that, and he seized on the opportunity to pound home his theme that heeding Whitefield's siren call was suicidal for Carolinians. Garden published a response to Whitefield's criticisms, but he avoided reciting the most inflammatory sections of Whitefield's description of southern slavery. Whitefield's remarks unwittingly raised an alarm across the South; they accurately exposed the brutal truths of southern slaveholding. To Garden and his colleagues, this meant that the letter must be banned and denounced. Rather than provoking thoughtful response and careful reform, Whitefield's letter and Garden's counterattack stifled the Great Awakening in the South. Still reeling from the catastrophic Stono Rebellion and lingering rumors of more revolt, Garden and his friends circled their wagons and fought back, with one exception: in direct response to the evangelical critique of southern polite society, they also did an astounding about-face on slave education and established what could have been a magnificent blessing to slaves. They founded a slave school.

By rebuffing Whitefield's critique of southern slaveholding, Garden recommitted himself to South Carolina's polite society and lost an opportunity to join his voice to the small but growing chorus of critics skeptical of American forms of slavery. By supporting Garden's slave school, an institution unheard of in the southern colonies because of the social dangers it represented, South Carolina polite society placed in Garden's hands the very reins of social control. Garden prevented evangelicals from savaging his moral leadership—it was he and not evangelicals who put moral theology into daring practice. At the same time, the slave school assuaged whites' guilt concerning slaveholding practices while maintaining firm control over slaves. Alexander Garden accomplished a trifecta: by gambling his popularity when he dared to oppose George Whitefield, he and his colleagues suppressed revivalist evangelicalism, burnished the moral gilding of their own polite leadership, and saved slavery in the South. The marriage between Garden and his slave society was complete; it was not an arrangement of convenience but one of survival.

The slave school should have been instituted many years earlier. From its organization in London in 1701, the Society for the Propagation of the Gospel urged Carolinians to Christianize their slaves. The SPG sponsored hundreds of missionaries around the Atlantic and incorporated in its founding objectives the preaching of the Gospel to the Indians and slaves of the British colonies. The "Instructions for the clergy employed" by the SPG included "Directions to the Catechists for Instructing Indians, Negroes, &c."[1] The SPG's first missionary in South Carolina, the schoolteacher Samuel Thomas, met with some success working with slaves before he died in 1706, and he predicted that "many [slaves] might be brought into the folds of Christ" with proper instruction.[2] His successor, Francis Le Jau, carried on his work until his death in 1717. Le Jau, who wrote frequently to the SPG about his zealous efforts to catechize and baptize slaves, was careful "always to Act by the Consent of the Masters," whose frequent objections he would "endeavor to answer as [he] had opportunities," and he succeeded enough to report encouraging numbers of black attendees and communicants at his services. "Our baptized Negroes with Several others that came to be Instructed in the Principles of our holy Religion have behaved themselves very well upon all occasions, so as to disarm and silence Envy itself," Le Jau reported with pride.[3]

The SPG confronted the plight of slaves in other colonies as well. When in 1710 a wealthy planter bequeathed to the society a plantation in Barbados and approximately two hundred slaves, plans were laid to build a college for slaves that would serve as a model of the civilizing potency of the Gospel by turning out educated but docile slaves. Slave owners elsewhere were to take notice. The brutal realities of running a plantation as a profit-making enterprise where slaves could survive disease and hard labor long enough to attend school delayed its opening until the mid-1740s, but this was not for lack of effort.[4]

The leaders of the SPG in London may have exercised considerable zeal for Christianizing slaves, but conditions on the ground in the colonies inhibited evangelization. Masters prohibited missionary access to slaves, and enthusiasm among missionaries for reaching nonwhite southerners waxed and waned considerably. Slave masters feared that Christianization would foster rebelliousness or that somehow slaves might leverage baptism to sue for emancipation on the grounds that the Bible forbade Israelites from enslaving other Israelites. When Antiguans in the West Indies uncovered a massive slave conspiracy in 1736, they mustered "all white Men, without distinction, above 16" to militia duty. A "Gentleman" reported the news to a Carolinian friend, who published his letter in the *Gazette,* and laid most of the blame on "favorite Negroes" who were "capable of Writing and Reading and had been taught the Christian Religion conformable to the frequent Admonition of our worthy Diocesan the Bishop of London." The lesson was clear: such rebellion could "be expected from Converting Negroes."[5] The Reverend Richard Ludlam, Anglican minister at St. James Goose Creek Parish, got to the heart of the matter when he perceived that masters were not "so unwilling as afraid to bring their slaves over to Christianity."[6]

Because of white colonists' resistance to slave evangelization, the SPG confronted from its earliest days many of the excuses used by slave owners to prevent SPG missionaries from accessing slaves, and within two decades the society had worked out appropriate theological responses. The experience of Elias Neau in New York provides the most thorough example of how SPG leaders in

London could work with willing missionaries to counter slave master protests. The SPG recruited Neau, a French Huguenot schoolteacher made famous by his religious zeal in championing Protestantism in Catholic France, to be an Anglican schoolteacher in New York City. In 1703 he set about his work with fervent determination to reach slaves with a Christian education. Encountering resistance from slave masters, Neau turned to the SPG to promote the passage of a law obligating masters to educate their slaves in New York, which in turn prompted an effort to obtain such a law for the entire British Empire.[7]

To accomplish this feat the SPG needed to clarify two primary theological questions posed by slave owners. First, Neau and the SPG emphasized the biblical command for servants to be obedient to their masters. They reassured slave owners that educating and Christianizing slaves would only make their human property more complaisant, not rebellious. Neau noted that the catechism he used for slaves stressed "the two great Articles, Faith and Obedience."[8] Second, Neau and the SPG emphatically denied that Christian baptism released converts from bonds of slavery. The 1706 SPG annual sermon declared that there was nothing in the Christian religion that necessitated the freeing of slaves upon conversion, because Christian masters in the Bible were not ordered to emancipate their Christian slaves. The SPG failed to secure the desired imperial regulation, but members of the SPG were involved in procuring the Yorke-Talbot opinion issued by the imperial attorney general in 1729 and declaring that baptism did not alter the slaves' temporal state. Neau succeeded in obtaining a proclamation from New York governor Robert Hunter encouraging masters to send their slaves to Neau's school and a colonial law that encouraged baptism of slaves without any necessary emancipation. Neau's slave school survived until his death in 1722, at one point attracting a student population of over a hundred.[9]

In 1720, therefore, when Alexander Garden arrived in the Carolinas, the SPG had already worked around key theological obstacles to evangelizing slaves.[10] Proponents of evangelization and education had for nearly two decades publicized with some success arguments against the two primary objections posed by slave owners. Legal precedents for and practical examples of slave education existed in several parts of the British Empire, including South Carolina. Garden could have pointed to the work of Neau, Thomas, and Le Jau as models of effective mission work among slaves. He might have used SPG, imperial, and New York colonial declarations to counter any complaints among his parishioners that education and baptism would necessitate emancipation, at worst, or render slaves unmanageable, at best. For over twenty years he did nothing of the sort.

Occupying the office of commissary of the bishop of London obligated Garden to convey to his ministerial cohort the bishop's periodic scolding of southern planters for failing to evangelize their slaves. Occasionally Garden reminded his colleagues of their formal duties toward nonwhites, such as when he relayed the bishop's 1727 "Pastoral Letter, To the Masters and Mistresses of Families in the English Plantations abroad; Exhorting them to encourage and promote the Instruction of their Negroes in the Christian Faith."[11] Otherwise there is no evidence that Commissary Garden actively promoted the instruction of slaves in the Christian faith.

As a slave owner married to a member of one of the slaveholding and slave-trading families prominent in the South, Garden exhibited little enthusiasm for spreading the Gospel among slaves. By 1740 his brother-in-law John Guerard had established himself as a leader in the slave trade. Most of the wealthiest slave merchants and plantation owners in the colony were Anglican and worshiped in the churches headed by Alexander Garden and his clergy friends. Councilman Joseph Wragg, who sponsored more slave ships and paid more in slave import duties than any other single person in the period 1735–75, sat in St. Philip's on Sundays.[12]

Garden's reluctance to push for the education of slaves changed with the onset of the Great Awakening because of the attacks George Whitefield lodged against Garden and his polite friends. Whitefield published "A Letter to the Inhabitants of Maryland, Virginia, North and South Carolina," with the date-line Savannah, January 23, 1740, not three weeks after his arrival in Charles Town. It began with a statement of sympathy that evoked Whitefield's sense of the common humanity of whites and blacks: "As I lately passed through your provinces, in my way hither, I was sensibly touched with a fellow-feeling of the miseries of the poor Negroes." However much one might appreciate his honesty and frankness—and rue the fact that he would later back away from the letter's most radical implications—the letter also indicated that as an evangelist who hoped for a harvest of souls in Charles Town, he grossly misjudged the nature of his audience. Indeed he indicated that he was aware of the possibility that his letter would offend many southerners when he wrote, "How you will receive" the letter "I know not; whether you will accept it in love or be offended with me, as the matter of the damsel was with Paul for calling the evil spirit out of her, when he saw the hope of his gain was gone, is uncertain."[13] This was a reference to the sixteenth chapter of Acts in the New Testament, which describes the imprisonment of the Apostle Paul for converting a young slave whose skills at prophesying had been a source of profit for her masters. By castigating southern opposition to evangelization in biblical context, Whitefield's—at least rhetorical —concession that he was unsure of himself diminished further the possibility of a positive reception of his letter.

Whitefield then blasted southern slave owners for their "abuse of and cruelty to the poor Negroes." He recounted how masters treated their dogs and

horses better than their slaves and forced slaves to grow their own food after
their miserable work in the masters' fields. He also had "been informed by an
eye-witness" that slaves had been, "upon the most trifling provocation, cut with
knives, and have had forks thrown into their flesh: not to mention that numbers
ha[d] been given up to the inhuman usage of cruel taskmasters, who by their
unrelenting scourges ha[d] ploughed upon their backs, and made long furrows,
and at length brought them even to death itself."[14]

If Whitefield was living dangerously at this point, he then proceeded to
plunge over the line of permissibility by invoking the specter of slave rebellion
as a form of moral justice. He wondered, "considering what usage they commonly me[t] with . . . that we have not more instances of self-murder among
the Negroes, or that they ha[d] not more frequently risen up in arms against
their owners," though "Virginia ha[d] been once, and Charles Town more than
once, threatened in this way. And though I heartily pray god, they may never
be permitted to get the upper hand; yet should such a thing be permitted by
providence, all good men must acknowledge the judgment would be just." To
suggest that slave rebellion was understandable and even justifiable, especially
during the immediate aftermath of just such a terror from which whites had not
yet recovered, was a strategy either naive, stupid, or unusually brave, or perhaps
all three. Whitefield continued, pointing out that in the Bible God responded to
the cries of oppressed slaves. Whitefield referred to the Gibeonites in 2 Samuel
21, who were "slaves like yours." God sent plagues on the Israelites for their ill
treatment of the Gibeonites, and southerners could expect no less. The blood of
the African American slaves "will ascend up to heaven against you" and incur
the righteous judgment of God. It would be a dull southern wit who could not
perceive at least some measure of danger in the letter by this interloper.[15]

Whitefield was not finished. Particularly discouraging to the evangelist
was the unwillingness of masters to teach their slaves the ways of Christianity: "Enslaving or misusing their bodies, comparatively speaking, would be an
inconsiderable evil, was proper care taken of their souls: but I have great reason
to believe, that most of you on purpose keep your Negroes ignorant of Christianity; or otherwise, why are they permitted through your provinces openly to
profane the Lord's day, by their dancing, piping, and such like?" Notice how the
evangelical concern with allegedly worldly entertainment meshed with southern treatment of slave labor. That Whitefield most certainly did not understand
the African and often religious roots of slave dance was irrelevant to the point
he was making regarding the seeming moral laxity of masters who tolerated the
paganism of their slaves.[16]

Whitefield rightly connected this reluctance to evangelize slaves to the common concern that exposing slaves to the Christian Gospel of freedom would
inspire them to press for earthly freedom and equality: "I know the general

pretence for this neglect of their souls, is, that teaching them Christianity would make them proud, and consequently unwilling to submit to slavery." To Whitefield, however, this reflected badly on the ethical "precepts of Christianity" they held dear. "Do you find," he challenged masters, "any one command in the Gospel, that has the least tendency to make people forget their relative duties? Do you not read that servants, and as many as are under the yoke of bondage, are required to be subject in all lawful things to their masters, and that not only to the good and gentle, but also to the forward?" Besides, Whitefield continued, if teaching Christianity to slaves would have "such a bad influence upon their lives," why were masters "generally desirous of having [their own] children taught? Think you, they are any way better by nature, than the poor Negroes?" Whitefield did not, and he argued that "if born and bred up here, I am persuaded [Negroes] are naturally capable of the same improvement" and that adult slaves could also "be brought effectually home to God."[17] The reader should not be distracted by the paternalism of Whitefield's comparison and miss how much it struck at the slave owner's identity by blurring the distinction between the souls of white children and those of black children. While Whitefield's spiritual egalitarianism should not be misrepresented as a cry for social leveling, it could be—and was—easily construed as corrosive to the social hierarchy.

By chastising southerners—and their clergy—for not Christianizing slaves and by denouncing his fellow Anglican clergy for their lack of New Birth spiritual vitality and condemning the polite entertainments in which many in St. Philip's congregation indulged, Whitefield struck at the very foundations of Garden's leadership. Whitefield insisted that Garden's pastoral care was illegitimate. How could Garden provide spiritual guidance to Christians when he himself failed the test of true Christianity: a testimony of inner conversion accompanied by outward manifestations of a Spirit-filled life? How could Anglicans follow a leader who had failed to mobilize southern missionaries to reach the very people to whom they had been commissioned to preach in the first place, slaves and Indians? Putting George Whitefield's sermons against unconverted clergy alongside his letter against southern slaveholders illuminates the implicit but pointed personal attack against Garden that the commissary could not and did not miss: Rev. Alexander Garden was a polite, slave-owning, luxury-loving, religious fraud who manifested no concern for the welfare of the weak.

George Whitefield's ministry manifested a genuine strain of spiritual egalitarianism, if perhaps also a bit of youthful naïveté about the true nature of colonial slavery and social hierarchy. He was an Englishman whose colonial base of Georgia would not be a slave colony until 1750 and who spent a considerable portion of his time in the middle and northern colonies. He would become a slave owner himself because of his chronic need for financial support of an orphanage he founded in Georgia, apparently conceiving of slavery in strictly economic terms as merely one form of labor. However, Whitefield also preached unabashedly to the poorest and most oppressed in the colonies, including blacks. His journals recorded the many times that he directed his homilies and counseling to black hearers, at times spending evening hours visiting with the personal slaves of his hosts. For instance, shortly before arriving at Charles Town, he stopped at the home of a white settler in North Carolina and, as was his custom, counseled "the negroes belonging to the house." The prayers of two slave children convinced him that "Negro children, if early brought up in the nurture and admonition of the Lord, would make as great proficiency as any white people's children."[18] At one point he proclaimed that he "doubt[ed] not, when the poor Negroes are to be called, God will highly favour them, to wipe off their reproach, and shew that He is no respecter of person, but that whosoever believeth in Him shall be saved." Among those who hindered slave evangelization, the idea that God was calling slaves to salvation implied disobedience. Even in New England, as the historian Harry Stout pointed out, Whitefield's call for the salvation of black souls could be seen as progressive, for he submitted to print the "first journalistic statement on the subject of slavery" in the northern colonies. Prompted by Whitefield, the press discussed the souls of slaves for the first time, establishing "a precedent with awesome implications."[19]

One of those implications of the notion of black souls was the acceptance of blacks into the body of Christ. To be converted meant to share in the divine nature of God on an equal basis with all other believers, as Whitefield explained in a sermon on the sanctifying power of Christ's righteousness: "And O what a privilege is this! To be changed from beasts into saints, and from devilish, to be made partakers of a divine nature; to be translated into the kingdom of God's dear Son! . . . to put on the new man, which is created after God, in righteousness and true holiness!"[20] Whitefield made clear the egalitarian nature of these fabulously expansive works of God in human souls when he finished one of his most popular sermons, "The Lord our Righteousness." He turned directly to blacks in the crowd and declared that he did not mention them last because he "despised" their souls but because he wanted to make "the deeper impression" on their hearts. To the crowd, including his print audience, Whitefield affirmed that "in Jesus Christ there is neither male nor female, bond nor free; even you may be the children of God, if you believe in Jesus."[21]

Many slaves responded with appreciation to Whitefield's recognition of their humanity and possession of souls. Whitefield's popularity among slaves is well documented. For instance, Phillis Wheatley, an African slave in Boston, wrote a famous poem that memorialized Whitefield's death. In it she reminded fellow Africans that Whitefield applied the Gospel to "every one" and that if slaves would respond to the invitation, God would make them "sons, and kings, and priests to God."[22] This was radical thinking for the eighteenth century. Slave masters were not accustomed to conceiving of their slaves as kings and priests to God.

George Whitefield's profoundly egalitarian (for that time) ministry, even absent his letter against slaveholders, clashed against southern racial conventions. While Whitefield folded this concern for slaves into his attack on pastoral delinquency, he also busied himself in philanthropic work of his own. It must have annoyed Garden that Whitefield pointed repeatedly to tangible evidence of his own piety: his orphanage in Georgia, called Bethesda. Whitefield began planning for his orphanage during his first visit to the Americas in 1738. By January 1740 the orphanage was caring for approximately twenty children, a promising start to what would become one of the most important social and economic institutions in colonial Georgia.[23] Whitefield took to ending his homiletic exhortations to forgo worldly attractions for the sake of God's kingdom with an appeal for donations to the orphanage. The link between "the benevolent heart of Mr. Whitefield" and "the idea of building an Orphan House" was not lost on his hearers. The connection here came from the pen of the religious skeptic Benjamin Franklin, whose wit in his autobiography provided an entertaining account of how effective Whitefield's fund-raising could be. His curiosity piqued by Whitefield's popularity, he decided to attend one of Whitefield's sermons. Before arriving he "silently resolved" not to give money for the orphanage, believing that the enterprise was poorly planned. Alas, Whitefield's benevolent pleading overcame Franklin's famous anticlericalism enough to empty the deist's pockets of gold, silver, and copper coins into the collection for Bethesda.[24] Meanwhile in the South, Whitefield's friends pointed to Bethesda as evidence of Whitefield's "Compassion to the Souls and Bodies of Men," thus linking the minister's spiritual message of mercy to its earthly manifestation, and the legitimacy of his spiritual leadership to evidence of his own piety.[25]

Garden could not let these evangelical attacks on the foundations of southern society and his own leadership go unanswered. He responded to Whitefield's open letter about southern slavery in a letter of his own printed at the end of July 1740. In this letter, published just after a slave had revealed that some 150–200 slaves were conspiring to break open the armory in Charles Town and equip themselves for rebellion, Garden highlighted the terrible social dangers Whitefield's critique of southern slavery could catalyze.[26] Garden agreed with Whitefield that "the little or no proper Care taken by Owners of the Souls of their Slaves" was "too sad a Truth" and "a sore Evil indeed!"[27] He also claimed, however, that "the Generality of Owners use their Slaves with all due Humanity" and that Whitefield's attack simply demonstrated his utter ignorance. In some places, warned Garden, Whitefield could be sued for "slander" and "indicted for Meddling . . . which may endanger the Peace and Safety of the Community."[28]

That he recognized the peril in Whitefield's justification for slave rebellion was demonstrated by his partial quotation of the most inflammatory passage of Whitefield's letter, the part justifying slave rebellion: "'And indeed, considering what Usage they commonly meet with,' &c.—I suppress the remainder of this, and the next following Paragraph of your Epistle, as judging it both sinful, and dangerous to the publick Safety to reprint them."[29] Garden worried that while most slaves could not read the paper, they could listen to other readers, white or black, and be incited to rebel.

More important than instigating Garden's printed protest, Whitefield's persistent pointing to the potent example of his personal piety, Bethesda, forced Garden to change his mind about slave education. Garden and his friends met fire with fire: after more than two decades of doing nothing to alter the spiritual, emotional, or material situation of slaves in South Carolina, Garden mustered his friends to the difficult work of founding a slave school in Charles Town. Unlike Whitefield, Garden was acutely aware that implementing slave education, especially after the calamitous Stono Rebellion, necessitated controlling the slave population and buttressing white power. He correctly perceived that he could exploit the egalitarian strain in Whitefield's evangelical ministry as a threat to the survival of southern white society by preempting Whitefield's philanthropic efforts with a slave school of his own. Garden devised a masterful strategy to use the issue of slavery to demonstrate the social dangers inherent in evangelicalism's seemingly irrational enthusiasm and to show the legitimacy of his own Anglican, polite social leadership. It worked. Not only did Garden's ministry emerge from the Great Awakening stronger than ever, but in addition he forced Whitefield to moderate his social critique and shift his evangelical ministry elsewhere.

Garden's strategy to use the slave school to defend rhetorically the legitimacy of polite leadership, including his own, revolved around proving that the school was more socially responsible than Whitefield's orphanage. First, Garden compared the "happiness" of southern slaves to the supposed ill treatment of orphans at Bethesda. Second, Garden organized the school upon principles conducive to discipline and social order, principles familiar to Garden's southern audience but allegedly foreign to the itinerant English minister. Third, men who had already earned public approval as responsible leaders oversaw the school, which was not the case for the orphanage. Fourth, while Garden and his friends continually castigated Bethesda as a financial scam, his school, they tried to demonstrate, operated as a truly philanthropic enterprise. Garden's benevolent work would be reported in the *Gazette,* leaving no doubts as to his superior spiritual leadership.

Garden claimed that slaves actually were "far . . . from being miserable." In a defense that presaged the arguments of nineteenth-century slavery apologists,

Garden favorably compared the "happy and comfortable" lives of southern slaves to those of "three fourths of the hired farming Servants, and Day Labourers, either in Scotland, Ireland, or even many Parts of England, who not only labour harder, and fare worse, but have moreover the Care and Concern on their Minds how to provide for their Families," a burden borne in the Carolinas by masters, not slaves.[30]

Garden compared—to his advantage—the treatment of slaves to that of Whitefield's orphans, noting the need for adequate discipline in both regards. Claiming that just as Whitefield based his accusations of southern mistreatment of slaves on hearsay, so Garden could repeat rumors of Whitefield's "abuse and cruelty to the poor orphans . . . not only in pinching their bellies, but giving themselves up also to task-Masters and Mistresses." Would it be fair, demanded Garden slyly, for him to repeat those accusations in a published "Letter" to Whitefield and suggest that God would approve if the orphans "put an End to their own Lives, or Yours, rather than bear such Usage?" Garden reminded Whitefield that "there must be due Discipline, or Rod of Correction exercis'd among Children" that might "and often is misrepresented for Cruelty and bad Usage." In the same way, "Discipline and Correction must be observed among every Parcel of Slaves . . . which in like Manner, may be, and often is [*sic*] misrepresented in the same Light."[31]

The fact that discipline in the cause of moral order constituted Garden's concern regarding proper treatment of slaves became even more evident in the method Garden advocated for Christianizing slaves. He rejected Whitefield's recommendation of education as "a poor Remedy" for slave insolence, though he agreed that Christianizing slaves would not make them more rebellious, as long as it was done properly: "I believe the Reason of their being so kept [in ignorance], is the want of one certain uniform Method of teaching them, and which I hope will soon be established with success."[32] This could be supplied by the 1727 pastoral counsel for the Christianization of slaves received from the bishop of London and recommended by the commissary in the introduction to his reply to Whitefield.

The pastoral letter from the bishop lamented the limited progress made "towards the delivering [of] those poor Creatures from Pagan Darkness and Superstition," but ultimately it affirmed the prerogative of masters in dealing with slaves. The bishop understood that the resistance of masters stemmed from "mistaken Suggestions of the Change which Baptism would make in the Condition of the Negroes, to the Loss and Disadvantage of their Masters." He reassured them that God would make up the difference in labor lost to religious instruction and that "the embracing of the Gospel, does not make the least Alteration in Civil Property, or in any of the Duties which belong to Civil Relations." What of the argument that Christianization bred discontent and rebellion? To be sure, "humanity forbids all cruel and barbarous Treatment of our Fellow-Creatures," but at the same time, "Christianity takes not out of the Hands of Superiors any Degrees of Strictness and Severity, that fairly appear to be necessary for the preserving Subjection and Government." Garden exhorted masters to try to be reasonable and compassionate but allowed that in some cases incorrigibility demanded a severe response, and "of this Necessity" slave masters should always "remain the Judges." In other words, baptism compelled no amelioration of discipline or deference; masters would "be in no Danger of suffereing" because of the Christianization of their slaves. Ironically, in justifying such severity Garden implicitly affirmed the notion that Christianization might inspire slaves to resist suppression, for in the next breath Garden asserted that the brutal suppression of a Christian slave could never outweigh the slave's gain of eternal life: "the greatest Hardships that the most severe Master can inflict upon them, is not to be compared to the cruelty of keeping them in the State of Heathenism, and depriving them of all Means of Salvation."[33] To the bishop and to Garden, the needs and wishes of the masters must take precedence. Theirs was a spiritual concern that was not to interfere in any way with the prerogative of the master to deal with his slave however he saw fit for the subjugation of the slave.

Thus the proper program for Christianization must accommodate to the needs of the colonists. Christianization must adhere to a uniform method and be free from the passing barbs cast by itinerant preachers. Foremost in this method was the maintenance of discipline and social order. Garden perceived that Whitefield's willingness to admit the justice of slave rebellion stood in stark contrast to his program to maintain order at all cost. Living in a society that teetered on the brink of rebellion and chaos, Garden understood in ways that Whitefield could not that a slavery-based society required that masters be allowed freedom to implement and manipulate rigorous social control. Dispensing with even the harshest of disciplinary methods, especially in the cause of some abstract morality or theology, would break the chains that connected blacks to whites and that held white society safe. For Garden, evangelicalism challenged not merely the religious status of slaves but also the social system of oppression and hierarchy that undergirded southern slavery.

Garden countered Whitefield's reckless call for slave evangelization with his own, presumably more socially responsible, plan. In June 1740 he responded to the bishop's inquiry as to "the most effectual Method for Instructing the Negroes and Indian slaves" in Christianity. He disingenuously announced—for the first time—that this had been "a matter of my long and serious attension."[34] He then listed his recommendations for the establishment of a school for slaves, and he offered to head up the organization of such a school according to his own design. His proposal did not address the sheer injustice of withholding the means to satisfy the intellectual and spiritual needs and desires of slaves, and it bristled with the social control so necessary in a colony outnumbered by slaves.

First, advised Garden, members of the society needed to start small so as not to meddle too much with slave masters' "property" by disturbing slave life and profitability. Rather than attempt the mass instruction of all the colonial slaves, they should approve the establishment of a slave school in Charles Town. Garden warned against sending a European to teach or do any other work for the school; he did not explain why, but perhaps, with Whitefield in mind, he felt that a European would be less familiar with slavery and less sensitive to the needs of southern slaveholders. Rather, a few slave "Males as should appear most capable and best disposed," between the ages of ten and sixteen, and "who shall appear to be of Sober docile Dispositions" would be selected for training as schoolteachers. They would be "Negro Schoolmasters home born and equally Property as other Slaves, but educated for this Service and employed in it during their Lives, as the others are in any other Services whatsoever." Slave masters would select these slaves, but the society should understand if a master declined this opportunity in light of "the loss of the Annual Profit from the labour of One slave." Garden had inquired of some legislators whether a law might be passed to compel a planter to comply with the society's wishes, but he had been informed that such a law meddling with "Properties" could not be passed, or "rather [legislators] would not do it being most of them Parties concerned." Garden had even considered "whether the Hon Society might not obtain his Majesty's Recommendation for the Passing such a Law in the respective Colonies" but had dropped the idea because colonists usually "evaded" such laws. Instead, Garden suggested that the society authorize the purchase of slaves for the purpose of training them to be the school's teachers.[35]

Other slaves would then attend the school under the slave teachers' instruction. The school would become what would later be called a "normal school" for the training of teachers. Garden recommended slave youths as pliable and expendable students. Slaves would convene in Charles Town and commence instruction and training as teachers. They would first learn "the Principles of the Christian religion, as contained in the Church Catechism, to read the Bible, and to make use of the Book of Common Prayer," after which they would return to their plantations as schoolteachers for the instruction of the other slave children. Interestingly, Garden wrote that "as among us Religious Instruction usually descends from parents to Children so among them it must at first ascend from Children to parents, from Young to Old." Why? Children did not normally instruct their parents. Indeed, Garden's wording appears more prescriptive than descriptive. Perhaps he felt that the content and character of the teaching could be controlled better if it were simplified and channeled through the children. In this way the young and relatively inexperienced minds of the children would mediate the knowledge as it passed to the older slaves who could challenge, alter, or redirect the social implications of the knowledge, although he did note that some of these educated children would grow to adulthood and continue the work. Or perhaps the school represented more of a response to the evangelical challenge than an acknowledgment of the demands of justice to lighten the burden of slavery; teaching children was simply much less intrusive in the exploitative colonial economy. A master could more easily do without the labor of a ten-year-old than a twenty-year-old. That the children would be left to try to teach their adult relatives at the end of the day when the adults returned exhausted from the fields, or on Sunday or "other spare times," would be of little consequence to Garden. He likely knew that slaves in South Carolina needed to use their "spare time" for the production of their own food supply.[36] Besides, children teaching adults—an arrangement that Garden recognized explicitly to be the reverse of the chain of command in white society—would fit nicely in a society that persistently attempted to rob slaves of human dignity.

Having begun small, Garden promised, the school would quickly advance under his guidance. This training of slave children required, of course, their learning of reading and writing, a process that could take "the Space of two years," but once these slaves returned to their home slave community, "a nation within a nation," instruction would multiply exponentially. Indeed, Garden predicted, "but for the space of Twenty years the Knowledge of the Gospel among the Slaves . . . would not be much inferior to that of the lower sort of whole People, Servants and Day Labourers (specially in the Country), either in England or elsewhere."[37]

To prove his sincerity and to maintain strict supervision by a proper colonial authority, Garden offered to take personal command of this endeavor.[38] The SPG must have concurred, for in May 1741 Garden reported that he and his longtime friends William Guy and Thomas Hasell planned to purchase two slaves for the society. Garden informed the society that he would provide for the "Maintenance and Education" of the slaves. He elaborated on his plan for the school. When the two slaves finished their instruction, one would, under the careful supervision of Garden and two other trustworthy persons, assume the teaching responsibilities of the other slaves sent by their masters to Charles Town. The other would settle in a country school and be paid five pounds sterling per year, a sum that could easily be provided by the parishioners.[39] Meanwhile in October 1740 Garden requested that Peter Timothy print the bishop of London's "Letter to the Masters and Mistresses of Families in English Plantations abroad" and "Letter to the Missionaries" exhorting them to train slaves in the Christian religion. It was the first time since the *Gazette* began publication in 1732 that Garden had publically sought to relay the bishop's desires for slave education and Christianization.[40]

By April 1742 Garden's plan for slave education was under way, two slaves having begun their teacher training. Andrew and Harry were fourteen and fifteen years old, respectively. Garden had purchased them from the estate of the deceased Alexander Skene, who earlier had been singled out by the missionary Francis Vernod when he noted to the SPG that "Scarce any body besides the Honourable Alexander Skeen Esq. and Mrs Hague take any care to instruct" their slaves.[41] Later that year Garden characterized one of the slaves as "an excellent Genius" who had already learned to read. The other slave was "of a somewhat slower Genius, but of a milder and better Temper and to the best of my Judgement will require less Authority and Inspection over him when he comes to the intended Service, tho possibly 3 or 4 months later than the former." Evidently, Garden preferred the "slower" but more tractable "genius."[42]

A year later, in October 1743, Garden announced to the society that the school in Charles Town was complete and had opened on Monday, September 12, "when several children (on publick notice, and some previous Discourses on the subject from the Pulpit) were sent thither for Instruction." Apparently Garden's "publick" solicitations worked wonders, for he expected the enrollment to increase to thirty in a short period, thus requiring more than one schoolmaster. Garden expected that the school should cost the society little, and "the Masters and Mistresses of the Children he instructs readily contribute such a Trifle." In fact, reemploying the language he had used against Whitefield in a phrase dripping with cruel irony, Garden noted that when it came to maintaining the school financially, "even the very Slave Parents themselves would gladly do it, tho they should pinch it off their own Backs, and out of their own Bellies."[43]

Garden submitted glowing reports on the school well into the 1750s. In 1744 he wrote, "The Societys negro School, under my Care, succeeds even beyond my first Hopes or expectation. Upwards of Sixty Negro Children are now Daily taught in it . . . and the number still gradually increasing so as sufficiently to employ both the societys youth to teach them."[44] By 1748 fifteen slaves had been "dischargd sufficiently instructed according to the design of the said school and 5 or 6 more are on the point of being dischargd as equally qualifyd."[45] In October 1752 Garden reported that the schoolhouse had blown down in a hurricane but that he "had another ready prepard for that Service; and the said School goes on with the Usual Success."[46]

Garden boasted about the triumphant success of the school for reasons that went beyond personal satisfaction with his work. Whitefield's attack on southern slavery had prompted this sudden interest in the welfare of slaves. As noted, Whitefield repeatedly referred to his orphanage for purposes of fundraising and to legitimize his claims to greater piety. Garden's friends began calling into question the financial integrity of the institution as a means of tainting Whitefield's ministry with scandal and shoring up their own polite leadership, resting as it did on a base of social responsibility and benefaction. The founding of a slave school, then, could serve two crucial interests for Garden: his need to answer Whitefield's attack on slavery and encourage public disparagement of Whitefield's orphanage and ministry; and his personal desire to shore up his standing as a legitimate member of Charles Town's social elite.

In mid-1743 the *Gazette* reprinted a pamphlet from New England that claimed that Whitefield had chosen Georgia for his orphanage because it was a distant, failing province that attracted little attention from responsible men who could keep an eye on Bethesda. The writer took advantage of the fact that the English colony, having been settled the previous decade, was still in a primitive state. In language that had to make the aspiring gentlemen of Georgia cringe, the author identified Bethesda's location as "a remote Place, where none of us can control [Whitefield's] Accompts, a frontier Colony, in the most dangerous Situation; under such an unfortunate Constitution; or such wretched Management, that 'tis already half desolate." No wonder, the writer continued, Whitefield used as references for his orphanage "Persons quite unknown to us, and, with all their sounding Titles, of no greater Distinction, than Clerk and School-Master of one of our Hospitals."[47]

The pamphlet also challenged Whitefield's financial stewardship of Bethesda in a way that questioned his entire ministry. The pamphlet writer wondered how some ministers could encourage "this vain empty conceited Stroller, in sponging, by a Mask of Religion, upon so many well meaning People, both for himself and his phantastic Project, no better than one of the Bubbles in the South Sea Times," a reference to an infamous failed investment scheme in the 1720s.[48] Another author claimed that Whitefield had collected money specifically and explicitly for the orphanage but that he pressured several major donors to allow him to appropriate it "for his own use." Whitefield's criticisms of luxurious living rang hollow for this author, for "did not [Whitefield] appear as much like a Prigg of a Parson as any ever did" by wearing "the best Purnelle and finest Hollands with Wiggs of Five Guineas a Piece?"[49] The author thought so, and so he used Whitefield's appearance to paint the evangelical censure of polite fashion as hypocrisy, perhaps merely a tool to provoke class resentment and gain a following by using what amounted to eighteenth-century populist rhetoric. Who could trust their charitable giving to such hands as Whitefield's?

Whitefield's critics could produce little evidence of malfeasance, and historians have uncovered no damning evidence, but the accusation against Whitefield's financial integrity proved to be useful rhetoric. Early in the contest a writer in the *Gazette* dismissed Bethesda as an extension—and victim—of Whitefield's diabolical Calvinist teaching: "having damn'd us without grudging," Whitefield was "reduc'd . . . T'accept beneath a thousand Pound/Towards founding Georgia's Orphan . . . For coining Dupes and catching Fools."[50]

By 1743 antirevivalists had claimed to have evidence of Whitefield's financial misdeeds. "Publicola" published a letter to the managers of the orphanage demanding full financial disclosure and offering in the meantime an audit of unclear origin, declaring that Whitefield's financial statements were "imperfect, unvouched, nor any wise attested Ones." The letter made a half-hearted attempt at objective responsibility out of concern for the public purse, claiming that Whitefield's continued "begging" demanded his highest integrity. Publicola reiterated previous attacks: the orphanage was a "Nest or Receptacle of idle vagabond Fellows" under the cover of a few orphans; it was a "Protestant Popish convent, of Men and Women, Boys and Girls"; the evangelicals used it to make themselves rich; Whitefield had not supported it with any of the money given to him for that purpose; and after he left the colonies the orphanage had had to fend for itself, with the "poor, dear Lambs . . . reduced again to a Starving Condition." The "account" then listed several orphans whose age or wealth called into question their status as dependent minors, or who were not being employed or trained in any useful occupation. This was followed by a financial statement showing no money received from Whitefield and no money generated from the hard work of the orphans. Meanwhile, Whitefield "indulged his own frail Tabernacle, [ate] and drank, and wore of the best."[51]

A year later Publicola published another open letter to the overseers of Bethesda, this one claiming that he still "waited with Impatience" for a satisfactory response. He accused Whitefield of duplicity for the purpose of financial gain and of playing himself off as "a stanch Churchman in Old England, a thorough Independent in New England, an Anabaptist 'mong Anabaptists . . . becoming all Things to all Men, not that he might gain some, but make some Gain of All!"[52] After Whitefield's on-site orphanage manager, James Habersham, curtly responded in the next issue that, not wishing to "render Railing for Railing," he would wait until Whitefield returned from England to give an account of all financial transactions in England and in the colonies, another southerner posted a poem that recalled when the "Whitefieldian Fever was at its Height in Charles Town." After Whitefield went about sowing discord "through each quiet State . . . / To rob weak Men, and their poor Wives beguile," and charitable people gave him money, the Calvinist preacher turned around to declare, "Our best of Actions, with all solemn Pray'res / Are ev'n sinful, in th'Almighty's sight."[53] Here was a mixture of theology and material concerns, with the Calvinist rejection of good works as efficacious in the attainment of God's favor characterized as counterproductive to the Christian teaching of charity and social responsibility.

Garden erected his own school in full public view in order to illuminate how it differed from Whitefield's orphanage. Garden published notices of his school's fund-raising in the *Gazette*.[54] The school would be closely supervised by upstanding members of Charles Town's elite class. These men had enough faith in his enterprise to fund it as well. Readers of the *Gazette* could peruse a list of donors, confirmed by the vestry, that named such leading men as Charles Pinckney, John Wragg, Robert Pringle, Jacob Motte, and Benjamin Smith.[55] Likewise the vestry maintained oversight of Garden's school.[56] Perhaps most important, less than eight months after Publicola called for a full financial account of Bethesda, Alexander Garden voluntarily published an account of his expenses, including the exact amount paid to named recipients for specific work done on the school and the precise amount of money donated by named persons. An accompanying statement verified that the account had been "audited and examined by the proper Vouchers, and approved by the Vestry of the Parish of St Philip, Charles Town, and signed by William Smith, Clerk." Next to this was a statement that "The above Accompt was sworn to, by the Reverend Mr. Garden, before me this 12th Day of December, 1743. James Wright, J.P."[57] Four months later Publicola renewed his demands for a full account of Bethesda's finances, this time using Garden's language in reminding Whitefield of "The Publick's reasonable Expectation and Demand of your Accompts, your full, faithful, sufficiently vouched, sworn to, authentickly audited, and attested Accompts of the said House."[58] With his eye on Bethesda, Garden clearly positioned his school as an ethically superior model of Christian charity and responsibility.

In sum, while confirming the leadership credentials of his own polite cohort, Garden sought to expose Bethesda as a philanthropic scam perpetrated by a religious heretic bent on social mutiny. In the words of the antirevivalist pamphleteer noted previously, "Let one but cant boldly about Religion, make the most impudent, barefaced boasting of his own Attainments, and Spirituality, and Orthodoxy, and give them proper Objects to vent their Wrath upon, and gratify a latent Vanity and Pride, and by bespattering all who differ from himself, and them, as cursed, damned Hereticks; and by insinuating great and general Contempt of their regular Ministry, as Men of no true spiritual Experience, or Ability, or Soundness; and the Populace will believe him in any Thing; even tho' be asserted, that the best Place for a British Orphan-House was the Peak of Teneriffe."[59] What is most remarkable is that this school was built after two more incidents involving slave rebellion that shook Carolinian society in the early 1740s. One month after Garden signed his May 1740 letter to the society conveying his recommendations for evangelizing slaves, a slave revealed that some 150–200 slaves were conspiring to raid the armory in Charles Town and arm themselves for rebellion. This conspiracy, according to the historian Peter Wood, had "the Appearance of greater Danger than any of the former" and "originated . . . in the very Heart of the Settlements" in St. John's Berkeley

Parish. Forewarned, a militia laid a successful ambush, 50 slaves were hanged, and the slave informant received "a new wardrobe and 20 pounds in cash."[60]

More infamous to historians of colonial evangelicalism was another threatened rebellion, this one in late 1740 and early 1741 and involving a wealthy planter and close associate and recent convert of Whitefield's, a self-proclaimed evangelical prophet named Hugh Bryan. Following a massive fire that destroyed over three hundred buildings in Charles Town, Bryan published an open letter in the *Gazette* that castigated the moral leadership of Anglican clergy with the typical evangelical ire directed against southern polite society. He excoriated ministers who, while "nourishing and indulging themselves in the same Passions, Tempers, and Delights as other Worldly minded men," nurtured "no Bowels of Love, no Pity for poor perishing Souls," especially among the slaves.[61] In 1741, probably with Whitefield's encouragement, Hugh and his brother Jonathan, among others, began educating and evangelizing slaves on their plantation while continuing to issue colorfully dire warnings to their white neighbors of God's imminent judgment upon their licentiousness and cruelty. Fearing slave rebellion, the colonial government sent officers to arrest Hugh Bryan, and before long he repented of his behavior and sought forgiveness. When it was discovered that Whitefield had edited the letters for Bryan, the itinerant was arrested too. Like Garden's attempt to silence Whitefield, the case quietly faded away after Whitefield posted bail and left a few days later for England.

By 1742 the colonial assembly was sufficiently worried about the "frequent and great Assemblies of Negroes" organized by the Bryans that it authorized an official investigation, which ultimately led to an indictment of Hugh Bryan for endangering public safety. During the investigation Bryan sent to William Bull Jr., speaker of the Commons House, a copy of prophecies predicting that God would use slaves to inflict his wrath upon the colony in judgment for ungodly behavior. The Commons House promptly issued a warrant for Bryan's arrest. Before he could be reached, however, Bryan experienced some sort of mental breakdown. Believing himself to be a Moses figure, Bryan attempted to part the waters of a river with a stick but succeeded only in falling in and nearly drowning himself. The episode snapped Bryan to his senses. He wrote a letter of retraction and apology to Speaker Bull that was published in the *Gazette,* and the incident melted away.[62]

These events have caught the attention of historians not because of what Bryan accomplished toward the goal of freeing slaves—he failed in that regard—but because of their long-term effects. Leigh E. Schmidt characterized the Bryan-Whitefield affairs as the first of "early evangelicalism's challenge to the [Anglican] establishment and slavery in the colonial South."[63] True, this episode did deeply disturb the colony, but the challenge to the establishment, which

Schmidt described almost solely in terms of Anglican clergy, reached back to the second visit by Whitefield, almost a year or more before the Bryan incidents, and involved more than simply an attack on slavery. The threat was not to slavery per se, especially since Whitefield never condemned the institution of slavery itself and would advocate strenuously for the legalization of slavery in Georgia by 1750—the government of Georgia had prohibited slavery since its founding in the 1730s—but to the slave-based culture specific to the southern colonies.

Indeed the fact that Garden's school, which on the surface appeared to satisfy the demands of the evangelicals, was built in the immediate aftermath of alarm complicated the evangelical challenge and demonstrated that the conflict turned on social control, not on a simple disagreement over the morality of slavery or the desire to care for the spiritual welfare of slaves. The school hinted at the way that issues of slavery connected to the most basic problems and prevailing solutions of colonial society by reflecting the desire of white colonists to redefine and inculcate the Christian virtue of submission among the black population while assuaging their moral guilt for keeping their slaves in unenlightened "paganism." What appeared as a simple attack on slavery by Whitefield revealed in actuality a wide disagreement over the repercussions of Christianizing the "wrong way." To get it wrong was to risk the apocalyptic rebellion that colonists feared so greatly. To get it "right" would serve the interests of the planters and the clergy, who would benefit from the reinforcement of their leadership authority not only among slaves but also among whites who looked for the manifestation of social responsibility and liberality among their betters. The historian Alan Gallay has brilliantly demonstrated how a chastened and humbled Bryan continued to evangelize and educate his slaves in a way purged of its most radical tendencies. Gallay located "the origins of slaveholders' paternalism" in this more conservative and oppressive evangelical slave reform.[64] If the southern evangelicals did develop a new form of slaveholder paternalism, though, they got the idea from their neighbors in the Church of England.

The timing of the end of the Great Awakening in South Carolina also spoke to the attention commanded by the revivalists and the social power of the antirevivalists. Judging from the reported size of the crowds and their excited responses, and the appearance of the first serious opposition to Whitefield, the peak of the Great Awakening in this colony occurred in mid-1740. In January 1741 Whitefield still wrote with thankfulness about the donations he received in South Carolina, but he also noted that "some have fallen away."[65] Indeed Whitefield seemed most excited in his journal about a reprint of letters he received relating the great work of God begun in colonial society. However, the letters were from correspondents in Boston, and they wrote of New England, not the South. There is little evidence that Whitefield received a response as fervent in Charles Town after 1740. After 1741 the antirevivalists held the upper hand—almost the only hand—in the newspaper debate. Apparently even Whitefield's most ardent defenders had grown wary of a too uncritical affirmation of his message. On August 30, 1742, one of Whitefield's Carolinian critics used the *Gazette* to mock the decline of revivals in Charles Town: "Considering how Whitefieldism has raged and rioted in some other Colonies to the Northward . . . we have great Reason to thank God, that it has so favourably subsided in this." He claimed that Whitefield's "zealot Disciples" in the town "are so reduced here, as if there were none remaining." That was wishful thinking, for evangelicalism continued to be at least as strong as before the Great Awakening. Yet the writer's bold assertion suggested that revivalism had not merely declined by 1742 but had already died out entirely.

Time Line of the Great Awakening and Great Anti-Awakening

---

### 1738

| | |
|---|---|
| May 7 | George Whitefield arrives in Georgia for the first time. |
| Aug. 28–Sept. 9 | Whitefield in Charles Town before leaving for London. Alexander Garden friendly to Whitefield on the evangelist's first visit to Charles Town. Great Awakening in South Carolina begins. |

### 1739

| | |
|---|---|
| | While in the British Isles, Whitefield preaches against politeness and "unconverted" clergy. |
| Sept. | Stono Rebellion in South Carolina. |
| Oct.–Dec. | Whitefield arrives in Pennsylvania on Oct. 30 and makes his way south toward Georgia. He continues to preach against politeness and "unconverted clergy." |

### 1740

| | |
|---|---|
| Jan. 5–7 | Whitefield in Charles Town. Garden absent. |
| Jan. | Whitefield arrives in Savannah on Jan. 10. He establishes Bethesda orphanage. He publishes in Philadelphia his letter, datelined Savannah, Jan. 23, criticizing southern slaveholders and justifying slave rebellion. Letter probably is not seen in Charles Town until spring. |
| Mar. 14–20 | Whitefield in Charles Town area. Great Awakening strong in lowcountry. Blowup between Garden and Whitefield at Garden's house on Mar. 14. |

| Mar.–July | Garden corresponds with Whitefield in letters he would later publish as *Six Letters to the Rev. Mr. George White-field*. |
| June | Slave conspiracy involving 150–200 slaves exposed. |
| July–Aug. | George Whitefield in lowcountry. His journals report great success. |
| Sept.–Nov. | Whitefield in New England and mid-Atlantic colonies. |
| Sept. | Garden publishes his *Six Letters to the Rev. Mr. George Whitefield* in Charles Town. The final letter of the set, dated July 30 and probably made public in August, emphasizes the dangers of Whitefield's perceptions of slavery. |
| Oct. 30 | Garden publishes bishop's letters in support of slave education. |
| Nov. 18 | Great Fire breaks out in Charles Town. |
| Dec. 9 | Whitefield arrives in Charles Town. |
| Dec. 10 | Whitefield preaches in Charles Town that the fire was God's punishment of polite behavior. His journals do not report a positive response to his preaching. |

**1741**

| Jan. | Hugh Bryan and Whitefield publish letter justifying slave rebellion. Whitefield reports some converts have "fallen away." Drop in enthusiasm for Charles Town in Whitefield's journals. Momentum in newspaper war shifts to antirevivalists. Great Awakening in Charles Town is waning. |
| May | Garden reports to the bishop that he, William Guy, and Thomas Hasell made plans to purchase slaves to train as teachers for a slave school. By April 1742 the slaves Andrew and Harry begin training. The school opens with slave students by Oct. 1743. |
| June | In a letter to the bishop, Garden outlines his plans for a slave school. |
| July 13 | Garden with reference to the Dutartres family preaches the sermon he would later publish as *Take Heed How Ye Hear*. |

This makes sense given George Whitefield's stance on slavery, on which so many whites depended. Recall the events during the second half of 1740: Garden's most scathing sermons, spoken and published; the onset of other newspaper attacks; the devastating fire; and Garden's open letter to Whitefield rejecting Whitefield's antislavery letter. Garden's letter of July 30, 1740, represented the first public revelation of Whitefield's ignorance of slavery and the threat to southern slave society posed by the evangelical message.[66] Coming after the slave conspiracy of June 1740 and followed by Whitefield's involvement in Hugh Bryan's letter sympathetic to slave rebellion in January 1741, Garden's letters, and especially his refutation of Whitefield's criticisms of southern slaveholding, must have done serious damage to evangelical efforts in the South. Bryan's inflammatory prophecies and his subsequent meltdown in 1742 would have destroyed any doubts among most white Carolinians that Whitefield's evangelical message represented an intolerable threat to southern society. Revealingly, when Whitefield next spoke publicly on the issue of slavery, it was to advocate for the legalization of slavery in Georgia. Never again would Whitefield take on southern slavery, and it would not be until the revolutionary era of the 1760s and 1770s that evangelicals would speak out against the southern system of slavery. Even then they would speak only briefly and mainly among the Methodist and Baptist populations of the frontier west where the slave population was much smaller. Whitefield's first public criticism of southern slavery had cost him his audience, and the hazardous implications of the evangelicals' social message had put an end to the First Great Awakening in the South.

Meanwhile, Garden offered the slave school as a viable option to evangelical-style Christian philanthropy, particularly Whitefield's Bethesda. Southerners bothered by the utter dehumanization of African slaves in the lowcountry could take comfort in the Christianization efforts of Garden and his polite cohort via their slave school. Garden personally fared rather well in this public contest. After figuring large in the defeat of the revivals in the Carolinas, his St. Philip's Church continued to grow, ultimately splitting into two and sharing the religious life of Charles Town with St. Michael's, established in the early 1750s. Garden personally prospered and enjoyed the high life with friends in the slaveholding and slave-trading elite class. When he retired in 1754, his church honored him with a gift and a letter of appreciation signed by seventy-five of the most prominent men in Charles Town.[67] His polite parishioners and their descendants remained leaders of the colony into the revolutionary era and beyond.[68] Garden's school endured as a source of pride for years. Garden passed away in 1756, but the school survived until it closed in 1764 for reasons not entirely clear. It appears that nobody ever bothered to name it. Probably due to the disruption of the Revolution, formal slave education in Charles Town would not begin again until sometime around the turn of the nineteenth century.[69]

Choosing to follow Garden's lead carried an immense cost to southern society for many generations to come. Yielding to Garden's call for a slave school as a way to answer evangelical censure of southern spiritual negligence and lack of piety relieved southerners of the burden of reconsidering the earthly dimensions of southern slaveholding, particularly those having to do with discipline. Garden helped save southern slavery by making it morally defensible in the eyes of his eighteenth-century peers. They could go on becoming extraordinarily rich from exploiting slave labor using whatever means they felt necessary, confident that their good friend in Charles Town had their spiritual obligations covered. In that sense, the school represented a lost opportunity.

Telling counterfactual history—musing on what might have happened in place of what actually happened—is always a dangerous business for historians, but one cannot help wondering about the course of American antislavery and slavery had Garden used Whitefield's criticisms of slavery as an opening for reflection. Garden may be excused for embracing slavery, given how entrenched the institution had been for millennia all over the globe, but there were enough people in his own time who raised serious questions about the nature of eighteenth-century American slaveholding that one might hold him accountable for not mounting a more vigorous protest of his colleagues' brutal treatment of slaves and moving the Anglican Church in South Carolina toward a social stance more critical of southern moral norms. Most Anabaptists, an increasing number of Quakers throughout the colonies, and Garden's own predecessors in the SPG, including Samuel Thomas and Francis Le Jau in South Carolina, either refused slavery altogether or rejected its American forms, occasionally in print. An outspoken Lutheran pastor, John Martin Bolzius, had already voiced principled opposition to slavery in Georgia by the time of the Great Awakening, as had a group of Scots who had settled in what is now Darien, Georgia. The Boston Congregationalist Samuel Sewell published a tract arguing against the morality of slavery in 1700.[70] Given his considerable cultural influence, as demonstrated by his ability to found a slave school and shut down the evangelical revivals, who knows where a greater, more forthright conversation, led by Garden, might have taken slavery by the time of the American Revolution. One can never know, because Garden chose to reject evangelical critiques and reaffirm polite society in the lowcountry.

Yet the fact that Garden succeeded in establishing the first successful formal school for Africans in the slave society of the American South should not be discounted. Previous work among slaves in South Carolina never achieved such planter support, the SPG's work in Barbados failed, and Neau's efforts in New York City took place in a city and colony not nearly as dominated by slavery. Coming as it did after a period of particular unrest among slaves, culminating in the Stono Rebellion, and as whispers circulated among Garden's neighbors of an even larger conspiracy in the works, Garden's conversion to chief promoter of slave education was astounding. That he managed to found a stable and productive slave school with the money and public approval of Charles Town's merchants and planters most entrenched in the institution of slavery demonstrated how deeply he had embedded himself among their ranks. After years of ignoring the bishop and excusing his friends' neglect of the spiritual and intellectual lives of slaves, the man in charge of southern religion changed his mind and the minds of the members of a polite class who had vehemently refused to entertain the thought of slave education. The fact that Garden woke from his decades-long slumber at precisely the moment that Whitefield attacked southern slaveholding underscores the seriousness with which he took Whitefield's attack, the sensitivity among the southern elites to their status as New World slavers, and the potency of the evangelical message in the southern religious climate—or in light of the ultimate evangelical failure in the South, the *impotency* of the message in the face of southern slaveholding power. It was a seismic shift in the long and otherwise evolutionary history of Anglo-American perceptions of slave education. However much one might bemoan the fact that he missed an opportunity to present a more comprehensive and hard-hitting critique of slavery from his position of considerable strength in St. Philip's, the school was a resounding accomplishment.

The school sealed the relationship between Alexander Garden and South Carolina in a marriage both conservative and radical. As always, the goal in mind was social order, the maintenance of the racial, economic, and social status quo, but the method struck out in a radical new direction. Stepping away from their traditional and deeply ingrained mistrust of slave education and Christianization, Carolinians placed an astounding level of trust in their Anglican rector to do both and do them right, which in their minds meant the amelioration of the worst moral flaws of bondage without getting everyone killed. His ideas were not totally new—the SPG and others had argued for something similar for decades—but Garden proved that he could implement them to meet the actual conditions on the ground. He had earned the trust of his polite fellows through two decades of standing resolutely by their side against the scruples of ministerial newcomers, marrying into their ranks, joining them in their commercial and social endeavors, and carefully tailoring the church to meet the demands of southern life by trimming and adjusting moral concerns so as not to disturb the social hierarchy already threatened by such massive disturbances as epidemic diseases, hurricanes, wars, and revolts. The wealthy merchants and planters who signed their names as sponsors of the slave school trusted Garden's cool, pragmatic, experienced, and rational leadership.

Garden exhibited great trust in his fellow Carolinians as well. Simply to raise the possibility of a slave school could have sabotaged his career, bringing him under sharp suspicion at a time when he was already under severe attack from within the Church of England. Even so he did, trusting that they would take his ideas seriously and would even make the school financially possible and practically feasible by withdrawing enough slaves from the fields to "waste" their time learning church doctrine. He trusted planters' abilities to maintain order over an educated slave population. Most remarkably, to put this in breathtakingly crass eighteenth-century terms, Garden trusted in the abilities of African slaves to learn—and even to teach!—while keeping their instincts subdued enough not to rebel or become too unruly to work profitably for their masters. This last point is racist, but it should be remembered that three hundred years ago most white people doubted the intellectual abilities of slaves. In Garden's world, steeped in social hierarchy, where polite superiors doubted the abilities of even their white-skinned inferiors to manage without their sophisticated leadership and where nearly everyone thought of Africans as mere chattel damned by God to a life of abject service to a more advanced society, the notion that slaves possessed any sort of claim on education occurred to precious few. Garden's ideas were radical, and he dared to risk his career to advance them at a precarious time in his career. He committed himself to his society with the same degree of trust that they placed in him. The risks were immense, from the standpoint of eighteenth-century conventional wisdom. If education not only inspired Africans toward armed resistance but also gave them the tools of literacy to help make rebellion happen, another bloody slave uprising far worse than the Stono Rebellion, perhaps more reminiscent of the cataclysmic Yamassee War, would be inevitable. That Garden and his polite friends fought hard against evangelical criticisms of polite entertainments and luxury is nothing surprising. That they sought to conserve the status quo by engaging in a radical enterprise of slave education is nothing but startling. The marriage between Alexander Garden and his colonial culture truly was "till death do us part."

Most important for the history of South Carolina, the South, and the future United States, Garden and his friends fashioned a founding myth for South Carolina and the slaveholding South. Unlike the city-on-a-hill myth that animated and guided New England, this was an earthy myth with a religious veneer: to thrive in the inhospitable environment of the South, white colonists needed to exploit slave labor fully and without regret or hesitation, and to survive in a community built so thoroughly on slavery, whites needed to construct and enforce a rigid social hierarchy maintained and guarded jealously by the polite slaveholding elites. The church not only was part and parcel of this hierarchy, but it also presided over it spiritually and sanctified even its most carnal modes of behavior. Ministers preached no jeremiads in South Carolina because there was no myth of a godly founding generation to reflect upon but also because Garden and his peers saw little to criticize in their culture, for they created it and owned it. This was Garden's greatest achievement: to take the establishment of the Church of England and give it cultural meaning and authority. The myth of religious toleration bestowed upon the colony by its first proprietors still guaranteed a religious pluralism that weakened the Church of England numerically and politically, but socially, economically, and culturally the church had no rivals. Of course, not everyone applauded this marriage between Garden and his culture. It came at tremendous cost to a majority of the Carolinian population: slaves.

The founding of the slave school could be considered the crowning achievement of Alexander Garden's career. Was that how slaves perceived it, though? How did slaves view Alexander Garden? Unfortunately, slaves wrote precious little of their thoughts about anything during the eighteenth century, primarily because the law forbade them to learn how to write, and few masters cared enough about them to let them set aside their labor long enough to learn anyway. In the last half century, though, historians have done a remarkable job teasing out and piecing together bits of information from the records left behind by white writers and the material artifacts uncovered by archaeologists. Consequently the story of slavery and slaves' stories have undergone significant revision, resulting in a much clearer picture of how slaves in Charles Town might have viewed Alexander Garden.

Two generalizations from this literature are particularly useful in thinking about how Harry and Andrew, the two young slaves acquired by Garden to become schoolteachers, might have viewed their new master. The first is that even while masters exhibited great reluctance to allow slaves access to formal education and Christianization, slaves demonstrated a willingness to grasp both when given the chance. The fact that widespread Christianization of slaves did not occur until after the American Revolution is inexplicable without understanding this: slaves did not change their views of Christianity; rather, whites' willingness to allow them access to the Christian Gospel changed. It was not as though slaves suddenly reconsidered their attachment to African traditional religion or Islam or Portuguese Catholicism and made the switch. Missionary letters from South Carolina to London revealed a surprising number of reports of slave conversions. Francis Vernod of St. George's Dorchester Parish reported in 1732 that he had been able to baptize twenty-one slaves and one African child.[71] The Reverend Richard Ludlam of St. James Goose Creek Parish surmised that "either negro or Indian Slaves such as are brought up in their owners houses are very Capable of being made Christian Converts."[72] Stephen Roe counted forty-eight white communicants and fifteen black communicants in St. George's Dorchester Parish in 1741.[73]

Of course, not all slaves responded positively to Christianization or formal white education or anything else they viewed as imposed upon them by white masters. Slaves resisted exploitation in wide-ranging and creative ways. It may be that Harry and Andrew both accepted and resisted Alexander Garden and his educational enterprise. According to Garden, they "were both Baptized in their Infancy, and could Say the Church Catechism, when we purchased them, but knew not a Letter of the alphabet."[74] Harry quickly impressed Garden enough that the commissary praised him to the SPG, calling him "an excellent Genius" who could "(in the space of 8 months) read the N. Testament exceeding well." Garden expected that Harry would soon "be thoroughly qualified for the intended Service, and by that Time with God's Blessing, I shall have a School-house ready near my own and everything necessary prepared for his entering upon it here at Charleston, and make no Doubt, but by this time 12 Month, I shall be able to acquaint the Society of a very considerable number of negroe Children under his Tuition, regulated by my own Care and Direction." Garden was not so sanguine about Andrew, whom he judged "a somewhat slower Genius, but of a milder and better Temper." Andrew promised to "require less Authority and Inspection over him when he comes to the intended Service, tho possibly 3 or 4 months later than the former."[75] Alas, by late 1743 Andrew, the less academically inclined slave, was still "not yet sufficiently qualified to teach by himself," so Garden decided to try to "employ him as an Assistant in this School for his Improvement." The other teacher, apparently, was doing well, although the number of students was increasing "so as I soon expect more than one Master can well manage."[76] By 1744 Garden had given up on Andrew's ability to learn and teach. "Tho an exceeding good nature and willing Creature," Garden wrote, he "yet proves of so weak an understanding that I'm afraid he will not be soon Qualified to Teach alone and wish the society would give a discretionary Power to sell him and Purchase another of better Genius for Learning in his Room."[77] The SPG recommended that Garden send him to the SPG slave plantation in Barbados and purchase another candidate for the teaching position.[78] However, for whatever reason, Garden waited until 1750 to sell Andrew, for "five hundred pounds currency."[79]

So Harry took to the school and became a teacher, while Andrew "failed" out and was sold out of the school and disappeared from the records. Did Andrew truly not have the intellectual capacity to perform as Garden's schoolmaster? He had been selected because of his brightness and skill, so his "slowness" seems to have been a bit odd. Did he feign a lack of intelligence in order to withhold his brain from Garden's purposes, much as some slaves withheld their physical capabilities? Perhaps he resented being separated from his home plantation community. Maybe he sensed early on that Garden had designed the school and the curriculum to maintain the exploitative nature of slavery. If so, he took his place in the long line of slaves who resisted enslavement quietly, cleverly, and effectively, just enough to prevent exploitation but not enough for outright punishment.

What about Harry? Did he naively submit to Garden's purposes because he had a sharp intellect but not much intuitive ability to discern Garden's ulterior motives? Or did he make a calculation that learning to read was worth some submission of the intellectual kind? Perhaps he recognized the utility of literacy to the cause of resistance and figured that if he could help participate in the eventual emancipation of his own family, or future generations, he should submit to Garden's authority for a while. Or maybe he made a calculation of another kind, recognizing that teaching students in Charles Town was a far better lot in life than draining swamps and processing indigo. After all, Andrew got sold to Barbados and Harry did not, and since Andrew had now been labeled intellectually slow, chances are he ended up back in the fields. Such calculations were made by slaves every day.

How did the scores of slaves educated in Garden's school view the commissary? If Andrew and Harry were indicative of the possibilities, some saw the commissary as merely another taskmaster unworthy of their obedience, while others saw him as a means to get out of the hot sun and feed their intellectual curiosity. Perhaps, in an ironic turning of the tables, Garden became an unwitting tool for a potential future rebellion, this time by a more prepared, informed slave population, and Harry became the clever one. In any case both African men emerged from the story as at least partial agents of their own future, capable of making decisions according to their own calculus of self and community interests. Garden perhaps did not look so clever and powerful to them.

*Chapter 7*

# TILL DEATH DO US PART

When the dust settled from the Great Awakening and the Great Anti-Awakening after 1741, Garden stood fully in charge of his churches and his reputation. From then until his death in 1756 Garden diligently served the church and the community to which he had committed his life. He counseled parishioners and baptized them, married them and buried them, attended vestry meetings, corresponded with the bishop, managed his slaves, tended his estate, and distributed material relief to those less fortunate than himself. He retired as commissary in 1749. By 1750 he was in his mid-sixties and continued to struggle with poor health, and so he retired from the rectorship of St. Philip's in 1754. It was time for him to step aside and let other, younger men take the helm. He did, and they would, but not before saluting him for his years of faithful and steady service. At his passing, the colony was sturdier than it had been upon his arrival over thirty-five years earlier. The Church of England in the colony, which had been surviving but barely relevant in 1720, enjoyed a position of authority and good favor when he retired. His legacy has been forgotten today, which is unfortunate for he had contributed religiously to a cultural and political tradition, a foundational myth of slave labor, racial hierarchy, and polite leadership, that would persist through the Revolution and beyond, ending only with the Civil War.

From the end of the Great Awakening until his retirement, Alexander Garden continued with his normal routine as the most powerful and well-situated minister in South Carolina. He faithfully attended meetings of the vestry and church wardens of St. Philip's. It appears from vestry minutes that they attempted to convene every month, although some weeks they would gather several times, especially after vestry elections, and some months they would not meet at all. Their work consisted mainly of the mundane tasks of daily colonial life: investigating requests for and administering poor relief; contracting with doctors for the care of the indigent sick; authorizing repairs to the church and glebe house; overseeing the renting of pews in the church; and assigning orphans to caretakers.[1] Without a modern bureaucratic welfare system, the church was the second, after family, and last line of defense in warding off poverty. Almost all of the people to whom the vestry distributed food, cash, clothing, or other provisions were widows, orphans, or the physically disabled, for the vestry saw little excuse for a man not to take care of himself or his family. Poor laws prohibited aid to the able-bodied, and families were expected to tend to their own. When Nicholas Mattyson, probably an older man unable to work any longer, appealed to the vestry after his son refused to take care of him, the vestry ordered the clerk to remind the son of his duty and that "in Case of his refusal the Vestry will take such Measures to Compell him thereto as the Law directs."[2] Similarly the vestry took action when it appeared that their assistance was being abused. They sent the carpenter Andrew Physick "to the Workhouse" for "Provision, and the Doctor of the Workhouse was Order'd to cure his Sore Leg." Six months later, having heard that "by his drinking his sore leg was grown something worse," the vestry called him to their meeting and "Order'd that he should refrain [from] drinking for the future."[3]

The vestry intervened in a wide array of affairs of personal and public interest. In one case the vestry agreed to provide for a slave woman whose master had contracted leprosy. In another the vestry "agreed to pay for the passage of Margaret Shoonemgrober a poor Palatine woman and her four Small Children to Philladelphia where she has friends." In addition the vestry arranged for care for James Butler's "very bad Venereal Disorder." Occasionally cases of mental illness came to the attention of the church, such as when Peter Calvert, "much disordered in his senses," began "firing Pistols out of his Window at Night to the Danger of Peoples Lives." He had become "a Terror to the Neighborhood" and to himself, for it appeared he would squander all means to provide for himself. The vestry appealed to the governor to appoint a guardian. By 1754 the vestry began plans to build an "Apartment . . . for reception of People disorder'd in their Senses."[4] Unfortunately they were too late for Anne Le Bresseur, "a prime Disciple of Mr. Whitefield's" who grew anxious for heaven and "shot herself with a Pistol." She had "recommended the Care of her Child to the Rev. Mr. Garden," but that should not be taken as a confession that she had religiously gone astray and wanted to return to the Church of England before she died: Garden would have officially received any such abandoned child and assigned her or him to another caretaker.[5]

Some of the cases appearing before Garden must have moved him at heart. At one meeting in early October 1740 the vestry agreed to pay for "Mrs. Miller and her Children's Passage" to New York or Boston. The poor family never made it out of the colony. The parish register noted for October 30, 1740, "Then was Buried Prudence Miller at the charge of the Parish." Consequently, during the vestry's first November meeting, Garden and his lay colleagues took responsibility for "David Miller a Boy of about Thirteen Years old," "Prudence Miller a Girl of about Three Years old," and "an Infant named Joshua Miller about Ten days old." Then on December 4 the secretary wrote in his register, "Then was Buried Joshua Miller a Boy at the charge of the Parish." Seven months later, acting as a colonial version of today's foster care agency, the vestry transferred Prudence to another caretaker.[6] One wonders about the story behind this family and how it must have affected Garden and the vestrymen. Was the social gap between Garden and this indigent family narrow enough that their plight reminded him of his own loss of a wife and young daughter?

The responsibility for the church's maintenance also fell upon Garden and his fellow church officers. They called Mr. John Harris to account for not keeping the church clock in working condition and admonished Mr. Saltur to "behave himself with more reservedness, and endeavor to regain ye favor and Goodwill of ye Inhabitants."[7] People preferred "Burying People late in the night by Candlelight" to capture the symbolism of the end of a day, and so, to prevent setting the town on fire, the vestry decreed that funerals must take place during daylight hours, or if that were not possible, only three lit candles were permitted.[8] They also wrote a letter to the "Captains of the Watch in Charles Town" to "prevent the Negroes from making a noise" and disturbing church services on the "Lords Day."[9]

The natural disasters that periodically afflicted the colony especially taxed the vestry. The vestry met daily to hear appeals for relief from "such poor People who have been Ruined by the late dreadful fire" of 1740. People seeking help appeared before the vestry personally, and their names and amounts given were recorded in the vestry minutes. When the fund ran dry, wealthy individuals, whose names the secretary duly noted in the minutes alongside their beneficiaries and who included at least one wealthy woman, "Madam Sarah Trott," gave money to be distributed each day.[10] Beginning Friday, November 21, and excepting Sundays, the homeless met before the church to ask for money. By the second week of December, when the number of poor diminished, the vestry began to meet only two or three days per week. Most often the poor received monetary assistance, but when the church wardens of St. George's Dorchester Parish sent barrels of rice, St. Philip's vestry began distributing that food in place of or in addition to the cash.[11]

Garden witnessed in his own community the ordinary poverty that increasingly plagued many coastal towns and cities along the Atlantic coast. Ironically the problem, at least as the vestry saw it, had to do with the Atlantic commerce that was making them so rich. In 1735 the vestry recorded the following petition submitted to the colonial government: "Whereas a Number Idle, Vagrant and vitiously-Inclined People, either brought in by Shipping, or on Various Pretences, resorting hither from divers Parts of the Provinces And by Drinking and other Sorts of Debauchery Speedily reducing themselves to Poverty and Diseases, have of late years become a great and dayley increasing Burthen on this Parish," they sought permission to build a "Publick Workhouse and hospital."[12] The assembly did grant permission, and two years later the vestry ordered "all the Poor that are at present on the Parish" to take up residence in the workhouse, where they would labor for the bread the vestry would assign them.[13] From that point on the church wardens and vestry managed the workhouse themselves, referring the indigent—"Mrs. Hogg was Order'd to go to the Workhouse and to be kept to hard Labour"—and hiring doctors and food suppliers for the daily maintenance of the sick and dependent.[14]

Garden gave no indication of how he participated in these meetings. Perhaps he enjoyed flexing his power when the church judged people worthy or unworthy of relief or correction or when they awarded a contract for work on the church. Perhaps the meetings bored him. The work must have gotten tedious at times; at one point the vestry "Ordered that if Mary Griffeth come anymore to Trouble the Church Wardens, that Application be made To Two Justice's of the Peace to Punish her as the Law Directs."[15] Such a comment rarely appeared in the minutes, and it is more accurate to the historical record to assume that compassion for the unfortunate kept Garden to his task. Most of the time the vestry, church wardens, and Garden issued orders for the maintenance of widows, orphans, and the sick with expedition and compassion, and it appears that they denied few applicants. When they did withhold assistance, they noted that it was conditional and temporary, such as when they "were of Opinion, that at present" Mrs. Hughs was "not a proper Object of Charity—but in Case of Sickness," they would provide help.[16] In fact, though the vestry's obligations extended only to the inhabitants of St. Philip's Parish, they approved relief to so many transients that the colonial assembly periodically scolded them for their generosity. In part because of this fact, historians have judged Charles Town's public relief system, under the supervision of Alexander Garden, to be the most liberal in the American colonies.[17]

The duties of a colonial minister afforded him plenty of other opportunities to keep busy. A sense of the types of pastoral responsibilities that would have consumed Garden's daily energy as a minister in the deadly lowcountry climate can be gained from a letter he wrote to the bishop in 1732: the "Distemper with a violent Fever" broke out in early July and by the middle of the month "raged in such manner, & proved so mortal, that every House almost looked like a Hospital, & the Whole Town as one single House of Mourning." Garden's associates, fearful of catching the disease, refused to help him, and so Garden labored alone visiting the sick and burying the dead: "This, my Lord, Employed all my Time and Attention. The Sick Chamber or Church-yard were my constant Stations from Morning to Evening." By August 3 the disease had laid him low, causing partial paralysis and a difficulty in writing that he believed the bishop could discern from his letter, written three months later.[18] In fact his letters do suggest that the disease rendered his hands weak and shaky. (See figure 4.) Garden again proved his devotion to his flock during the 1739 yellow

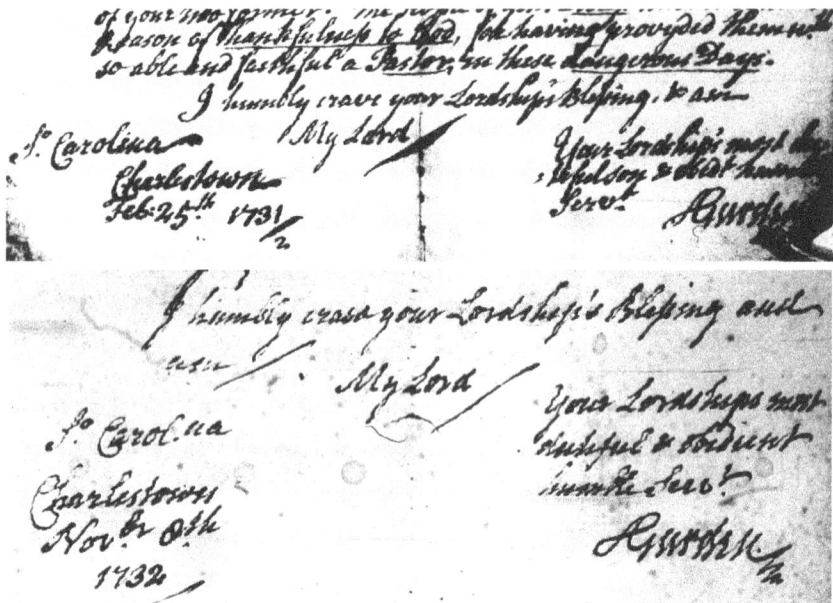

FIGURE 4. *Top:* Alexander Garden to Bishop Gibson, Charlestown, February 25, 1732, in Fulham Papers at Lambeth Palace Library, American Colonial Collection, 9:262–63. *Bottom:* Alexander Garden to Bishop Gibson, November 8, 1732, in ibid., 9:266–77.

fever epidemic. Robert Small from Christ Church Parish, the only minister who agreed to help him visit the sick and assist with the funerals—"from 4 to 12 Funerals of a Day"—died after a week in Charles Town. Then Garden fell ill, and he could not write "in guarding the People of my Charge," he wrote the bishop of London, "against the fascinating Gibberish of Young George Fox, alias Whitefield.[19]

Garden's work with the vestry and in tending faithfully to the sick, and risking his own life in the process, may link his ministry to his shadowy pre-colonial upbringing and lend strength to the theory that he was born under disreputable circumstances. Recall from chapter 1 that, aside from a brief mention of his college degree, Garden entered the historical record in 1720, when he arrived in Charles Town. Nothing was recorded of his parents, but there are several possibilities, one being that he was born out of wedlock. Such an ignominious beginning may have prompted him to leave Scotland and England and seek his fortune in the colonies. It may also have steered him toward the ministry out of compassion for the suffering and inspired him to persevere when others withdrew from the horrors of epidemic disease. Perhaps memories of his mother living with the pain of disrepute cultivated sensitivity toward suffering widows and his own experience as an "illegitimate" child softened his heart to the orphans who sought his help. However much his past drove him to America and motivated him to seek the comfort of wealth and public approval, it probably also fostered a kindness toward the less fortunate that guided him through his career in South Carolina.

Curiously, few records illuminate Garden's work with the other two colonies under his jurisdiction, North Carolina and the Bahamas. What does exist might explain this paucity of evidence. Apparently the distances between the colonies removed Garden from immediate oversight enough that his counsel was sought only as a last resort. Settlement in North Carolina took place more as an extension of Virginia than of South Carolina, even though the two colonies shared governments until well into the eighteenth century. Hence religious life in North Carolina reflected Virginia's influence more than South Carolina's, and Garden was consulted only when formally required. In 1737 Garden passed on a letter he had received about a drunkard minister who was caught on a Sunday "dead Drunk and fast asleep, on the Great Road to Virginia, with his Horse's Bridle tyed to his Leg" in Edenton, North Carolina. Garden believed the reports because of the reputation of the letter writers and because he had heard gossip of that sort when he passed through the colony a couple of years earlier. During that visit he did not have with him his commissary commission, which would have authorized him to make a formal inquiry, and besides, he noted, he had to hurry home before winter set in. Now, he said, the four hundred miles made it impractical for him to inquire in person. Therefore he simply forwarded the letter to the bishop and recommended that the bishop take action.[20]

Nassau, the main city of the Bahamas, lay over five hundred miles from the reach of Charles Town. Church records from both colonies rarely mentioned Garden and the Bahamas in the same place to any substantive degree. The two primary occurrences suggested that the islands did not capture much of Garden's attention or respect. In 1731 he reported to the bishop that William Guy had visited the islands to perform religious services. Guy preached, relayed the bishop's pastoral messages to the people, baptized, "married two or three couples, buried one woman, & christened upwards of 130 children." The inhabitants requested a full-time minister, but Guy reported to Garden that maintaining one could be difficult due to the poverty of the "extremely indolent and lazie" parishioners, who cared only to pillage offshore shipwrecks. Political gridlock stymied the passing of laws necessary to support a minister, and anyway, noted Guy, what minister would want to live under the supervision of the governor's "unhappy Temper" and obstinacy in refusing to get along with his subjects? With that, Garden moved on to more local concerns.[21]

Garden had good reason to avoid getting pulled into affairs in the Bahamas. The only other time Garden had dealt with the church's situation there predated Guy's visit in an episode that Garden appears to have dismissed with perhaps a bit of annoyance. In 1725 a long and sordid struggle between a minister and his parishioners erupted on New Providence Island. Thomas Curphey had officiated there since approximately 1723. There was some question about Curphey's qualifications as a minister and consequently the state of the souls he had baptized if, in fact, he was unqualified to perform the sacrament. That ordination papers were eventually found did not satisfy some on the island, and by 1727 doubts that he had been properly ordained plagued him enough that he left the island to seek employment in South Carolina. Once he was gone, two men, Edward Lease and Thomas Sackerson, swore they had witnessed Curphey consorting with Sarah Lawford, the wife of a gentleman merchant, Samuel Lawford, at whose home the two men were doing work. Samuel had been away on business. Why the two men were watching the house and peering into her bedroom in the early morning hours was left unclear. Upon his return, Samuel Lawford sorrowfully wrote to the bishop of Sarah and Curphey's "Criminal Correspondence." According to Samuel, Sarah "confessed the facts" and now believed herself to be pregnant with Curphey's child. Samuel "hastened" his affairs and sailed to Charles Town. There, Lawford said, Curphey confessed and "in ye Humblest Posture offered to beg My Pardon on His Knees."

However, when Lawford took Curphey to Garden, Curphey denied not only the affair but also ever having confessed or apologized for it. Curphey denied the charges to the bishop in a letter of his own, claiming that Lawford "can be prov'd to have been a Pirate, and is also accus'd with the Barbarous Murder of Several Men" and that Lease and Sackerson had "been frequently accuse'd and punished for Infamous and Scandalous practices, the one whipt about the Town for Perjury, and the other not much less wicked and vile." Curphey claimed that Lawford was simply trying to blackmail the minister, keeping it secret from everyone else on the small island, which, said Curphey, would have been difficult to do had the allegations been true. That story seems dubious, considering that Curphey's poverty made him an unlikely target for blackmail. A more likely explanation came from the pen of Woodes Rogers, governor of the island, who surmised in a letter to the bishop that the two laborers had made up the story to deceive both Lawford and Curphey into paying them off. His words, in their entirety, about the episode were as follows: "My Lord I hope that Affair your Lordship was troubled with hence and which you was pleased to Shew me from Mr Samuel Lawford was abuse to both the Reverend Mr. Curphey and Mr. Lawford who now lives comfortable with his Wife."[22] It seems that the two laborers had bullied Sarah into her confession in order to get money from the rich merchant at the expense of a harried and vulnerable minister.

Whatever happened, Garden never bothered to offer any other opinions to the bishop. It would not have been his responsibility in 1728 to adjudicate the affair, for he had not yet been appointed commissary. However, even before he became commissary he already felt free to insert himself in business not of his own in Charles Town, and in 1730, when he did write as commissary to report the sad state of support for the ministry on the island, just a few months before Rogers sent his comments on Curphey and Lawford, Garden said nothing about the situation.[23] Most likely he saw nothing of importance to himself in the contest and chose to ignore it so that he could settle matters closer to home. Ultimately his correspondence with the bishop concerning the Bahamas was comprised only of this letter and the 1731 letter regarding Guy's visit to the island.

Such negligence seems strange given Garden's reputation then and now as a hard-nosed disciplinarian. Historians have often painted him as either the right man for his office because of his diligence in enforcing propriety and the canons of the Church of England and promoting Anglican interests in the colonies, or as an ecclesiastical tyrant ignorant of true spirituality. In July 1728, before Garden became commissary, Rev. John Winteley complained to the bishop of disorder among the clergy, whose meetings were "more like Billingsgate," London's fish market known for its profanity and chaos, "than an Assembly of the Clergy."[24] No minister said that after Garden became commissary a year later. Winteley would feel the heavy hand of his lead minister by the end of 1729.

However, Garden's reputation for being a stickler for rules can easily be overdrawn. Brian Hunt, after being deposed in South Carolina for performing a marriage disapproved of by Alexander Garden, who charged Hunt with breaking church laws regarding marriage, retorted that "few of the Canons of the Church are observ'd by the Carolina Clergy." He spelled out several instances of ministers conducting weddings under circumstances similar to the one that got him in trouble and concluded that "no man breaks the Canons offner than the Minister of Charles Town."[25] Garden probably learned to bend the rules early in his career. In 1725 he asked the bishop to admonish the Reverend John LaPierre for baptizing children of St. Philip's Parish in their homes immediately after Garden had refused to perform the sacrament at church because of some irregularity in attendance. "I had," Garden told the bishop, "brought my Parish to tolerable good order and conformity in most things to the Laws and Rules of the Church" before LaPierre showed up. LaPierre's willingness to oblige independent-minded parents undermined Garden's authority and, Garden said, "tends to create a Dislike of my Parishioners towards me, as one too stiff and punctilious, not of an obliging enough temper and disposition (i.e.) not so complying with their Humours as Mr. LaPierre has shewn them I might be."[26]

Nothing remains to indicate that the bishop corrected LaPierre, but Garden did adjust his own course. Several years later Garden, when contending with

Andrew Leslie, a minister who had a difficult time getting elected in St. Paul's Parish, admitted to the bishop that he had warned Leslie against too strictly enforcing the forty-ninth canon concerning baptism, which stipulated that a child candidate for baptism must be sponsored by a communicating member of the church. Garden noted that there were too few communicating members in some rural parishes and that, given the tendency of sudden and fatal diseases to sweep away children's lives, parents were concerned that their children could die before an appropriate sponsor could be found. So, said Garden, the ministers agreed that they would not uphold "this Canon in all Cases, but a prudential only" and counseled Leslie "to follow the example of his Brethren."[27] Leslie relented, but years later he still could not persuade the vestry to hold an election. "Prejudices are easily excited but very hardly allay'd," Garden observed, and he then noted that there were "still some leading men" in the parish who were "pretty sanguine against him." They considered Leslie "stiff and assuming" with an attitude "more like that of a young, conceited Collegian than of a prudent Clergyman."[28]

Garden showed similar restraint when confronted with Rev. Francis Guichard, a French, Anglican minister who conducted his services in a Calvinist manner. Unwilling to disrupt a friendly relationship with his French neighbors and parishioners, Garden chose to look the other way.[29] Garden forged an impressive career out of such prudence; he had learned his lesson well. He could be firm with his peers—Hunt, Winteley, Whitefield, and many others could attest to that—when he sensed the need to defer to his polite friends. The "prejudices" so "easily excited" among the leading men factored into Garden's sense for determining which church policies he would enforce and which he would not.

Not all of his duties involved serious questions and contentions. Some of his activities he likely enjoyed as a respite from his urban obligations. Garden served as host for new settlers and assisted their transition to the colony. When a minister arrived without a call to a specific parish, Garden, upon verifying his credentials, could send him off to a vacant pulpit. If a minister had a call from a parish in hand, according to the Reverend Charles Boschi, it "was customary to wait at Charles Town until the vestry would send for their minister."[30] It would have been natural for Garden to host such a minister waiting for his vestry. Garden may have also hosted other visitors and immigrants. In 1733 Garden guided some Swiss immigrants to the Savannah River, where they found friends waiting.[31] Although no other accounts of Garden showing immigrants around the colony exist, it is likely, given the way ministers traveled to fill pulpits and in light of Garden's landholding interests in the countryside, that this was not an isolated incident.

These duties represented a considerable workload for a minister in any state of health and age but especially for a frail man in his fifties or sixties. Several times over the years Garden and his vestry pleaded with the bishop of London to send him an assistant. He requested help even before he became commissary. In 1724 he warned of needing to return to England if the bishop did not send aid. In 1736 he claimed to be so sick that he was "Scarce able to write my name. I hope by this time your Lordship has appointed an Assistant for this parish," though "when he arrives, whether he may not find a Vacant parish instead of an Assistant place, God only knows."[32] In 1736 the vestry and the assembly together took action on Garden's behalf, claiming that "The Great and dayly Increasing Number of Parishioners of this Parish hav[e] rendred the Pastoral Duty of the Same very difficult if at all Practicable for One Clergy man to Perform as it ought to be with Safety to his health and Constitution."[33] Usually the bishop complied, but his efforts must have seemed Sisyphean. Garden continued asking for an assistant because his assistants kept leaving in one way or another. In the 1720s Thomas Morritt was too busy teaching school. John Lambert died in 1729. In 1740 William Orr departed "on some private Affairs," and the minister who helped out Garden in the interim caught "the Distemper" and died. The next year Orr left for a parish of his own. In 1748 Garden lamented that his assistant was too much a "sickly and infirm person" to offer much help. When Garden retired, so did his latest assistant, Alexander Keith.[34]

The safety of his fellow ministers' health and constitution weighed on Garden, especially since he bore the responsibility of filling empty pulpits. Many ministers died, and many others left in fear of death. In the first half of the eighteenth century, a third of the SPG's missionaries to the colony died within ten years of their arrival. Many others fled the colony to recover their health. In fact, according to one recent study, "only four survived in the colony more than twenty years."[35] Consequently the bishop regularly received letters from Garden and from vestries pleading with him to send more ministers. In the meantime surviving ministers, Garden included, weakened their own health by often traveling to perform services in depleted parishes.

In spite of his own poor health and the odds against him, Garden found this work fulfilling enough to stay at his post for over thirty years. In 1734 he warned the bishop that a recent fever epidemic had "so impair'd" his health that he feared for his life. Only his love of his people and his work kept him in South Carolina: "as I am naturaliz'd, as 'twere, though not in my Constitution to the Climate, yet in my Affections to the People of the Place, and flatter myself of some share of theirs in Return, I am exceeding loth quite to give up the Charge, and rather choose to hold it as long as God" allowed.[36] This was a revealing passage. Although he was forced to battle ill health for his entire tenure, Garden remained in the colony because he enjoyed the people and felt their approval. Garden had found his home, and he chose to live in a state of almost perpetual physical weakness rather than give it up.

The nature of his work explained his close relationship to the people. Certainly he became keenly aware of the economic, spiritual, and social state of the colony, probably, in fact, more than anyone else in the colony. Most of the time the vestry, church wardens, and Garden knew enough about the applicants for poverty relief that they would hear some appeals and issue orders for support without investigations. Occasionally they requested character references or inquiries into the particular situations of appellants, such as when Garden and two others were commissioned to investigate the situation of Mrs. Hargrave, who said she was "in great Necessity her Goods being seized for Rent and having nothing to redeem them or even to support her." Garden was to determine what would be the best way to "relieve her present Exigency's and Support her for the future."[37] He probably went on other such visits, for when the vestry commissioned "the Clerk" to persuade Nicholas Mattyson's son to take care of his father, they meant Alexander Garden, clerk and rector. Perhaps the vestry felt that the reverend wielded more compelling moral authority with which to persuade parishioners of their ethical and legal duties.

Garden knew the political life of the colony as well. Many assemblymen and councilors, not to mention the governor, worshiped at St. Philip's. Under his supervision vestrymen and church wardens were elected by his parishioners assembled in the church building, at which time they also held elections for such lower political offices as "Commissioners for the High Way" and "Commissioners for the Work house and the Market."[38] Individuals sometimes served multiple terms as vestrymen and church wardens, but none of them came close to the duration of tenure that Garden did as rector, and none of them could have known Charles Town's inhabitants better than he. Garden rubbed shoulders with the colonists in the highest and the lowest echelons of society. He heard their stories of hardship and suffering, baptized their young and buried their old, wedded the love-struck and picked up the pieces after an abandonment, received their gifts to the church, and listened to the vestry complain about the rich who would not pay their bills to the church for poor relief. Garden knew his people so well because he was, quite literally, in the center of many of the most important economic, political, religious, and social events of the colony.

His familiarity with the people included at least some of slaves and the social institutions that bound them. Slaves often did the repair work on the church and his parsonage house. Garden had to have been aware that it was a slave who "blew" the church organ for at least six years, supplying it with the air pressure needed to produce sound for the services.[39] On December 10, 1739, the vestry drew over one hundred pounds to pay "Revd Mr. Allexander Garden in full for the hire of his Negroes in the Service of the Church." What work did they do? Unfortunately no description of their services followed in the minutes, but if

Garden treated the transaction as did nearly all other colonists who hired out their slaves for labor, he would have kept at least most of the money for himself.

Not all of Garden's activities concerned the church, of course. Garden endured his share of family tragedy, particularly with the early passing of his wife in 1737, but he also had good family times. In 1751 Garden witnessed the wedding of his oldest daughter, Martha, to "Mr. Sampson Neyle, merchant." In the eighteenth century world, where marriages represented the primary means of a woman's material maintenance, the match must have gratified Garden as a father and as a stakeholder in polite society, although it may be that Neyle benefited similarly from his marriage. He appeared in the admittedly incomplete records as a merchant of note only after his marriage. He began as a seller of "pins, tapes, and assorted goods," renting space from the prominent merchant Othniel Beale, but around the time he became engaged to Martha, he moved to his own place, where he sold "dry goods." Neyle did well enough for himself to secure business partnerships with the assemblyman and St. Philip's vestryman Francis Bremar, brother-in-law to the renowned Henry Laurens, and engaged in two ventures into the Atlantic slave trade.[40]

Garden no doubt also prided himself that daughter Martha was no social slouch. The *South Carolina Gazette* marriage announcement described her as "a very agreeable and accomplished young lady of distinguished merit, with a handsome fortune." Along with comments about accomplishments and beauty, these were boilerplate descriptors often used in the *Gazette* to honor brides, but they seem to have been selected carefully and with some discernment by the writers. Miss Mary Child was "an agreeable young lady and heiress; reputed the richest in this province." Miss Susanna Seabrook brought with her "a fortune of £15,000." The governor's sister, Miss Glen, was "a lady of celebrated beauty and merit," while the anonymous "relict of the late Mr. Kenneth Michie" was simply "a lady possessed of all the amiable"—but presumably unidentifiable— "qualities that promise uninterrupted felicity in the marriage state." Hence one could infer from the stock phrases selected in Martha's announcement that she was wealthy and accomplished in the ways of society but not eye-catchingly beautiful. That the entry in St. Philip's marriage register labeled her a "spinster" at the age of twenty-four says more about social customs of the time than her age.[41] Her father had the pleasure of conducting the wedding service, and approximately nine months later of welcoming a grandson, Philip Neyle, into the world as his first grandchild.

It is a truism that all good things must come to an end. At a vestry meeting on April 16, 1753, Alexander Garden delivered to his friends a letter he had written and signed. It read as follows: "I Alexander Garden Clerk, Rector of the Parish of St. Philip Charlestown, give the Vestry of the same, this timely Notice, that being now broken with Age & often Infirmities, & greatly disabl'd from executing the Duties of my Office, I am therefore determin'd to Resign my present Charge of this Parish, at the Expiration of One Year, commencing from 25th March last past; or as much sooner as both Parishes now in Charlestown, shall be provided with Ministers; & which I hope they both will be, within the said Time limited, Viz 25th March 1754; for, God giving Life to that Period, I shall, at all Events, then Resign. Given under my Hand this 16th day of April 1753."⁴²

Then, "on Sunday, March 31, 1754, Mr. Garden preached his Farewell Sermon to a crowded Audience at St. Philip's Church, from Romans X.i." What can be known of his last sermon as rector of St. Philip's came from the pen of the early nineteenth-century Episcopalian historian Frederick Dalcho, who, thankfully, preserved the last and most personal portion of the sermon. It is the clearest window available into the heart of Alexander Garden. The text that Garden chose from Romans hinted at what he would talk about when he finally bid them farewell. In Romans the Apostle Paul sought to explain how it could be that Gentiles of any sort could enter the family of God through Jesus Christ without converting to the Jewish religion. However, being a Jew himself, Paul also made it clear that God was not done with the Jews. Paul explained his own love for his Jewish people with touchingly personal language in chapter 9: "I speak the truth in Christ—I am not lying, my conscience confirms it through the Holy Spirit, I have great sorrow and unceasing anguish in my heart, for I could wish that I myself were accursed and cut off from Christ for the sake of my people, those of my own race." Then, in the first verse of chapter 10, Garden came to his chosen text: "Brothers and sisters, my heart's desire and prayer to God for the Israelites is that they may be saved." Here, said Paul the theologian, deep in the middle of a sophisticated treatise on election and sanctification, is my heart for my people.

In like manner Garden opened his heart one last time to his flock. Most of the records he left behind, including the few sermons he published and the letters he sent to the bishop and the SPG, yielded an impression of an ambitious and businesslike administrator. In his final farewell sermon beat the heart of compassion that helps explain why his vestry was the most generous in the colony. The sentiment in his final sermon was almost palpable. "I come now to the last and hardest part of my present task, viz. to bid Farewell to you, my beloved Congregation," he began. "It was always in my heart to live and die with you," he continued, and he acknowledged how many times over the years he had approached death. Nonetheless he had persevered for many happy years. He felt "as much Honor and Esteem, as any Minister can expect, wish for, or desire" and attributed that feeling to his congregation's graciousness. As with Paul's devotion to the people of his own time, Garden pointed out that he had "not wilfully either neglected or deserted you at any time, or omitted to declare the whole Will of God to you to the best of my knowledge and capacity." It was true that "the unruly and ruder sort" did not always appreciate his adherence to the "Laws and Rules of the Church of England," but "the more knowing, virtuous, discreet, and prudent" did, and any slight he perceived from the lower sort would "quickly vanish away." There he hinted at his preference for polite company and a rather startling dismissal of the nonpolite, but such statements were more easily pronounced in the eighteenth century, when even many poor people took for granted the necessity of paternalist leadership by the elites. Besides, leaders often spoke like this. If conceit was their vice, their virtues were frankness and transparency of sentiment: they believed that they were better and told people so. For these reasons, likely nobody gasped at Garden's elitism, for it did not come off as such to his hearers. Rather, they believed, as he did, that he had justly and righteously cared for all of his parishioners, with deference to the polite and paternalist condescension toward the rest.[43]

In a generous acknowledgment of the religious pluralism of his community, he included among his supporters non-Anglicans, "with whom," he said, "I have always lived in all peace and friendship; and who have always treated me with Civility and decent regard." True, he wished that all were "united in the same communion of the Church of England," but that did not prohibit him from seeking to "live in Peace, friendship and charity towards them." Indeed, like Paul, his "hope, and earnest desire of my heart, and prayer to God for them also is, that they may be saved." Then, with emphasis—and one can almost hear his voice raise—he "declare[d], that there is neither Man, Woman, nor Child in the whole Province of Carolina, with whom I am not in perfect Charity, and to whom I do not heartily and sincerely wish all happiness, both temporal and eternal." Were these just words? Was this an attempt at healing old wounds and setting his relationships in order before he passed on? Likely not, for the last time he had confronted anyone with great zeal had been during his contest with George Whitefield in the early 1740s. Perhaps that scuffle had worn him out. More likely, after working hard in the 1720s and 1730s to claim his place and the place of the Church of England high in the social hierarchy of South Carolina, he spent his last decade in peace, prosperity, and harmony.[44]

Then came the climax, and it was remarkable for its openness and expressions of affection. It is worth reading whole and unbroken by any commentary, slowly, and keeping in mind his years of service, of counseling, of administering material relief to sufferers of fires and hurricanes and comfort to the many men, women, and children widowed and orphaned by disease. With the many years of sickness and health, poverty and wealth, in good times and bad, for better or worse in mind, the old stalwart of the pulpit proclaimed,

To return to you my peculiar charge: My peculiar affection must natu-rally be towards you. How many of you have I christened! How many of you have been my Catechumens, and brought up from your Infancy, under my weak, though always sincere and well-designed Ministra-tions! How then can it otherwise be, but that I must regard you as my children in the Lord, and my Affection towards you be truly paternal?

Though I am now on the Point of Departing from you, yet think not (my Brethren) that I shall straitway, or ever forget you. No; assure your-selves, you'll seldom be out of my thoughts, and never omitted in my prayers: Tho' absent from you, yet wherein soever I may be capable to serve you, please only to lay your commands on me, and see, whether I shall not cheerfully and faithfully obey them. Wherever I am, there you'll always have a stedfast friend, a true and faithful Servant. Tho' absent from you in Body, I shall be present with you in Spirit. My Spirit will be always hovering in your assemblies, hovering in this sacred Mansion, and 'specially about this holy Altar, where I have so often administered the Mysteries of God, the symbolical Body and Blood of Christ, and been so often Partaker of them, to the great Comfort, Strenthening and refreshing of my Soul! But I must have done.

Once more (my beloved Brethren) farewell! May the very God of Peace sanctify you wholly; and preserve your whole Spirits, and Souls, and Bodies blameless, unto the coming of our Lord Jesus Christ.

May all the Blessing of Heaven descend upon all the Inhabitants of this Province in general;—those of Charles-Town in particular;—but more especially on you the beloved People of my late charge.—May the ever blessed and glorious Trinity bless you in the City, and in the Field; in the fruit of your Body, the fruit of your Cattle, and the fruit of your Ground; Bless you in your Basket, and in your Store, and in all that you set your Hand unto:—Bless you with all the temporal Blessings, of Health, Peace, and Prosperity; but above all, and as the Source of all, bless you with truly faithful and obedient Hearts, and finally conduct you safe to the Blessed Regions of Glory and Immortality.[45]

One can imagine some tear-filled eyes among his audience. The vestry judged the sermon "Excellent," requested his permission to publish it, and presented him with a commemorative plate resembling an alms basin to represent his selfless service to his parish.[46] They also issued a resolution of appreciation and gave him a thank-you letter commending him for his many years of service conducted "with Piety, Authority and Steadiness; and offered as a small Testi-mony of the great Esteem for that Constant, Upright Behavior, of which many have been eye-witnesses." Then they told him that "with hearts full of affection towards your Person, we return you our warmest thanks and acknowledgments, for your long, painful, and distinguished labours amonst us" as well as "your excellent farewell Sermon."[47] Reading what they chose to highlight suggested that Garden's verbal expressions of his love in his farewell sermon may have been unusual for his pulpit ministry: he probably was not a man given to emotional outpouring of personal feeling, and he was known as a person more of diligence and authority than sweetness and affection. Nonetheless his heartfelt love for his people shone through his sermon, and the vestry returned his affection on behalf of the congregation. It was a moving close to a distinguished career.

The vestry enlisted three South Carolinian gentlemen, Benjamin Smith Esq., Charles Pinckney, and James Crockatt Esq., who were visiting London at the time, for assistance in finding Garden's replacement. When Smith returned to Charles Town in the fall of 1753, he brought news that the Reverends Richard Clarke and John Andrews had agreed to make the trip from the Old World to the New. Garden's sense of urgency in all of this is nearly palpable, for at the same meeting when the new ministers were announced, Garden requested that his letter of resignation be reworded to reflect his intention to retire as soon as his pulpit was filled. The original language indicated that he would wait until a minister could be found for the pulpit in St. Michael's as well. The vestry accommodated his request, and he retired.[48]

Garden made haste to England. He preached his final sermon on March 31, 1754; the church presented him with his gift and letter of gratitude on April 10, noting that "the day fixed for your departure from this Province being So near at hand"; and by May 27 the vestry was already working up a letter to him in England asking for his help in finding a new assistant minister for St. Philip's. Garden's assistant John Andrews had returned to England in order to recuperate from poor health.[49] Garden continued serving the church with the same diligence and sense of responsibility that had propelled him through over thirty years of service in the Carolinas. In June 1755 he wrote a letter to the bishop noting a request from the vestry at Prince William's Parish in South Carolina for his help in finding a suitable minister for their pulpit. He convinced "the Reverend Mr. Jenkin Lewis" to make the trip to the Americas. At the same time he reported his plans to leave England immediately and offered his services to the bishop: "if your Lordship shall think fit to charge me with any Commands, relating to religion, the Church of England, or Clergy there, that I am capable to execute, you may depend on the due Execution of them to the Utmost of my Capacity and Power."[50]

Garden left England as abruptly as he had come. England's climate disagreed with him. He told the bishop that as "The Cold Climate of Great Britain proves so disagreeable to my health and Constitution, after having been so long accustom'd to the Warmer one of South Carolina," he would take a ship out at "the first good Opportunity."[51] Remember that he had written to the bishop thirty years earlier wondering if his constitution could ever be "reconciled" to the more tropical lowcountry climate but determined to "venture the Tryal for sometime longer."[52] Perhaps now the problem was reverse acclimation, or maybe it was simply hard for him to acknowledge that his ailments now stemmed primarily from old age.

Something else probably explains Garden's hasty visit to England. Most likely Garden had gone to England to rescue his son John from financial problems and, that proving impossible, was ready to return to his home. The young Peter Manigault, son of Garden's good friend Charles Manigault, while at school in London wrote to Judith Wragg, widow of Councilman Joseph Wragg of Charles Town, that upon reaching Britain Garden had gone straight to Exeter, where he hoped to meet up with his oldest son, John. Instead he discovered that John had forged a letter and "had got £20 upon his Father's Account, & made off towards Bath with it; & had not since been heard of." Manigault noted how "the good old Gentleman" took his son's misbehavior "so much to heart." So despondent was Alexander Garden that he "will not come to London; because he says his Son's Misconduct affects him so, that he cannot see his Friends with any Pleasure."[53] This was pitiful, to be sure, but also ironic, for it was Garden's ministerial predecessor's financial malfeasance that had created an opening in St. Philip's pulpit thirty five years before when Garden arrived in South Carolina. Recall that when William Wye left England for the ministry in Charles Town he absconded with a carriage and the money from three rented horses that he had illicitly sold. The crime caught up to him in South Carolina and cost him his rectorship at St. Philip's, clearing that pulpit for Garden. His father, Dr. Wye, "a very worthy man," according to one friend, became "unhappy in some of his Children and greatly oppressed in his Circumstances by their wickedness and ill Managmt." Dr. Wye, said an acquaintance, "resolved as far as he can utterly to forget so abandoned a wretch."[54]

Garden apparently reached the same conclusion about his own recalcitrant son. He wrote his will soon after he returned to Charles Town and allowed John, his oldest son, "the Sum of One hundred pounds Lawful Money of Great Britain and no more to him and his heirs and Assigns forever." He left much more, eight hundred pounds, to his son Benjamin; a thousand pounds to his daughter Anne, who was unmarried at the time; ten pounds to his daughter Martha Neyle, to buy a suit for his burial, in addition to "the Fortune already paid into the hands of her . . . Husband"; and the rest of his estate, including land, to be split among the three younger children, excluding John. As Dr. Wye had done with William, Alexander Garden resolved to wash his hands of his son John.[55]

It would not be long before Garden's "Loving Friend Francis Bremar and my Loving Son in Law Sampson Neyle of Charles Town Merchants Executors and my Loving daughter Ann Garden Executrix" would gather to execute his will. Given the notice taken of his retirement, Alexander Garden's obituary, published in the *South Carolina Gazette* on Saturday, October 2, 1756, read as an anticlimactic ending to his illustrious career in South Carolina: "Last Sunday Morning [September 26] died, in the 71st Year of his Age, the Rev. Mr. Alexander Garden, formerly Rector of this Parish, and on Wednesday Morning he was privately interred agreeable to his own Request." His epitaph is similarly reticent: "Here lies the remains of the Rev'd Mr. Alexander Garden who was rector of this parish 34 years / he departed this life the 25th day of Sept anno domini 1756 age 71 years." His wife, Martha, and daughter Mary are buried there with him and share his gravestone, as does John. Carved into Alexander and Martha's gravestone are the names of two of their children: Mary, who died in 1736; and John. It identifies July 14, 1755, as the day of John's death, more than a year before Alexander's. Could Garden have buried his own son? In a letter dated June 23, 1755, Alexander notified the bishop that he was looking to leave England for South Carolina as soon as he could. He likely arrived in Charles Town in July or August 1755. This suggests that Alexander could have, in fact, found his son—or at least his lifeless body—and they returned together to South Carolina. However, on March 5, 1756, Garden amended his will but did not alter John's inheritance of one hundred pounds. He must not have known that John had died. Curiously, the register of St. Philip's Parish, which recorded Anglican births, including John's, marriages, and deaths, did not mention John's death or burial. It is most likely that John died in obscurity in England and that his body was only later identified and returned to its final resting place next to his already-deceased father. The reunification Garden had sought was accomplished after all, in body if not in spirit.

Nothing else is known of Alexander Garden's passing. The old minister exited quietly, perhaps too quietly for a man of his stature. A few historians, concerned mainly with his impact on the development of evangelicalism in South Carolina, have interpreted the solitude of his later years as an admission that social change had passed him by. One claimed that already by the 1740s "times were changing," with experiential, revivalist evangelicalism displacing the old Anglican guard, leaving Garden frustrated and on the sidelines. Others have noted that pluralism eroded Anglican superiority, implying that Garden could not have maintained the level of control over religion in South Carolina that he did in the 1730s and 1740s.[56] In these accounts Garden slipped away in a fashion befitting what they saw as a fleeting imprint on the colony.

There is some truth to these assessments. In many ways evangelicalism did win out in the South. Southerners had demonstrated great interest in evangelical, revivalist preachers during the Great Awakening. Even Garden's congregation approved of their more emotive language and preaching style, and Garden knew it. In 1748, as he made one of his periodic pleas to the bishop to send an assistant, he noted that the position could command a £150 annual salary, a tidy sum in those days, and "to a Popular Preacher it will be worth more," indicating that he recognized the advantages of eloquence.[57] The animated, charismatic Richard Clarke took over Garden's pulpit in St. Philip's and enjoyed great success. The politics of the Revolution may have interrupted the religious development of British North America, but it has been convincingly demonstrated that even then political rhetoric took on an evangelical tone when Patriot leaders used plain language accessible to the masses and attributed millennialist urgency to political crises.[58] After the Revolution, the Church of England felt it wise to change its name to the Protestant Episcopal Church in an attempt to rid itself of its nominal attachment to England, but its staid formality—relative to evangelical spontaneity—proved more of a hindrance to growth. Methodists and Baptists carried the day during the Second Great Awakening of the first half of the nineteenth century and swamped the Anglicans numerically. People liked to listen to dynamic preachers who spoke their vernacular—Garden knew that—and evangelicals had plenty of such orators to go around after 1800.[59]

For Garden, though, it was never about numbers.[60] Personally he found in South Carolina what he was looking for when, in his mid-thirties, he crossed the Atlantic to a dangerous colony recovering from war and in the midst of a political revolution. Freed from the family restraints that held him back in the British Isles—politico-religious demands, financial embarrassment, a disreputable birth—Garden found freedom, fortune, and family in the far reaches of the British Empire. His marriage to Martha brought him cherished companionship and five children, two of whom survived as his "beloved" daughters in his old age. His marriage also lent him great wealth and access to the upper levels of society that had shut him out in Scotland and England. He made friends, established business partnerships, and rose to the highest ecclesiastical position in the British American colonies: the office of commissary. All the while he grew to know and love the people around him, and they loved him back.

Garden also achieved a long-lasting legacy in South Carolina. He left the colony in much better condition, at least for white people, than he found it, and as he was the chief religious figure allied with the major economic, social, and political figures, part of that prosperity should be attributed to his using his office to bolster and harness polite power. He helped planters and merchants establish control over a volatile population by reining in contentious ministers. He lent his pulpit and his church to polite rhetoric and ritual. He ended the revivalist threat during the Great Awakening, and he sanctified polite slaveholding by publicly tending to slave education and Christianization. In sum, he inherited a church whose power consisted of a legal establishment printed on a page and turned it into the dominant religious force in the colony. It was

Alexander Garden who made establishment mean something, even if it had to exist in a pluralist environment; or, to make his accomplishment more evident, it was Alexander Garden who made establishment mean something *in spite of* a pluralist environment.

This power lasted for many generations, as did the society he left behind. This was no small achievement considering it was built on the powder keg of plantation slavery. South Carolina's delegates to the 1787 Constitutional Convention, Pierce Butler, Charles Pinckney, Charles Cotesworth Pinckney, and John Rutledge, all were Anglicans from Charleston—Charles Town's name was modified after the Revolution. South Carolinians chose Anglicans almost exclusively as governors in the 1770s, 1780s, and into the 1790s, and most of them were from Charleston. Charlestonians may have liked a rousing sermon now and then, but for quite a few years they preferred to keep social and political leadership in the hands of Anglicans, a legacy of Garden's triumph over Whitefield in the early 1740s.

So secure was the society Garden helped found that it lasted for over a hundred years after his passing. The black and white populations grew rapidly in the decades after Garden's death. The economy continued to boom, and by the Revolution, South Carolina had accumulated more wealth than anywhere else in North America, led by the same crops, rice and indigo, that dominated Carolinian agriculture in Garden's time. South Carolina survived the might of the British Empire during the 1760s, 1770s, and 1780s and wielded enough power in the new nation to silence antislavery efforts during the writing and ratifying of the Constitution. It was South Carolina that pushed the tariff and nullification crisis of the 1830s, and southerners celebrated secession in Charleston before their confederates in Richmond or Montgomery or Nashville. In sum, the basic outlines of the Carolinian society—a majority black, enslaved population ruled by a white minority, led by a polite elite class, and based on an export economy supported by plantation agriculture—in December 1860 remained the same as Garden had left it. In fact only cannons, rifles, and hundreds of thousands of human casualties could bring it to an end.

The myth of the Old South, a harmonious and just society based on slavery and a social hierarchy blessed by a religious system that headed it, survived into the twentieth century, though with an ironic twist: it was maintained most vigorously by Garden's old enemies, the evangelicals. The American Revolution reduced the cultural power of the Church of England, renamed the Protestant Episcopal Church in 1783, though it remained something of a religion of the elites for two centuries. Cultural leadership would pass to the Baptists and Methodists in the Second Great Awakening of the early and mid-nineteenth century. Then southerners sought and received spiritual sanctification for their endeavors, not in Garden's church, but in the upstart Baptist and Methodist communions, who like Garden and the Anglicans before them, succumbed to the siren call of social respectability and prosperity offered by the slaveholding elites. After initially going beyond George Whitefield by questioning not only the treatment of slaves but also the institution of slavery, the evangelical juggernaut these two denominations represented assumed cultural dominance by sacrificing their prophetic voice and came to defend slavery as not only morally defensible but also socially requisite for harmony and the survival of all involved. To them, as with Garden, social order was next to godliness to the benefit of all, white and black.[61] Even after the Civil War, Jim Crow could sit comfortably in the pews of many southern churches. Garden was right: southerners could get along quite well with evangelicalism once evangelicals quit being so divisive and critical of southern habits. The myth of the Old South, forged by Garden and his peers out of the remains of the Yamassee War, faded slowly.

Perhaps it is best to see Garden leaving the stage quietly but with dignity, a conqueror, a kingdom builder whose work was done. He was buried in the St. Philip's cemetery in the courtyard outside his church. His gravestone, lying horizontal to the ground, has been weathered down to the point that his epitaph is difficult to read. Nothing about it attracts attention to the grave, just one among many plots in a beautiful but unpretentious cemetery in the middle of Charleston. Garden rests in peace.

The colony that Garden left rested in peace for only a few more years before the tumultuous years of the American Revolution began. Many books, articles, and Web pages have been written about the colony, and there is even more material about the state that would lead the South into the Civil War. Much less has been written about Garden. In fact the commissary slipped quickly into obscurity in public memory and among historians. When the name Alexander Garden does get mentioned, more often than not the speaker is referring to a different man of the same name. So this story ends where it began, by noting that just as his ancestry is shrouded amid a clutter of Gardens in Scotland, so his memory has been confused by the fact that there were several other Gardens in eighteenth-century America, including at least two named Alexander. The first was his own nephew, who still dwells in his own blissful inconspicuousness outside of historical remembrance. The other was the great botanist Dr. Alexander Garden, who arrived on the Charles Town scene in 1752, just as the commissary Alexander was making his exit. The luster of that Alexander's scientific career—the gardenia is named after him—soon overcame the memory of his loyalism during the American Revolution and the religious fame of the reverend senior.

In fact only specialists have kept our Alexander Garden's name alive over the centuries. Church historians, particularly those who chronicled the development of the Anglican or Episcopalian Church in America, and historians of education, revivalism, or slavery still note his importance in each of those subfields. As with any subject, however, their treatments of him have differed across time. There are three distinct eras in the historiography of the commissary: the preprofessional church historians of the nineteenth century honored Garden as a likable, wise, and mature defender of church order and promoter of the Gospel; the first two or three generations of professional, secular historians in the first half of the twentieth century largely forgot him in their enthusiasm for all things Puritan; and in the second half of the twentieth century, evangelical historians re-remembered him, or rather they remembered his acrimonious opposition to the Great Awakening.

Garden fared quite well in the hands of nineteenth-century historians of American religion, most of whom wrote from within and about particular denominations. These Protestant faith traditions found themselves competing for public attention and influence in the new American republic, shorn of the privileges of official government support they had enjoyed under colonial governments. Their historians did their part to shore up their public authority by presenting their past as the story of how God had chosen their heroes of the faith to save the Christian church and introduce the world to the glories of freedom and democracy. The Constitution may have separated church and state when it came to taxation, but historians busily reunited them to explain how God had raised up their churches in their colonies and states for the purpose of triumphing over what they considered the paganism of the New World and the Catholic superstition of the Old.

Within this context the Charlestonian and Presbyterian David Ramsay in his 1808 portrayal of Alexander Garden set the terms for understanding the commissary for the next two hundred years. In the years after the Revolution, Ramsay chronicled how it was that such a glorious nation as the new American republic had come into being, and of his own state's contribution to the cause, so that the descendants of the first patriots would "learn, from their example to love their country and cherish its interests."[62] Accordingly he downplayed internal conflicts, and his treatment of southern religion took on ecumenical and irenic tones. To Ramsay, Garden's "strict morals and steady adherence to all the forms of the Episcopal church qualified him in many respects" to be the commissary, for he was "steady, strict, and impartial" and "methodical" in his approach to his ministerial duties. "His charity was in like manner measured by rule. The exact tenth of his whole income was regularly given to the poor," though how he knew of Garden's philanthropic habits Ramsay did not record. With Winteley, Hunt, and other ministers in mind, Ramsay wrote, "Improper conduct on the part of clergymen was immediately noticed, the delinquents brought to trial, and the canons of the church were enforced against them." Garden "was attentive to the religious education of his children and servants" and founded a thriving slave school.[63] Garden's intelligence, industriousness, integrity, and devotion to righteousness had carried his day during the founding generations of South Carolina.

Such positive characterizations of the minister posed a problem when describing his bitter conflict—to Ramsay, merely an "unpleasant controversy"—with George Whitefield, who was too well-loved and respected in America to dishonor on the pages of a history book. Therefore Ramsay hedged, admiring both men for their adherence to principle and duty, although one does sense a bit of distaste for the commissary on the part of the Presbyterian chronicler, who, as something of an evangelical himself, probably felt a stronger affinity for the itinerant Anglican than the one rooted in church tradition. Whitefield broke Anglican canons from "no selfish views nor improper motives," and the same held true for Garden when he enforced them. "Both were good and useful men, but in different ways." Garden "was devoted to forms," while Whitefield "soared above them. The piety of the one ran in the channel of a particular sect of Christians; but that of the other, confined neither to sect nor party, flowed in the broad and wide-spreading stream of Christianity." Writing during the early years of the Second Great Awakening of the nineteenth century, Ramsay sought to bridge sectarian divides and honor all divines.[64]

Episcopal historians followed Ramsay's lead. Frederick Dalcho, pastor at St. Michael's Episcopal Church in Charleston in the first half of the 1800s, praised Garden for diligence, uprightness, and integrity and added that people liked Garden: the commissary "was beloved by his people, and highly respected by the inhabitants generally, for his learning, piety, and zeal." Blame for the conflict with Whitefield lay entirely on the shoulders of the itinerant, whose "dereliction of duty" in breaking from proper Anglican forms forced the commissary's hand.[65] Writing at the end of the century, Charles C. Tiffany, an Episcopal clergyman and archdeacon in New York, likewise called Whitefield to account for his "loose ways and intolerant denunciations of his less ardent brethren," which Garden, "faithful rector," simply had to confront. "This most famous episode in Garden's life as commissary," Tiffany explained, "would give a wrong impression of him if it led one to infer that he was a mere ecclesiastical martinet, scrupulous as to the letter and unalive to the spirit of his office. He was himself earnest and devout in the work of the ministry." Overcoming great reluctance on the part of his fellow colonists, Garden demonstrated his love for religion and learning by founding the slave school, "and in such an exemplary life and earnest ministrations he gained and retained a strong hold on the hearts of his people."[66]

Nonevangelical nineteenth-century writers did not appreciate Garden's legacy of robust leadership. The Presbyterian chaplain A. S. Billingsley, in his 1878 biography of Whitefield, nearly dismissed the St. Philip's pastor, at one point even misspelling his name as "Gardner." In 1877 the Methodist minister and biographer of both Whitefield and John Wesley, Luke Tyerman, had nothing pleasant to say about Whitefield's antagonist. "Commissary Garden's replies" to Whitefield's early teachings and admonishments "were unworthy of his character as a gentleman and Christian minister. Mr. Garden, unfortunately, will turn up again," sighed Tyerman in his account, before moving to other of "young Whitefield's troubles." When Garden did turn up again in Tyerman's description of the commissary's trying of Whitefield in ecclesiastical court, "the commissary was angry, too angry, perhaps, to be prudent and dignified."[67]

Thus two sketches of Garden lingered in the minds of ecclesiastical historians: one of Garden as the dutiful Anglican pastor and the other of him as the angry antagonist of true experiential religion. Both would recur long into the twentieth century. Edgar Pennington, writing in the 1930s for the *Historical Magazine of the Protestant Episcopal Church,* at the time a quasi-scholarly but nonetheless denominational publication, lauded Garden for his "qualities best calculated to win popular esteem and affection." Garden was "one of the most stalwart figures in the history of the colonial church," a "leader in the province," and a fine disciplinarian always on the lookout for dangers to the church.[68] In 1951, and in the same journal, Quentin Keen characterized the commissary as "a man of piety, devotion and austerity" and asserted that "his faith in God and his devotion to the Church of England gave him the strength and perseverance to carry on."[69]

Such intermingling of objective history and devotional memory has occurred often in denominational historiography, although not always to Garden's benefit. Arnold Dallimore, another Whitefield biographer, this time from a decidedly evangelical Baptist tradition, could not vilify Garden enough. Garden represented "the offended churchmen and the angry planters" when, for instance, he "issued a violent tirade against" Whitefield and "laid plans to humiliate him further" by calling Whitefield to trial. Dallimore's account of the trial dripped with disdain for Garden: "This trial constitutes Garden's only claim to fame. Nothing else that he did in life has proved worthy of mankind's remembrance. Alexander Garden satisfied his ego with his little game of court and his masquerade as judge, but he himself stands judged before the bar of history, guilty of . . . seeking to hinder—to prohibit if he could—a ministry that was being used of God in an unparalleled reviving of Christianity on two continents."[70] Dallimore published this throwback to nineteenth-century evangelical hagiography in 1970.

Historians have continued to quote from Dallimore on occasion, perhaps because of the thoroughness of his biography of Whitefield. However, today they are far more likely to draw from and produce more secularized histories that seek greater objectivity in their characterizations of their subjects. That does not mean that histories produced in-house by members of a faith tradition writing about their own heroes do not serve an important purpose in remembering the past, but it does mean that the historiography of religious figures, including Alexander Garden, now flows well within the currents of mainstream scholarly research. This transfer from church halls to ivory towers occurred in the late 1800s.

The professionalization of historical inquiry occurred alongside the rise of other scholarly fields that are now taken for granted. By the end of the 1800s, the rapid increase in commercial competition and social complexity that accompanied industrialization and urbanization spawned new academic fields in the social sciences, such as sociology and anthropology, and professionalized the writing of history. Confident in their capacity to be objective and dispassionate, new academic professional historians sought to adapt the "scientific" analytical methods used first by German historians to the American context in an effort to ascertain the truth of the past. Specially trained and accountable to each other in the new departments of history at colleges that had reformed into universities committed to scholarly research, they published in each other's journals and fraternized at the annual meetings of the American Historical Association, founded in 1884.[71]

Secularization of the academy accompanied this process of professionalization of history. Religious topics moved to the religious studies departments, where they were dissected as one would any other element of human life. Historians increasingly eschewed providential tellings of history, wherein it was presumed that God had chosen English-speaking populations to save the rest. They forsook the narrative of history as the story of God working through Americans to redeem the continent and beyond from the clutches of barbarism and ignorance, in favor of more earthy grand narratives. Materialist explanations, whether in the form of full-blown Marxism or the more socially acceptable Progressivism, became fashionable. To them, previously unheralded masses moved society through history toward the triumph of the exploited over the exploiting. This may not appear immediately as irreligious, but the point of these histories was to demonstrate that economic forces, not divine ones, caused change over time. Besides, Americans were an increasingly diverse lot, with diminishing cultural space for spatting about religious differences. Historians, busily engaged in crafting the framework for professional, objective historical scholarship, neglected America's religious past. Politics, especially social democracy, not faith, became the tale to tell.[72]

What if historians could include religion in their stories without resorting to providentialist triumphalism? What if historians at secularized universities could explain America's religious past in a way that helped make sense of its economic, political, and social pasts? Those questions had surfaced by the

1930s with the impressive work of scholars of and in New England. The first wave of professional, American religious history explained in great detail how Puritanism went hand in glove with the advance of education, industry, and ambition in America. Led by the Harvard professor Perry Miller, these scholars pursued the religious past for its own sake and for what it could explain about change in American society over time, rather than to illustrate the righteousness of their own beliefs. Tellingly, Miller described one of his books as a "chapter in the history of ideas," rather than religion, and though he admitted that he "wholeheartedly admire[d] the integrity and profundity of the Puritan character," he also hastened to point out that his "interest in Puritanism has not been a matter of liking or disliking" but a matter of scholarly interest in the intellectual development of the Western world. "Puritanism is of immense historical importance," he wrote. "It was not only the most coherent and most powerful single factor in the early history of America, it was a vital expression of a crucial period in European development, and those who would understand the modern world must know something of what it was and what heritages it has bequeathed to the present."[73] Whatever their own personal persuasions—Miller subscribed to atheism—these men and the occasional woman wrote as scholars in pursuit of the facts. That some of the facts had to do with people in worship was a matter of reality, not divine favor or personal commitment on the part of the historian.

Unfortunately for scholars of the South, these historians focused their attention away from anything south of Virginia, forgetting Alexander Garden entirely in the process. Indeed, Virginia rarely made more than a cameo appearance in the larger story of America's New England heritage, and when it did, it stood representative of "the South" as a whole. William Sweet, in his otherwise admirable survey of American religion published in 1930, included South Carolina only to note that the colony suffered from "a dearth of clergymen"—end of story.[74] The 1960 Prentice-Hall textbook *History of Religion in the United States* favored New England but did devote seventeen pages to Virginia. South Carolina shared two and a half pages with North Carolina and Georgia.[75] Carl Bridenbaugh's seminal *Mitre and Sceptre* ignored the South until it reached the American Revolution, even when it dealt with the Church of England, which was established only in New York and the South. So customary was this neglect of southern religion that when the *Journal of Southern History* published a review of the book, it failed to mention this glaring disregard for its home territory![76] Even Sydney Ahlstrom's landmark *Religious History of the American People,* which graduate students in religious history continued to read decades after its publication, hurried through southern Anglicanism, barely acknowledged the Great Awakening in the South, and never mentioned Alexander Garden in its over one thousand pages.[77]

Again, it would take changes in the profession to initiate alterations in the telling of American religious history and of Alexander Garden's life. Beginning in the 1950s but more so in the 1960s and beyond, new generations of hetero-geneous scholars with fresh interests greatly enriched our understanding of the past with innovative methods and perspectives. Women scholars studied Mar-tha Washington alongside George, African Americans discovered the couple's slaves, and whites of middle-class background—rather than the sons of the upper-class intelligentsia—studied the craftsmen, sailors, and soldiers who paid the rents and taxes that kept the Washingtons in fashion. Sociology blended with history in the new social and then cultural histories as historians explored new techniques for uncovering and interpreting primary sources. The field of history splintered into a dazzling array of subfields and specialties.

The much-bemoaned casualty of this barrage of historical exploration and innovation has been the metanarrative, the grand unifying theme that could make sense of the past by constructing generalities out of all its details. Having rejected providential history, historians now look with skepticism at materialist explanations, even those that heralded the triumph of the democratized masses. Now there are historians of gender and/or sexuality, race, and class alongside and among the historians of religion, economics, or politics, but few believe in the explanatory power of any single historical perspective. Not that people do not try for some organizing theme or approach, "cross-," "inter-," and "multi-disciplinarity" being the latest buzzwords of the profession, but the few lump-ers who manage to publish still have a difficult time rising above the masses of splitters, and the next dominant synthesis lingers just around the corner.[78]

Happily, Alexander Garden has risen out of the wreckage of the providen-tial metanarrative to reappear in any number of the new subfields. Unhappily, age has not been kind to his memory. In 1966 Alan Heimert published an oft-critiqued examination of the role of religion in the American Revolution. Much can be said of the book's historiographical effects, but as far as Garden was concerned, it also restored something of his stature in the eighteenth century by way of asserting the importance of the revivals against which he argued. The author took as his subjects the revivalists of the Great Awakening, claiming that the evangelical antiauthoritarianism they cultivated in the colonies gave rise to the republican spirit of the American Revolution. As something of a recapitula-tion of the triumphalist providentialism of the nineteenth century, the book has not fared particularly well in today's academy. However, neither has one of its literary antagonists: unfortunately but unsurprisingly, Garden appeared merely as one of the adversaries of evangelical Progressivism. Heimert mentioned only his supposed bad temper: George Whitefield "provoked the wrath" of Alexan-der Garden, who provided the "first colonial criticism" of his ministry by way of his "attacks" on evangelical enthusiasm. The next year Heimert and Perry

Miller published an anthology of Great Awakening primary sources, and they noted that Whitefield "outraged" Garden, who appeared in the book only to stand against the tide of evangelicalism.[79]

For the next half century Garden's alleged anger dominated historians' memories of this important figure. One can predict with strong certainty how a book will portray the commissary. He will almost exclusively appear when describing Whitefield's adversaries. The story of Garden "throwing" Whitefield out of his house in 1740 is now legendary, as are Garden's attempts at legally suspending Whitefield from his ministry. On the pages of recent scholarship— and these are quoted almost verbatim—Garden railed and exploded against Whitefield, sneered at the young minister, flashed his hot anger, retaliated furiously against Whitefield's censures of unconverted clergy, and viciously attacked his opponent's Calvinism. He was livid, scathing, acerbic, and vehement in these feuds, the most violent and bitter of Whitefield's Anglican opponents. Occasionally a historian has cast Garden as a fool, duped by Whitefield's savvy for publicity in goading the commissary into persecuting the evangelist to the point of martyrdom.[80] None of this has flattered Garden's personality or leadership abilities.

Why have historians narrowed Garden's life down to one characteristic, his anger, based on only one episode that lasted only a few of his many years? It may be because evangelicals—writing as professional scholars and often in secular universities—have played an important role in putting the revivals back in play among historians. Whether or not they agreed with Heimert, scholars since Heimert and with some sympathy toward the revivals have argued for the importance of the Great Awakening to understanding the late colonial and revolutionary eras. It makes sense, then, that Garden would make his appearance only when needed to tell Whitefield's story. Furthermore, the culture in which these historians have done their work makes difficult the task of understanding Garden's role in the episode as anything but angry and contentious. Full-throated religious debate regularly spilled onto the pages of the newspapers and popular pamphlets. In the eighteenth century, religious people believed that there was one truth worth finding, and if it took bare-knuckled argument to find it, so be it. Nobody ever accused Garden or Whitefield of hate speech when they issued their startlingly frank moral polemics. Today, in an age when a person of any stripe risks being called a hatemonger, or worse, for vocalizing disagreement on matters of moral importance and when religious views increasingly appear out of place in public conversation, Garden's willingness to stand for something of potentially eternal importance inevitably comes off as vicious and intolerant. Historians of the nineteenth century understood what he was doing: if there were truth to be found, it was his responsibility as a religious leader to find it and take a stand on it. Such chroniclers of the past may not have perceived the moral problems with southerners' adamant support of the social undergirding of their slave society, problems that more recent historians have illuminated in painful detail, but they understood the advantages of seeking truth in the pursuit of moral rectitude.

Ironically, Whitefield's goading of Garden into establishing the slave school has ended up being Garden's saving grace among historians. Historians of education, slavery, and slave education have appreciated his philanthropic work among his enslaved neighbors. Largely writing outside the subfield of religious historiography, these historians have remembered not Garden's opposition to Whitefield but his work persuading southern slaveholders and merchants to support slave education. A few have been downright lavish in their praise of this endeavor. "Of all the many schemes for Negro education, under the institution of slavery," wrote Frank Klingberg in his important 1941 book on slavery, "none was more fundamentally wise, practical, far-seeing, than this comprehensive proposal for a plantation school system" that was "grounded so firmly in humanitarian ideas."[81] Some of them believed Garden's sincerity in the matter but took a more judicious tone, such as claiming that "Garden had faith in the Negroe's ability to succeed," while others stressed the paternalistic nature of the slave school, which educated slaves to obey the social norms that oppressed them. One labeled the school a "paternalistic fantasy" born of Garden's "rosy portrait of colonial slave holdings."[82] So, ironically, it was the slave school, not the slave society that Garden sought to protect, that kept the memory of Garden alive among historians not working on religion.

All of this pulling of Garden from the obscurity of the past is undoubtedly not the sort of resurrection Garden sought, with all of its distortions and omissions and hyperbolic depictions of his more unseemly traits. Perhaps, though, efforts to uncover the real Alexander Garden, with all of his blemishes and positive traits, make for a more useful resurrection, at least for people today. He probably did have an anger problem—think of his blowups with Winteley and Whitefield; he probably would not be a person with whom many today would like to drink a beer—to use an anachronistic yardstick of friendliness—and he almost certainly preferred to guard his polite status than to protect his clergy. He started a rather impressive slave school, but only after being prodded into it by Whitefield, and he structured it carefully to advance his own reputation and the needs of southern slaveholders. On a more positive note, he survived in all dimensions of life in which so many others around him failed: religiously, economically, socially, culturally, and—no small feat—physically. Rather than merely survive, he thrived, as did the people around him whom he loved so dearly and for whom he labored so diligently and compassionately. Their partnership —Garden and his community—was a match made, if not in heaven, in the eighteenth-century world they inhabited, with all of its gritty moral ambiguity, quests for gain, and battles for survival. Theirs was a world much different from today's in its rigid social hierarchy, brutal forced labor, and rampant disease, but it was their world, and historians are its visitors. Americans today are also the inheritors of its economic legacies and religious toleration, and in that regard, perhaps, Garden and his fellow colonists, black and white, should be looked upon with some sense of understanding and humility.

# *Notes*

PREFACE

 1. Myers, *Roger Lundin.*

CHAPTER 1: BIRTHPLACES

 1. For an outstanding exploration of the effects of suffering on colonists, see Donegan, *Seasons of Misery.*

 2. Kopperman, *Sir Robert Heath,* 276.

 3. For a concise history of the settlement of North and South Carolina, see Butler, "Early Settlement of Carolina"; Edgar, *South Carolina.*

 4. Dunn, *Sugar and Slaves,* 69.

 5. Dobson, *Scottish Emigration,* 67.

 6. Dunn, *Sugar and Slaves,* 230.

 7. Amussen, *Caribbean Exchanges,* 90–98.

 8. Dunn, *Sugar and Slaves,* 76. Dunn has estimated that 94 percent of the original settlers were male (ibid., 326), largely because of the gendered nature of the labor demands in Barbados. By the time white men sought women for wives, the reputation of the deadliness of the journey and of the islands discouraged women from taking their chances in Barbados (ibid., 76–77).

 9. Quoted in ibid., 77.

 10. Dobson, *Scottish Emigration,* 74.

 11. Quoted in Gragg, *Englishmen Transplanted,* 27.

 12. Ibid., 176–81.

 13. Ligon, *True & Exact History of the Island of Barbadoes,* 104–7.

 14. Dunn, *Sugar and Slaves,* xiv–xv.

 15. Ligon, *True & Exact History of the Island of Barbadoes,* 108, 117.

 16. Loftfield, "Creolization," 225.

 17. Beasley, *Christian Ritual.*

 18. Greene, "Colonial South Carolina," 195, 192.

 19. Lesser, "Barbados," 47–48; Lesser, "Lords Proprietors of Carolina," 566–68.

 20. Lord Ashley to Sir John Colleton, November 27, 1672, quoted in Edgar, *South Carolina,* 84.

 21. Lesser, "Yeamans, Sir John." See also Smith, "Sir John Yeamans," 152–56.

 22. Towles, "Goose Creek Men"; Edgar, *South Carolina,* 84. Roper, *Conceiving Carolina,* warned against exaggerating the Barbadian influence in the faction (45).

 23. Greene, "Colonial South Carolina," 197.

24. Ibid., 198. It is possible to exaggerate the importance of Barbados to the settlement of South Carolina, and the question of the degree of the island's importance has been the subject of some debate among historians. The exact ratios of Barbadians to people of other origins are not known, and when perusing shipping records it is easy to mistake Barbados as the place of origin rather than as a port of call in transit. Settlers did come from other Caribbean islands, other British North American colonies, and England. By 1700 many settlers had migrated from European countries and the flow of Barbadians had dwindled. See also Bull, "Barbadian Settlers," 329–39; Roper, *Conceiving Carolina.* For an excellent recent reassessment, see Roberts and Beamish, "Venturing Out."

25. Nellis, *Shaping the New World,* 26–31.

26. Carney, *Black Rice;* Wood, *Black Majority,* 59–62.

27. Snyder, *Slavery in Indian Country,* 48.

28. Gallay, *Indian Slave Trade,* 7.

29. Ibid., 299, where Gallay argued for a total range of twenty-four thousand to fifty-one thousand Indians traded as slaves.

30. The complicated and unfortunate nature of Indian trade with Europeans was much too expansive to be summarized here. See Ramsey, "Something Cloudy in Their Looks," for an excellent exploration of problems that plagued the trade.

31. Quoted in Gallay, *Indian Slave Trade,* 216–17, from which this assessment of the law and its failures was derived.

32. Clergy of South Carolina to Bishop Robinson, October 18, 1715, in Fulham Papers at Lambeth Palace Library, London, 9:49–50.

33. Ramsey, "Something Cloudy in Their Looks"; Gallay, *Indian Slave Trade,* 327–29.

34. Gallay, *Indian Slave Trade,* 338. I owe my summary and interpretation of the Yamassee War and its aftermath almost entirely to Gallay's award-winning book.

35. Weir, *Colonial South Carolina,* 86.

36. British History Online, "'New Pretended' Council."

37. William Tredwell Bull to the Bishop of London, May 13, 1728, in Williams, "Letters to the Bishop of London" (January 1977): 31; Williams, "Letters to the Bishop of London" (April 1977): 122.

38. Glasson, *Mastering Christianity,* 20.

39. Dalcho, *Historical Account of the Protestant Episcopal Church,* 40, 47.

40. Weir, *Colonial South Carolina,* 210.

41. These percentages were derived from Vernod's list of male inhabitants, whom he identified as either dissenters or nondissenters. See "Names and number of the inhabitants of St. Georges Parish So Carolina inclosed in Mr. Varnod's Letter dated 21 January 1725," in *Selected Pages Relating to South Carolina,* 19:104–12. In 1728 he indicated that many nondissenters were independents turned Presbyterians and Anabaptists ("Mr. Varnod to the Secretary [of the SPG], 3 April 1728," in *Selected Pages Relating to South Carolina,* 21:77).

42. Weir, *Colonial South Carolina,* 76–80, treated the establishment controversy from various perspectives. The controversy figured large in Brinsfield, *Religion and Politics,* in which the author argued that religious freedom and toleration were key

factors among settlers choosing New World destinations, as well as among colonists choosing sides in the Revolutionary War. A recent anthology has argued that the religious toleration of colonial South Carolina helped steer the new United States toward disestablishment and religious toleration during the revolutionary era: Underwood and Burke, *Dawn of Religious Freedom in South Carolina*. Sensbach, "Early Southern Religions," placed this religious diversity in an Atlantic context.

43. Friedlander, "Commissary Johnston's Report," 260–61.

44. The historian Rebecca Anne Goetz has provocatively suggested that because southern Christians were outnumbered by African and Indian non-Christians, we should imagine "a South where pockets of Christianity were surrounded by vast seas of other, non-European religions"; see Goetz, "Religious Diversity." Goetz's essay is an introduction to an informative roundtable on the historiography of early southern religion found at http://jsreligion.org/issues/vol14/, accessed February 7, 2017.

45. For a recent survey of the history of American Baptists beginning with their roots in Europe, see Kidd and Hankins, *Baptists in America*.

46. Gardner, *Baptists of Early America*, 111; Townsend, *South Carolina Baptists*, 271.

47. Townsend, *South Carolina Baptists*, 280.

48. Ibid., 55.

49. Ibid., 280–81.

50. Ibid., 12.

51. "Church Wardens and Vestry of Prince Georges Parish, S.C. [to Secretary of the SPG], 12 May 1728," in *Selected Pages Relating to South Carolina*, 21:105–6.

52. For Huguenot migration to America, see Butler, *Huguenots in America;* Golden, *Huguenot Connection;* Van Ruymbeke, *From New Babylon to Eden*.

53. Quoted in Howe, *History of the Presbyterian Church in South Carolina*, 126.

54. See Sirmans, "Politics in Colonial South Carolina." Morton should not be entirely blamed for inhibiting Morgan's arrest. Morgan, born to a respectable family in Monmouth, Wales, garnered enough appreciation for his depredations against the Spanish that the British governor of Jamaica gave him a state funeral upon his death of natural causes in 1688. See Cordingly, *Under the Black Flag*, 42–43.

55. The establishment controversy has been ably described in Brinsfield, *Religion and Politics*, 16–37; Weir, *Colonial South Carolina*, 75–103; and Bolton, *Southern Anglicanism*, 16–28.

56. Edgar and Bailey, *Biographical Directory*, 5.

57. Congregationalist names were taken from *Record Book Independent* and compared to biographical entries in Edgar and Bailey, *Biographical Directory*.

58. For a useful overview of Catholics' experiences in South Carolina, see Miller, "Roman Catholicism in South Carolina."

59. Gideon Johnston, Commissary, to the Bishop of London, December 9, 1715, and April 6, 1716, in Williams, "Letters to the Bishop of London" (January 1977): 15, 16.

60. William Tredwell Bull, Commissary, to the Bishop of London, May 15, 1718, in ibid., 16–18.

61. Dalcho, *Historical Account of the Protestant Episcopal Church,* 28.

62. Friedlander, "Commissary Johnston's Report," 261.

63. Klingberg, *Carolina Chronicle,* 187–88, 195.

64. Dalcho, *Historical Account of the Protestant Episcopal Church,* 76.

65. Bolton, *Southern Anglicanism,* 29.

66. Ibid., 31–36.

67. The situation of the Puritan church establishment in New England has been treated masterfully in Conforti, *Saints and Strangers.*

68. Anderson, *Officers and Graduates,* 99; Anderson, *Roll of Alumni,* 51–52. An Alexander Garden graduated in 1706 and 1711. Peter John Anderson, who compiled and edited the university alumni records around the turn of the twentieth century, claimed that the 1711 Alexander Garden, "minister of the Gospel in South Carolina," received a doctorate in 1726. I believe he confused the 1711 Alexander with the 1706 Alexander, who was likely Alexander Garden the younger of Troup, who stayed in Europe. The South Carolina Alexander Garden never mentioned receiving a doctorate, and given his unremarkable position in South Carolina in 1726, discussed in the next chapter, it seems unlikely that his alma mater would have granted him a doctorate. It seems much more likely that the university would have forgotten about him by then.

69. Hill, "Law of Nature Revived"; Greene, "Latitudinarianism Reconsidered"; Rivers, *Reason, Grace, and Sentiment;* Holifield, *Theology in America,* 57–61; Spurr, "'Latitudinarianism' and the Restoration Church."

70. His gravestone lies observable in the cemetery adjoined to St. Philip's Church in Charleston.

71. Garden, "Letter from Rev. Alexander Garden." Gordon's errors are understandable. Perhaps he was taking after Whittemore, *Heroes of the American Revolution and Their Descendants,* 82–83, in which the entry for the botanist, the "son of Rev. Alexander Garden," was placed right after the entry for our "Rev. Alexander Garden," thus, intentionally or not, making the South Carolina botanist the son of the South Carolina minister.

72. Hawkins, "Alexander Garden," 60–62, quote from 61.

73. Bertie, *Scottish Episcopal Clergy,* 48.

74. Allardyce, *Records of Old Aberdeen,* xxvi.

75. The best biographical sketch of George Garden can be found in Macmillan, *Aberdeen Doctors.* His spiritual life is recorded by Henderson, *Mystics of the North-East,* a work upon which I have relied in this summary of Garden's spiritual life. For more on religion and politics in early eighteenth-century Scotland and England, see Bowie, "Popular Resistance."

76. Church of Scotland, *Acts of the General Assembly,* 306–7.

77. Macmillan, *Aberdeen Doctors,* 267–68.

78. Henderson, *Mystics of the North-East,* 209, 218.

79. Ibid., 219–20.

80. Dobson, *Scottish Emigration;* Devine, *Scotland's Empire;* Gingrich, "That Will Make Carolina Powerful."

81. Henderson, *History of the Parish of Banchory-Devenick*, 8–12; Burke, *Genealogical and Heraldic History*, 483, 482.

82. Dinnie, *Account of the Parish of Birse*, 110–11; Stuart, *Selections*, 283, 285.

83. Stuart, *Selections*, 214, 215, 228, 232, 237, 262, 275, 315.

84. Scott, *Fasti Ecclesiae Scoticanae*, 1:341; Bertie, *Scottish Episcopal Clergy*, 25.

85. Scott, *Fasti Ecclesiae Scoticanae*, 5:430.

86. Stuart, *Selections*, 226–27.

87. Michie, *Records of Invercauld*, 412.

88. Garden, "Letter from Rev. Alexander Garden," 117.

89. Macfarlane, *Genealogical Collections*, 36.

90. Brown, *Register of the Privy Council of Scotland*, 167–68.

91. Dobson, *Scottish Emigration*, 99. For turmoil pushing Scottish emigration and pull factors attracting them overseas, see Devine, *Scottish Nation*.

92. Dalcho, *Historical Account of the Protestant Episcopal Church*, 33.

CHAPTER 2: ACQUAINTANCES

1. Edelson, "Clearing Swamps, Harvesting Forests."

2. Coclanis, "Death in Early Charleston," 280.

3. Hart, *Building Charleston*, 38–44.

4. Weir, *Colonial South Carolina*, 105–11.

5. Letter 10, Wm. Tredwell Bull to the Bishop of London, August 10, 1723, in Williams, "Letters to the Bishop of London" (January 1977): 25.

6. Enright, "Account of Charles Town," 15.

7. Pinckney, "Eliza Lucas Pinckney to Mary Bartlett."

8. See the table of contents in Chalmers, *Account of the Weather*.

9. See Duffy, "Yellow Fever."

10. Weir, *Colonial South Carolina*, 40; Coclanis, "Death in Early Charleston," 290; Central Intelligence Agency, "Country Comparison"; The World Bank, "Death Rate."

11. Merrens and Terry, "Dying in Paradise," 542.

12. Weir, *Colonial South Carolina*, 40.

13. July 31, 1754, in Simpson, "Archibald Simpson Diary."

14. Alexander Garden to the Bishop of London, South Carolina, Charlestown, May 4, 1724, in Williams, "Letters to the Bishop of London" (April 1977): 125.

15. Alexander Garden to the Bishop of London, South Carolina, Charlestown, November 8, 1732, in Williams, "Letters to the Bishop of London" (April 1977): 146.

16. Williams, "Letters to the Bishop of London" (July 1977): 236. The historian Peter McCandles has offered a thorough examination of disease in the South and argued that rampant disease was unleashed by plantation agriculture (McCandles, *Slavery, Disease, and Suffering*).

17. Garden excerpted Pitcairn, *Works of Pitcairn*, 272–75. Garden published this excerpt in the June 1, 1738, edition of the *South Carolina Gazette*.

18. Klingberg, *Carolina Chronicle*, 196.

19. Mr. Wye's Testimonials, in "A Series Letter Books," A12:22–23.

20. Ibid., A13:140–42.

21. McCrady, *Historic Church,* 8–9.

22. South Carolina of St. Paul, September 25th: 1718, in "A Series Letter Books," A13:184.

23. Klingberg, *Carolina Chronicle,* 176.

24. Clergy of South Carolina to Bishop Robinson, Charles Town, May 31, 1716, in Fulham Papers at Lambeth Palace Library, London, 9:59–60.

25. Klingberg, *Carolina Chronicle,* 178, 194.

26. To the Church Wardens and Vestry of St. James's Goose Creek, August 14, 1717, in "A Series Letter Books," A12:173.

27. Klingberg, *Carolina Chronicle,* 3; "A Series Letter Books," A:138.

28. A Letter without Name directed to the Secretary Supposd to be from Governor Johnston, in "A Series Letter Books," A13:154.

29. To the Right Revd Father in God The Bishop of London and The Base and Humble Petition of John Smart and Wm Ordnay, in "A Series Letter Books," A12:30, 34.

30. To Governor Johnson, in "A Series Letter Books," A12:174.

31. A Letter without Name directed to the Secretary Supposd to be from the Governor Johnston, in "A Series Letter Books," A13:154.

32. To the Lords the Bishops of Rapho and Kittaloo and the Sovereign of Donleer, in "A Series Letter Books," A12:474.

33. Lord Bishop of Rapho to the Secretary, in "A Series Letter Books," A12:464–65.

34. To the Churchwardens and Vestry of Charles Town and To Governor Johnston, in "A Series Letter Books," A13:202.

35. Messrs Hasell, Jones, and Guy to the Secretary, May 13, 1719, in "A Series Letter Books," A13:224–26.

36. Mr. Jones to the Secretary, May 18, 1719, in "A Series Letter Books," A13: 229–32.

37. To Governor Johnston, November 24, 1719, in "A Series Letter Books," A13: 266.

38. Mr. Hasell to the Secretary, September 16, 1720, in "A Series Letter Books," A15: 54.

39. Mr. Varnod to the Secretary, March 21, 1725, in "A Series Letter Books," A19: 60.

40. Mr. Merry to the Secretary, July 1723, in "A Series Letter Books," A17:10.

41. Yonge, *Narrative,* 39.

42. William Tredwell Bull to the Bishop of London, August 12, 1720, in Williams, "Letters to the Bishop of London" (January 1977): 21–22.

43. Williams, "Letters to the Bishop of London" (April 1977): 123.

44. Ibid., 131–32.

45. Weis, *Colonial Clergy,* 93.

46. Alexander Garden to the Bishop of London, Queries to be Answer'd by Every Minister, April 15, 1724, in Williams, "Letters to the Bishop of London" (April 1977): 123.

47. For a useful geographic analysis of the development of Charles Town's importance to the colonial economy, see Lewis, "Metropolis and the Backcountry."

48. A Short Memorial of the Present State of the Church & Clergy in his Majesty's Province of South Carolina in America by Wm. Tredwell Bull, April 10, 1723, London, in Williams, "Letters to the Bishop of London" (January 1977): 25.

49. Dalcho, *Historical Account of the Protestant Episcopal Church*, 120–22. Vestries commonly designed and oversaw the construction of churches. See Upton, *Holy Things and Profane*, 23–34.

50. Bull, Memorial, in Williams, "Letters to the Bishop of London" (January 1977): 25.

51. Dalcho, *Historical Account of the Protestant Episcopal Church*, 122–23.

52. Quoted in McInnis, "Conflating Past and Present," 41.

53. Fraser, *Charleston*, 46–47.

54. For the basis of this description of the physical and social arrangement of the town, see Coclanis, "Sociology of Architecture"; and Calhoun, Zierden, and Paysinger, "Geographic Spread."

55. Williams, "Letters to the Bishop of London" (July 1977): 236.

56. Douglass, "Power of Attorneys," 10, 21.

57. Edgar and Bailey, *Biographical Directory*, 87–90, 409–10, 31; Douglass, "Power of Attorneys," 20.

58. Holcomb, *South Carolina Marriages*, 90.

59. There were exceptions. Retention of control of a woman's property in her own hands could be worked out legally in marriage arrangements, although in South Carolina this practice was not common in the 1720s. See Berkin, *First Generations*, 156–64; Salmon, *Women and the Law of Property*, 81–119; Kierner, *Beyond the Household*, 23.

60. Childs, "Petit-Guerard Colony," 9.

61. Nash, "Trade and Business," 8–10.

62. "Garden, Martha, Wife of Rev. Alexander Garden to Alexander Hext, Renunciation," Series S136009, vol. 1726, no. 00325, in South Carolina Department of Archives and History, On-line Records Index, 2000. http://www.archivesindex .sc.gov, accessed February 7, 2017.

63. Childs, "Petit-Guerard Colony," 10–11.

64. Calhoun, Zierden, and Paysinger, "Geographic Spread," 196.

65. *South Carolina Gazette*, July 2, 1737.

66. Salley, *Register of St. Philip's Parish*, 64, 70, 77, 249. Scholarship on remarriage among widowers is scarce, particularly for the lowcountry, but historians have generally assumed that colonial widows and widowers often remarried. See Anzilotti, *In the Affairs of the World*; Grigg, "Toward a Theory of Remarriage"; Higgs and Stettler, "Colonial New England Demography."

67. Manigault, Jervey, and Webber, "Peter Manigault's Letters," 149.

68. "[Last Will and Testament of Alexander Garden]."

69. Wood, *Black Majority*, 151.

70. Kelsey, "Swiss Settlers," 90.

71. Webber, "Presentment of the Grand Jury," 193–95.

72. Morgan, *Slave Counterpoint,* 59, 74–76.

73. *Conveyance Books,* G:148–49.

74. Mr. Morritt to the Secretary, July 8, 1726, in "A Series Letter Books," A19:320–22. See also Pennington, "Reverend Thomas Morritt."

75. Letter 15, Alexander Garden to the Bishop of London, May 4, 1724, in Williams, "Letters to the Bishop of London" (April 1977): 125–26.

76. Alexander Garden to the Secretary of the SPG, July 18, 1735, in "A Series Letter Books," A23:138. For his landholdings, see "Morritt, Thomas, Land Grant for 500 Acres in Craven County," series S213019, vol. 0001, no. 00437; "Morritt, Thomas, Land Grant for 160 Acres in Craven County," series S213019, vol. 0002, no. 00336; "Morritt, Thomas, Land Grant for 250 Acres in Craven County," series S213019, vol. 0002, no. 00373; "Morritt, Thomas, Land Grant for 500 Acres in Craven County," series S213019, vol. 0002, no. 00404; "Morritt, Thomas, Land Grant for 350 Acres in Craven County," series S213019, vol. 0003, no. 00294; "Morritt, Thomas, Land Grant for 1,000 Acres in Craven County," series S213019, vol. 0003, no. 00295, all in Index.

77. Salley, *Register of St. Philip's Parish,* 155.

78. Alexander Garden to the Bishop of London, May 26, 1727, in Williams, "Letters to the Bishop of London" (April 1977): 128–32.

79. Letter 12, William Tredwell Bull to the Bishop of London, May 13, 1728, in Williams, "Letters to the Bishop of London" (January 1977): 31.

80. Andrew Allen and Charles Hill to the Bishop of London, June 23, 1727, in Fulham Papers at Lambeth Palace Library, London, 9:200–201.

81. Letter 18, Alexander Garden to the Bishop of London, May 26, 1727, in Williams, "Letters to the Bishop of London" (April 1977): 129.

82. Mr. Hunt from the Common Prison in Charles Town to the Secretary of the SPG, February 1728, in "A Series Letter Books," A20:199–36.

83. Laing, "Very Immoral and Offensive Man," 28.

84. Alexander Garden and wardens and vestry of St. Philip's, Charles Town, to Bishop Gibson, June 26, 1728, in Fulham Papers at Lambeth Palace Library, London, 9:218–19.

85. Letter 12, William Tredwell Bull to the Bishop of London, May 13, 1728, in Williams, "Letters to the Bishop of London" (January 1977): 29–31.

86. Williams, "Letters to the Bishop of London" (April 1977): 132–34.

87. Weir, *Colonial South Carolina,* 206–7.

88. Berkin, *First Generations,* 146–48. The "consort" description comes from Alexander Garden's tombstone.

89. Ibid., 143–45; Morgan, *Slave Counterpoint,* 353–58; Kierner, *Beyond the Household,* 13–14.

90. Kierner, *Beyond the Household,* 37–43.

91. Ibid., 26–30.

92. Friedlander, "Commissary Johnston's Report," 264–65.

93. Ibid., 271.

94. Severens, "Johnston, Henrietta de Beaulieu Dering."

95. Klingberg, *Carolina Chronicle,* 29.

96. Cooper, *Statutes at Large of South Carolina,* 75.

97. Cohen, *South Carolina Gazette,* 54, 76.

98. *South Carolina Gazette,* postscript to March 3, 1742; December 4, 1740; April 10, 1742.

99. See, for instance, "Eliza Lucas Pinckney to George Lucas, January 1742"; "Eliza Lucas Pinckney to George Lucas, June 4 1741"; "Eliza Lucas Pinckney to William Murray, 11 November 1741"; "Eliza Lucas Pinckney to Mary Bartlett, [1742]" (two letters), in Schulz, *Papers of Eliza Lucas Pinckney and Harriott Pinckney Horry.* An excellent summary of her life and legacy is Bellows, "Eliza Lucas Pinckney."

100. For more on women's economic and social opportunities in colonial South Carolina, see Kierner, *Beyond the Household;* Anzilotti, *In the Affairs of the World;* Gunderson, *To Be Useful to the World;* and Winston, "Economic Power."

101. *South Carolina Gazette,* February 26, 1732; December 25, 1740; March 14, 1743.

CHAPTER 3: FRIENDSHIP

1. Quote from Landers, "Gracia Real de Santa Teresa de Mose," 13. Joel Berson too described the African exodus from South Carolina to Florida, and he linked it to the Stono Rebellion; see Berson, "How the Stono Rebels Learned."

2. *South Carolina Gazette,* May 19, 1733; August 23, 1740; September 13, 1740.

3. Morgan, *Slave Counterpoint,* xxii. See also Wood, *Black Majority,* 285–307. Robert Olwell dealt with slave resistance throughout *Masters, Slaves, and Subjects.*

4. Wood, *Black Majority,* 298–99, 220, 222.

5. Garden, *Six Letters,* 53.

6. Langford, *Polite and Commercial People;* Klein, "Politeness"; Klein, *Shaftesbury and the Culture of Politeness;* Isaac, *Transformation of Virginia;* Shields, *Civil Tongues.*

7. For an excellent examination of the display of politeness through home furnishings and other accoutrements in the society that Carolinians admired, see Vickery, *Behind Closed Doors.*

8. Hutchinson, "Private Character of Admiral Anson."

9. Bushman, *Refinement of America,* 51.

10. Thomas Dale to Rev. Thomas Birch, folio 53, November 17, 1732, in Dale, "Correspondence."

11. Cohen, *South Carolina Gazette,* 75.

12. Waterhouse, *New World Gentry,* 93.

13. Cohen, *South Carolina Gazette,* 29–30.

14. Davis, *Fledgling Province,* 171.

15. Cohen, *South Carolina Gazette,* 20, 76.

16. To Revd Mr Thomas Birch St. Johns Lane near Smithfield London, October 2, 1735, in Dale, "Correspondence."

17. Isaac, *Transformation of Virginia,* 131.

18. Hutchinson, "Private Character of Admiral Anson."

19. For an excellent examination of the way British industrialization revolutionized society and culture in the American colonies, see Breen, *Marketplace of*

*Revolution.* For a snapshot of the fashion that Carolinians aspired to, see "Fashion" in Waller, *1700,* 153–76.

20. Bushman, *Refinement of America,* 51.

21. Ibid., 52, 55–56, 57.

22. *South Carolina Gazette,* March 30, 1738.

23. Ibid., April 20, 1738.

24. Lovejoy, *Great Chain of Being.*

25. *South Carolina Gazette,* March 22, 1734.

26. Kingwell, "Politics and Polite Society"; Smith, "Great Reformation."

27. Church Wardens and Vestry of Christ Church to Secretary of the SPG, October 21, 1728, in "A Series Letter Books," A21:131–32.

28. Mr. Winteley to Secretary of the SPG, October 22, 1728, in "A Series Letter Books," A21:134. The brothers-in-law were William Capers, George Benison, and George Haddrell.

29. Winteley to the Secretary of the SPG, June 14, 1729, in "B Series Letter Books," B4II: 229.

30. No title, in "B Series Letter Books," B4II:230. Apparently this was a notation by the transcriber, as follows: "The sic affidavits which follow are mostly before J Bond JP and dated June 10 and 24. Four are by women, and two (as to his drunkenness) are by Thomas Boone before Bond, and by John Guerard and Alex Peronneau before Daniel Greene." Unfortunately the transcriber did not include the original affidavits. For Winteley's claim that the women who signed the affidavit were disreputable, see J. Winteley to Bishop Gibson, Charles Town, February 13, 1729, in Fulham Papers at Lambeth Palace Library, London, 9:229–30.

31. Winteley described the above account in Winteley to the Secretary of the SPG, June 14, 1729, in "B Series Letter Books," B4II:229.

32. Ibid.

33. See Weir, *Colonial South Carolina,* 109–10.

34. Edgar and Bailey, *Biographical Directory,* 90.

35. Winteley to the Secretary of the SPG, June 14, 1729, in "B Series Letter Books," B4II:229.

36. Alexander Garden to the Bishop of London, June 28, 1729, in Williams, "Letters to the Bishop of London" (April 1977): 134.

37. Keen, "Problems of a Commissary," 143.

38. Alexander Garden to the Bishop of London, November 24, 1729, in Williams, "Letters to the Bishop of London" (April 1977): 135.

39. Ibid., 134.

40. Weir, *Colonial South Carolina,* 108.

41. Winteley failed at St. Bartholomew's for reasons that are unclear. In 1731 Garden wrote to the society that Winteley had "stroll'd about soliciting the Members of the Assembly to recommend him" as the teacher for the Free School in town. In spite of his "same untoward Be[ha]vior," he was able to convince enough assemblymen to commend him to the trustees of the school. The trustees, Garden, and "four other prin[ci]pal Gentlemen of the Province" refused the recommendation but did suggest that the assembly provide "some Allowance from the Publick for his Subsistence."

Had Winteley been sufficiently chastened into obedience that he was able to gain the support of some members of the assembly? Was it an embittered Garden who convinced the trustees to reject Winteley? Garden reported in 1733 that Winteley had "behaved himself so as to be dismiss'd his Chaplainship of Savanah Garison." The assembly gave him "£40 Sterling to enable him to return home," but he died of "a Flux and Fever" before the end of the year. This pattern of quickly overstaying his welcome did not speak well of Winteley's character; however, that the society, according to a fellow minister, Brian Hunt, sympathized with Winteley's plight enough to restore the salary that had been withheld during his troubles in South Carolina does. See Alexander Garden to the Bishop of London, April 7, 1733, in Williams, "Letters to the Bishop of London" (July 1977): 214; Alexander Garden to the Bishop of London, April 20, 1731, in Williams, "Letters to the Bishop of London" (April 1977); Alexander Garden to the Bishop of London, December 28, 1733, in ibid., 218; Petition of Bryan Hunt and His Wife, April 14, 1730, in "A Series Letter Books," A23:394.

42. Fulton to the Secretary of the SPG, December 4, 1730, in "A Series Letter Books," A23:221.

43. Alexander Garden to the Bishop of London, April 7, 1733, in Williams, "Letters to the Bishop of London" (July 1977): 213.

44. Church Wardens and Vestry of Christ Church to Secretary of the SPG, May 18, 1734, in "A Series Letter Books," A23:93.

45. Mr. Fulton to the Secretary of the SPG, May 25, 1734, in "A Series Letter Books," A23:95.

46. The Apeal of John Fulton of Christ Church, missionary . . . to the Society and His Lordship the Bishop of London, May 25, 1734, in "A Series Letter Books," A23:125–26.

47. Ibid., A23:127–35.

48. Ibid., A23:125–26. Information on Barton was taken from Edgar and Bailey, *Biographical Directory*. In 1723 Barton had advocated against paper currency—the opposite of Thomas Boone's position. Apparently they had made peace by the early 1730s.

49. "A Series Letter Books," A23:127–35.

50. Alexander Garden to the Bishop of London, April 30, 1734, in Williams, "Letters to the Bishop of London" (July 1977): 227, 230.

51. "A Series Letter Books," A26:128–29; Williams, "Letters to the Bishop of London" (July 1977): 236.

52. Mr. Hunt to the Secretary of the SPG, November 5, 1725, in "A Series Letter Books," A19:80.

53. Mr. Hunt to the Secretary of the SPG, November 24, 1726, in "B Series Letter Books," B4II:215.

54. Mr. Hunt to the Secretary of the SPG, February 9, 1727, in "B Series Letter Books," B4II:196.

55. Thomas Thompson to the Secretary of the SPG, August 16, 1743, in Gambrill, "St. Bartholomew's Parish," 181, 178, 182.

56. Thomas Thompson to the Secretary of the SPG, January 30, 1744, in "B Series Letter Books," B10:213.

57. Charles Boschi to the Secretary of the SPG, October 30, 1745, in Gambrill, "St. Bartholomew's Parish," 184, 185.

58. Ibid., 188.

59. Ibid., 189.

60. Charles Boschi to the Secretary of the SPG, April 7, 1746, in Gambrill, "St. Bartholomew's Parish," 188, 189, 190–91.

61. "Way, Aaron, and William Way to Alexander Garden, Sale for a Town Lot in Dorchester," series S372001, vol. 00S0, no. 00240, in Index.

62. "Garden, Martha, Wife of Rev. Alexander Garden to Alexander Hext, Renunciation," series S136009, vol. 1726, no. 00325, in Index.

63. "Dwight, Christiana, Wife of Daniel Dwight to Alexander Garden, Renunciation," series S136009, vol. 1739, no. 00090, in Index. Curiously, this barony did not appear in Smith, *Baronies of South Carolina*, which, though by no means an exhaustive study, is the most complete treatment of baronies in South Carolina. Smith did, however, point out that though the title of barony was intended to refer specifically to a grant of land of twelve thousand acres as part of a seigniorial system, in South Carolina it eventually came to include any piece of land of twelve thousand acres.

64. Morgan, *Slave Counterpoint*, 43.

65. Note in "Garden, Alexander (1686–1756)," 2 MSS: DS, April 7, 1743; and MP, February 4, 1901, South Caroliniana Library, University of South Carolina, Columbia.

66. "LaRoche, Daniel, of Craven County, to the Reverend Alexander Garden, Rector of Saint Philip's, Charles Town, Bond for Payment of the Sum of Six Hundred Pounds," series S213003, vol. 002I, no. 00230, in Index; "LaRoche, Daniel, Andrew DeLavillette, and David Montaigut, Merchants of Georgetown, to the Rev. Alexander Garden of St. Phillips Parish, Bond for Payment of the Sum of One Thousand Five Hundred Pounds," series S213003, vol. 002I, no. 00235, in Index.

67. There were three Alexander Gardens in mid-eighteenth-century South Carolina: the commissary Alexander Garden; his nephew; and a botanist. To ensure that I was correctly identifying Alexander Sr., I checked the actual documents (as opposed to the online index) for all of Garden's transactions. The botanist arrived in the colony in 1752 and lived in Charles Town. The reverend's nephew too was a minister, and he lived in the parish of St. Thomas and St. Dennis. Since both ministers were well known in the colony, records from the time distinguished between the two by designating Jr. and Sr., a distinction that is usually confirmable in the records by the location of the transaction. The botanist arrived in the colony toward the end of Alexander Sr.'s life, so most of his business was carried on after Alexander Sr. had left the scene. Finally, the records usually denote Alexander Sr. as "Rector of St Philip's." The four instances of power of attorney were as follows: "Osborn, Thomas, Bookseller of London, to Reverend Alexander Garden and George Seaman, Power of Attorney to Receive Money Owed by William Logan and Lionel Chambers, Merchants of South Carolina," series S213003, vol. 002I, no. 00353; "Bull, William Tredwell, to Alexander Garden, Power of Attorney to Sell his Estate in South Carolina," series S372001, vol. 00D0, no. 00205; "Society for

the Propagation of the Gospel in Foreign Parts to Rev. Alexander Garden, of St. James Goose Creek, and William Guy, of St. James Goose Creek, Clerk, Power of Attorney to Recover from William Dry, of St. James Goose Creek, Every Part of the Estate of Rev. Richard Ludlum, of St. James Goose Creek, to Dispose of the Estate for the Largest Monetary Gain Possible for the Society, and to Revoke the Letters of Administration of William Dry," series S213003, vol. 002G, no. 00412; and "Society for the Propagation of the Gospel in Foreign Parts to Reverend Alexander Garden of Charles Town, Rector of St. Philips Parish, Power of Attorney to Sell a Negro Slave Named Andrew," series S213003, vol. 002H, no. 00250, all in Index. Garden was also involved in at least two lawsuits, one on behalf of work done on St. Philip's Church: "Meek, John vs. Alexander Garden, Judgment Roll," series S136002, box 025A, item 0046A; and one apparently to recover a small debt for himself: "Garden, Alexander vs. John Brand, Judgment Roll," series S136002, box 017B, item 0011A. The eight land transactions were the three mentioned above along with "Mitchell, John and Wife to Alexander Garden, Lease and Release for Part of Town Lot no. 115 in Charlestown," series S372001, vol. 02Qo, no. 00115; "Trott, Nicholas and Wife, Sarah to Alexander Garden and Joseph Wragg, Lease and Release for Land in Berkly County and Charlestown," series S372001, vol. 02Oo, no. 00279; "Rawlins, Lydia, Wife of Robert Rawlins to Alexander Garden, Renunciation," series S136009, vol. 1739, no. 00649; "Rose, Beulah, Wife of Thomas Rose to Alexander Garden, Renunciation," series S136009, vol. 1743, no. 00134; and "Wood, Alexander to Alexander Garden, Mortgage of Lease and Release for 200 Acres of Land in St. James Goose Creek," series S372001, vol. 02Mo, no. 00233, all in Index. Garden was also involved in at least two other land transactions on behalf of the SPG: "Marian, James to Alexander Garden and Henry Izard, Attys for Society for Propagation of the Gospel, Mortgage of Lease and Release for 425 Acres in Goose Creek," series S372001, vol. 02Do, no. 00015; and "Bryan, Hugh to Society for the Propagation of the Gospel by Rev. Alexander Garden and William Guy, Attys., Mortgage for 300 Acres of Land in Granville County," series S372001, vol. 00So, no. 00063, in Index. The eight debt agreements were the ones listed above as well as "McKenzie, John, and Matthew Roche, Merchants of Charles Town, to Alexander Garden, Clerk, Rector of St. Phillips Parish Charles Town, Bond for Payment of the Sum of Three Hundred Nineteen Pounds," series S213003, vol. 002I, no. 00229; "Christie, Henry to Alexander Garden, Mortgage of Lease and Release for part of Town Lot no. 268 Charlestown," series S372001, vol. 02Ho, no. 00026; "Croft, Childermas to Alexander Garden, Mortgage of Lease and Release of 81 Acres of Land on Charlestown Neck and a Town Lot in Charlestown," series S372001, vol. 02No, no. 00486; "Sheed, George Jr. to Alexander Garden, Mortgage of Lease and Release for Part of Town Lot no. 199 in Charlestown," series S372001, vol. 02No, no. 00365; "Pinckney, Charles and Wife to John Williams and Alexander Garden, Mortgage of Lease and Release for 2 Town Lots in Charlestown," series S372001, vol. 02Ho, no. 00018; and "Watson, Ann to Alexander Garden, Mortgage for Part of Town Lot no. 28 in Charlestown," series S372001, vol. 02Fo, no. 00266, all in Index.

68. "An Inventory of Sundry Effects belonging to the Estate of the Revd Mr Alexander Garden Senr deceased taken and appraised by us in Charles Town the 15th

to the 19th October 1756," inventories of estates, vol. 84 (original vol. S), 1756–58, S213215, South Carolina Department of Archives and History, Columbia. Richard Waterhouse has analyzed all 4,443 of the surviving estate inventories for the period 1736–75, a sample that included primarily the wealthy since the poor left few probate records. He provided a chart of estate values in Waterhouse, *New World Gentry*, 64. The wills from which Waterhouse derived the values and rankings noted only the value of nonreal property.

69. Weis, *Colonial Clergy*, 79. The quotation is from Mr. Guy to the Secretary of the SPG, January 22, 1727/28, in "A Series Letter Books," A20:110–14.

70. William Guy to the Secretary of the SPG, March 26, 1740, in "B Series Letter Books," B7:239–40.

71. "Society for the Propagation of the Gospel in Foreign Parts to Rev. Alexander Garden, of St. James Goose Creek, and William Guy, of St. James Goose Creek, Clerk, Power of Attorney to Recover from William Dry, of St. James Goose Creek, Every Part of the Estate of Rev. Richard Ludlum, of St. James Goose Creek, to Dispose of the Estate for the Largest Monetary Gain Possible for the Society, and to Revoke the Letters of Administration of William Dry," series S213003, vol. 002G, no. 00412, in Index.

72. Mr. Hunt from the Common Prison in Charles Town to the Secretary of the SPG, February 1727/28, in "A Series Letter Books," A20:119–36.

73. Brian Hunt to the Bishop of London, March 20, 1727, in in Transcripts of South Carolina Records of the Bishop of London, 1710–1767, Lambeth Palace Library MSS South Carolina, no. 154, microfilm, South Carolina Department of History and Archives, Columbia, South Carolina.

74. Letter from the Commissioners of the Free School, December 2, 1726, in "B Series Letter Books," B4II:217.

75. Alexander Garden to the Secretary of the SPG, May 20, 1741, in "B Series Letter Books," B9:124.

76. "Guy, William, Land Grant for 1,000 Acres in Granville County," series S213019, vol. 0001, no. 00203; "Guy, Rev. William, Plat for 500 Acres in Berkley County," series S213184, vol. 0004, no. 00008; "Guy, Rev. William, Plat for 500 Acres in Berkley County," series S213184, vol. 0004, no. 00013; "Guy, William, Land Grant for 500 Acres in Berkley County," series S213019, vol. 0003, no. 00130, all in Index. See Moore, *Abstracts of Wills*, 2:125.

77. "Vernold, Francis, Memorial for 3 Tracts . . .," series S111001, vol. 0005, no. 00325, in Index. The spelling of the name Vernold was a typographical error.

78. Moore, *Abstracts of Wills*, 2:36.

79. Edgar and Bailey, *Biographical Directory*, 41–42, 430.

80. Ibid., 262.

81. Ibid., 275.

82. Constantia Hasell married John Pagett, and Ann Hasell married Samuel Thomas. See ibid., 499–500, 668.

83. Weis, *Colonial Clergy*, 76.

84. "Dwight, Daniel, Memorial for 100 Acres in St. John's Parish . . .," series S111001, vol. 0003, no. 00247; "Dwight, Daniel, Land Grant for 60 Acres in Craven

County," series S213019, vol. 0002, no. 00019; "Dwight, Daniel, Land Grant for 1085 Acres in Craven County," series S213019, vol. 0002, no. 00073; "Dwight, Daniel, Land Grant for 500 Acres in Craven County," series S213019, no. 0041, no. 00094; "Dwight, Daniel, Land Grant for 315 Acres in Craven County," series S213019, vol. 0002, no. 00426; "Dwight, Daniel, Land Grant for 42 Acres in Craven County," series S213019, vol. 0002, no. 00424; "Dwight, Rev. Daniel, Memorial for Two Tracts in Prince George Parish . . .," series S111001, vol. 0007, no. 00404, all in Index.

85. Laing, "Very Immoral and Offensive Man," 28.

86. Levi Durand to the Secretary of the SPG, October 29, 1741, in "B Series Letter Books," B10:157.

87. Levi Durand to the Secretary of the SPG, April 23, 1747, in "B Series Letter Books," B13:171.

88. Levi Durand to the Secretary of the SPG, October 15, 1744, in "B Series Letter Books," B12:107.

89. Moore, *Abstracts of Wills,* 3:55.

90. Fraser, *Charleston,* 55. Charles Town was actually the fourth largest town in North America at this time.

91. A classic work of cultural history relevant to this book is Isaac, *Transformation of Virginia.* Agnew, "Main Currents," and Banner, *Century of American Historiography,* provide an excellent overview of the evolution of the historiography of American cultural history.

92. Isaac, *Transformation of Virginia,* 58–65. See also Nelson, *Beauty of Holiness,* 309–29.

93. Witzig, "Beyond Expectation."

94. *South Carolina Gazette,* December 28, 1738.

95. November 27, 1738, in "Minutes of the Vestry, St. Philip's Parish." The workhouse was built by order of the vestry and maintained under the guidance of the vestry who also kept track of all who were "taken in and victualled" (May 1740).

96. "C Series Letters," box 7, 117.

97. For the importance of slave merchants to the plantation economy, see Coclanis, "Hydra Head of Merchant Capital."

98. Morgan, *Slave Counterpoint,* 79–95.

99. See Littlefield, "Charleston and Internal Slave Redistribution."

100. Higgins, "Charles Town Merchants and Factors."

101. Some traders, particularly those whose first and last names were recorded, who occupied vestry or trustee positions, or who baptized their children in an Anglican church, can be identified with much greater certainty than others. Partnerships were usually titled only by the last names of the partners, in which cases I counted them as probable identifications based on the commonality of the names among particular denominations' records, even where the uniqueness and prominence of a last name would strongly suggest a particular identifiable colonist. For instance, Pringle of the Pringle and Inglis partnership was most certainly Robert Pringle since Robert was virtually the only prominent Pringle to appear in colonial records during this time and the chances of there being another Pringle active in slave trading was

small. Anglican records oftentimes included records of marriages and births of non-Anglican colonists within the parish and therefore are not reliable markers of religious preference, but baptisms could be performed by anyone and thus would not likely appear in Anglican records unless the parents preferred an Anglican baptism. Occasionally I included as a probable identification someone whose family name frequently appeared in places of importance within a particular denomination and only within the records of that denomination. Edgar and Bailey, *Biographical Directory,* pointed out that "it was not unusual for dissenters to be elected either a vestry-man or churchwarden" (5). I have not noticed this, particularly in the Charles Town churches. I suspect that it probably occurred in the parishes where dissenters lacked sufficient buildings and ministers to support their own denomination. SPG missionaries in the outlying parishes often spoke of dissenters who attended the established church, occasionally breaking off when they either had the resources or became too upset with the Anglican services. Besides, that a dissenter would agree to serve as vestry or warden of an Anglican church indicates a rather lukewarm attachment to nonconformity. One can hardly imagine many New England Congregationalists taking positions in the Church of England. Evidence of that sort of denominational particularity can be seen in the statement describing the dissenter Othniel Beale, who maintained cordial relationships with various Anglicans. That he never became a vestryman or a warden—he most certainly had the reputation and wealth to attract those offices—may owe to what the Anglican minister Charles Woodmason described as Beale's "Bigotted Zeal for Independency" (quoted in Edgar and Bailey, *Biographical Directory,* 63).

102. I was able to glean names of prominent Presbyterians in Charles Town from Howe, *History of the Presbyterian Church;* and E. T. H. Shaffer, *Bethel Presbyterian Church,* which included some elders' minutes. Since church leaders and traders came from the same upper ranks of wealth in society, it is likely that any Presbyterian traders would have shown up in these histories. In other words, even a short but incomplete list of prominent Presbyterians such as from these histories should capture the names of Presbyterian traders. Therefore it is highly doubtful that the unidentifiable traders were exclusively or even predominantly Presbyterian.

103. Names and number of the inhabitants of St. Georges Parish So Carolina inclosed in Mr. Varnod's Letter dated 21 January 1725, in "A Series Letter Books," A19:104.

104. Petition of Bryan Hunt and his Wife, April 14, 1730, in "A Series Letter Books," A23:394.

CHAPTER 4: DALLIANCE

1. The literature on the Great Awakening and George Whitefield is large and increasing every year. A short list should include Bonomi, *Under the Cope of Heaven;* Butler, "Enthusiasm Described and Decried"; Gallay, *Formation of a Planter Elite;* Gallay, "Origins of Slaveholders' Paternalism"; Goff, "Revivals and Revolution"; Heimert, *Religion and the American Mind;* Hoffer, *When Benjamin Franklin Met the Reverend Whitefield;* Kenney, "Alexander Garden and George Whitefield"; Kidd, *Great Awakening;* Lambert, *Pedlar in Divinity;* Lambert, *Inventing the "Great*

*Awakening"*; Mahaffey, *Accidental Revolutionary;* Stout, *Divine Dramatist;* Witzig, "Great Anti-Awakening."

2. Alexander Garden to the Bishop of London, April 24, 1740, in Williams, "Letters to the Bishop of London" (October 1977): 296.

3. For an excellent examination of definitions and history of evangelicalism in America, see Noll, *American Evangelical Christianity,* esp. 29–43.

4. Garden, *Doctrine of Justification,* 14.

5. Allison, *Historical Theology,* 498.

6. Little, *Origins of Southern Evangelicalism,* 2013, xiii; Smith, *Cautious Enthusiasm.*

7. The definition and characterization of evangelicalism are from Bebbington, *Evangelicalism in Britain;* Noll, *American Evangelical Christianity.*

8. Garden, *Six Letters,* 12, 33–35.

9. Garden, *Regeneration,* 2.

10. The biblical reference to Paul's conversion and the thief on the cross can be found in Acts 9 and Luke 23:32–43.

11. Garden, *Regeneration,* 10, 12.

12. Ibid., 12.

13. Whitefield, *Select Sermons,* 52.

14. Benedict, *Christ's Churches.*

15. Garden, *Doctrine of Justification,* 10.

16. Garden, *Regeneration,* 7.

17. Garden, *Doctrine of Justification,* 16–19.

18. Ibid., 21.

19. Ibid., 25.

20. Ibid., 52.

21. Ibid., 56.

22. Ibid., 61.

23. Garden, *Six Letters,* 13–14.

24. Ibid., 35–36.

25. Ibid., 20.

26. Ibid., 19.

27. Garden, *Take Heed,* 31a.

28. Whitefield, *George Whitefield's Journals,* 165.

29. Gillies, *Memoirs of the Rev. George Whitefield,* 33.

30. Whitefield, *George Whitefield's Journals,* 165.

31. Whitefield's theatrical preaching style and the crowd's hearty approval of it were described in Stout, *Divine Dramatist.*

32. Ibid., 36–48.

33. Garden, *Regeneration,* 25.

34. Garden, *Take Heed,* 18b–19b.

35. Ibid., 19.

36. May 3, 1753, in "Minutes of the Vestry, St. Philip's Parish," 180.

37. Alexander Garden to the Bishop of London, April 23, 1745, in "B Series Letter Books," BII:80; Weis, *Colonial Clergy,* 73.

38. A useful description of a minister comparable to Alexander Garden can be found in Welsh, Skaggs, and Enholm, "In Pursuit of the 'Golden Mean'"; Finke and Stark, "How the Upstart Sects Won America"; White and White, *Sounds of Slavery*.

CHAPTER 5: ENGAGEMENT

1. Whitefield, *George Whitefield's Journals*, 400–401.

2. *South Carolina Gazette*, July 14, 1739; August 11, 1739; September 1, 1739.

3. Little, *Origins of Southern Evangelicalism*, 116–17.

4. Whitefield, *George Whitefield's Journals*, 384–85.

5. Ibid., 384.

6. Ibid. The amount of time he spent in South Carolina can be calculated using his journals.

7. Whitefield, *Letters of George Whitefield*, 345, 103, 385.

8. Whitefield, *George Whitefield's Journals*, 241.

9. To Mr.—, at Philadelphia, May 21, 1740, in Whitefield, *Letters of George Whitefield*, 176, 55.

10. George Whitefield to the Rev. Mr. T., November 10, 1739, in Whitefield, *Letters of George Whitefield*, 93, 320–21, 135, 69.

11. Whitefield, *Three Letters*, 12.

12. Whitefield, *George Whitefield's Journals*, 401.

13. *South Carolina Gazette*, January 4, 1739.

14. Weir, *Colonial South Carolina*, 121.

15. Quoted in Duffy, "Yellow Fever," 194.

16. Fraser, *Charleston*, 46–47.

17. Wood, *Black Majority*, 313.

18. Quoted in ibid., 310.

19. *South Carolina Gazette*, July 28, 1739.

20. Ibid., August 18, 1739.

21. Quoted in Wood, *Black Majority*, 319.

22. This chronology and the quotations were taken from ibid., 321.

23. "B Series Letter Books," 7:243, American Material in the Archives of the United Society for the Propagation of the Gospel, 1635–1812, British Online Archives, http://www.britishonlinearchives.co.uk, accessed February 7, 2017.

24. Morgan, *Slave Counterpoint*, 386.

25. Cooper, *Statutes at Large of South Carolina*, 7:416.

26. Wood, *Black Majority*, 301, 308–26, remains the best account of the rebellion, although important aspects of the event have been described in Smith, "Remembering Mary"; and Thornton, "African Dimensions." For the aftermath of the rebellion, see also Wax, "Great Risque."

27. *South Carolina Gazette*, November 17, 1739.

28. Ibid., November 17, 1739; May 26, 1739; July 14, 1739; February 1, 1739; February 8, 1739.

29. Whitefield, *George Whitefield's Journals*, 384–85.

30. *South Carolina Gazette*, January 12, 1740.

31. Ibid., February 16, 1740.

32. Ibid., July 1, 1740.

33. Ibid., July 18, 1740.

34. Ibid., July 20, 1741.

35. See, for instance, Smith, *First Great Awakening*, 79.

36. For instance, he published his defense of Tillotson in the *South Carolina Gazette* on April 21, 1740, under his own name when the Great Awakening was going strong. Dr. Logan Mayfield, associate professor of computer science at Monmouth College, his research assistant Emma Vanderpool, and the author are using author verification technology to establish the likelihood that Garden wrote the Arminius letter. Early results strongly support the author's contention that Garden did not author the letter signed Arminius.

37. For a more complete evaluation of antirevivalism in South Carolina, see Witzig, "Great Anti-Awakening."

38. Garden, *Six Letters*, 9, 13, 16, 29, 32; Garden, *Take Heed*, 6; Garden, *Regeneration*, i.

39. Garden, *Regeneration*, 1.

40. Ibid., i, ii.

41. Garden, *Take Heed*, 4, 5, 11–13.

42. Ibid., 4, 17–19, 20–23.

43. Garden, *Six Letters*, 8, 43.

44. Garden, *Regeneration*, 1.

45. Ibid., 3, 15–17.

46. Garden, *Six Letters*, 9.

47. Ibid., 26; Garden, *Regeneration*, 3.

48. Garden, *Six Letters*, 32–42.

49. Ibid., 10.

50. Garden, *Take Heed*, 22–23.

51. *South Carolina Gazette*, November 29, 1738.

52. Garden, *Regeneration*, 49–50.

53. Garden, *Take Heed*, 63.

54. Ibid., 64–66.

55. This is by no means to argue that works of charity and piety counted for nothing in the evangelical world. Rather, to Whitefield and his fellow evangelicals, such works made evident to others the work in the soul that had already taken place as a result of God's election of grace. Works counted for nothing toward gaining salvation, though, as was made clear in his sermon titled "The Method of Grace." Here he preached the doctrine of unconditional election and asserted, "Before you can speak peace in your heart, you must not only be made sick of your original and actual sin, but you must be made sick of your righteousness, of all your duties and performances" (Whitefield, *Select Sermons*, 83).

56. Garden, *Take Heed*, 17–19.

57. *South Carolina Gazette*, February 9, 1740.

58. Ibid., May 24, 1740.

59. Ibid., July 12, 1740.

60. Ibid., October 16, 1740.

61. Garden, *Take Heed,* 29–30.

62. Ibid., 30–31.

63. Ibid., 32–34.

64. Ibid., 34–35.

65. Whitefield, *George Whitefield's Journals,* 442–43.

66. Garden, *Take Heed,* 6.

67. Ibid., 31–32.

68. *South Carolina Gazette,* July 25, 1740.

69. Stout, *Divine Dramatist,* 111.

70. Henchman, *Reasons Offered.*

71. Whitefield, *George Whitefield's Journals,* 440.

72. Garden, *Six Letters,* 21.

73. For a detailed analysis of antirevivalism in Philadelphia, see Witzig, "Great Anti-Awakening."

74. Griffin, *Old Brick,* 41, 55, 56.

75. Chauncy, *Dr. Chauncy's Sermon,* iii.

76. Ibid., 3, 5.

77. Ibid., 13, 15, 21, 27.

78. Nash, *Urban Crucible,* 68.

79. Whitefield, *George Whitefield's Journals,* 400–401, 440.

80. Ibid., 441–44.

81. Garden, *Six Letters,* 6.

82. Dallimore, *George Whitefield,* 2:209.

83. Christie, "Newly Discovered Letters of Whitefield," 248. A reader of the *South Carolina Gazette* had published affidavits from 1744 attesting that Whitefield had tried to prosecute his appeal of Garden's suspension. Following the affidavits, the submitter argued that the affidavits were not clear that Whitefield had tried to complete his appeal within a year after Garden's suspension, as he had promised Garden. Smith had likely written to Whitefield about this sudden appearance of the affidavits in the *Gazette* and identified the submitter as Garden. Why Garden chose to publish the affidavits in 1746 is not clear.

84. *South Carolina Gazette,* February 16, 1740.

CHAPTER 6: MARRIAGE

1. Dalcho, *Historical Account of the Protestant Episcopal Church,* 43, 47.

2. "Documents Concerning Rev. Samuel Thomas," 37. Thomas left the colony in 1705 but returned the next year, only to die in the yellow fever epidemic ("Documents Concerning Mrs. Samuel Thomas," 99).

3. Le Jau to the Secretary, July 14, 1710; Le Jau to the Secretary, February 9, 1711; Le Jau to the Secretary, March 19, 1716, in Klingberg, *Carolina Chronicle,* 81, 86, 174.

4. Comminey, "Society for the Propagation of the Gospel"; Watson, "Good Will Come of This Evil"; Glasson, *Mastering Christianity.*

5. *South Carolina Gazette,* April 30, 1737.

6. Mr. Ludlam to the Secretary of the SPG, March 22, 1725, in "A Series Letter Books," A19:62–63.

7. Material on Neau and the SPG's response to slave master resistance to slave education relied on Glasson, *Mastering Christianity,* 72–86.

8. Quoted in Glasson, *Mastering Christianity,* 84.

9. Ibid., 81–86. See also Glasson, "Baptism Doth Not Bestow Freedom."

10. Hawkins, "Alexander Garden."

11. Dalcho, *Historical Account of the Protestant Episcopal Church,* 104–12.

12. Or at least he claimed St. Philip's as his church. See Higgins, "Charles Town Merchants and Factors," 206; Salley, *Register of St. Philip's Parish,* 57, 58, 62, 69, 73, 76, 105, 106, 110, 117, 121, 124, 126, 217, 218.

13. Letter III, Letter to the Inhabitants of Maryland, Virginia, North and South-Carolina, concerning their Negroes, in Whitefield, *Three Letters,* 13.

14. Ibid.

15. Ibid.

16. Frey and Wood, *Come Shouting to Zion,* 13–14, 26, 30.

17. Whitefield, *Three Letters,* 14–15.

18. Whitefield, *George Whitefield's Journals,* 379.

19. Stout, *Divine Dramatist,* 123.

20. Whitefield, *Select Sermons,* 103.

21. Ibid., 138.

22. Wheatley, *Elegiac Poem.*

23. Cashin, *Beloved Bethesda,* 21. For another, earlier account of Bethesda, see Gamble, *Bethesda.*

24. Franklin, *Autobiography of Benjamin Franklin,* 83.

25. *South Carolina Gazette,* June 25, 1741.

26. Wood, *Black Majority,* 321–22.

27. Garden, *Six Letters,* text-fiche, 53.

28. Ibid., 51.

29. Ibid., 52.

30. Ibid.

31. Ibid., 53.

32. Ibid.

33. Dalcho, *Historical Account of the Protestant Episcopal Church,* 110.

34. Alexander Garden to the Secretary of the SPG, May 6, 1740, in "B Series Letter Books," B7:235.

35. Ibid., B7:236–37.

36. Ibid., B7:237.

37. Ibid., B7:236, 237.

38. Ibid., B7:237.

39. Alexander Garden to the Secretary of the SPG, May 20, 1741, in "B Series Letter Books," B9:124.

40. *South Carolina Gazette,* October 23, 1740.

41. Alexander Garden to the Secretary of the SPG, April 9, 1742, in "B Series

Letter Books," B10:138; Mr. Vernod to the Secretary of the SPG, April 3, 1728, in "A Series Letter Books," A21:77.

42. Alexander Garden to the Secretary of the SPG, October 24, 1742, in "B Series Letter Books," B10:139.

43. Alexander Garden to the Secretary of the SPG, October 10, 1743, in "B Series Letter Books," B11:204. Sale of slave in Alexander Garden to Secretary of the SPG, September 9, 1750, in "B Series Letter Books," B17:182.

44. Alexander Garden to the Secretary of the SPG, October 18, 1744, in "B Series Letter Books," B12:119.

45. Alexander Garden to the Secretary of the SPG, October 22, 1748, in "B Series Letter Books," B16:146.

46. Alexander Garden to the Secretary of the SPG, October 29, 1752, in "B Series Letter Books," B20:134.

47. *South Carolina Gazette,* August 1, 1743.

48. Ibid. For an excellent discussion of the "Bubble" and its immediate transformation into a series of Atlantic cultural myths, see Hoppit, "Myths."

49. *South Carolina Gazette,* October 3, 1741.

50. Ibid., May 24, 1740.

51. Ibid., July 4, 1743.

52. Ibid., postscript to August 27, 1744. Publicola here plays on the language of 1 Cor. 9:19–22 in the Bible.

53. Habersham's letter was in *South Carolina Gazette,* October 15, 1744, and the poem was in ibid., November 12, 1744. Neither was Publicola satisfied with Habersham's letter of delay. Claiming that he had been pleased to see Habersham respond, his "Joy was turned into Grief and Confusion" upon reading the letter, and even more when the next day he entered a conversation with others who were also dissatisfied with Habersham's letter and who bemoaned the persecution Publicola had met in response to Publicola's "good and honest Endeavors for the Good of the House!" (ibid., November 19, 1744).

54. See, for instance, *South Carolina Gazette,* March 14, 1743.

55. Ibid., April 2, 1744.

56. For instance, they removed one of the students to the "madhouse." See Rogers, *Charleston,* 91.

57. *South Carolina Gazette,* April 2, 1744.

58. Ibid., postscript to August 27, 1744.

59. Ibid., August 1, 1743.

60. Quoted in Wood, *Black Majority,* 322.

61. *South Carolina Gazette,* postscript to January 1–8, 1741. For more on the fire, see Scott, "Sufferers."

62. The story was described most fully in Jackson, "Hugh Bryan."

63. Schmidt, "Grand Prophet," 238.

64. Gallay, "Origins of Slaveholders' Paternalism"; Gallay, *Formation of a Planter Elite.*

65. Whitefield, *George Whitefield's Journals,* 502–4.

66. It is unclear when, exactly, the letter became public. According to a notice in the August 30, 1740, *South Carolina Gazette,* publication of the set of six letters, including the last letter (dated July 30) against Whitefield's criticism of slavery, would begin in early September. It is likely, however, given the close-knit nature of colonial society, that the contents of Whitefield's letter and Garden's response were public knowledge before the publication of Garden's response. The fact that Garden indicated in the preface accompanying his published *Take Heed* sermon that his first three letters were already "now before the World" (14) supports the theory that his letters were distributed as Garden wrote them and before the September printing.

67. Tuesday, April 9, 1754, in "Minutes of the Vestry, St. Philip's Parish."

68. For instance, Henry Laurens served as president of the Continental Congress, and Charles Pinckney served as president of the Provincial Congress in 1775.

69. Birnie, "Education of the Negro."

70. MacMaster, *Land, Piety, Peoplehood;* Durnbaugh, *Fruit of the Vine;* Marietta, *Reformation of American Quakerism;* Soderland, *Quakers and Slavery;* Cadbury, "Early Quaker Anti-Slavery Statement"; Cozma, "John Martin Bolzius"; Towner, "Sewell-Saffin Dialogue"; Peterson, "Selling of Joseph."

71. Francis Vernod to the Secretary of the SPG, May 6, 1732, in "A Series Letter Books," A23:331.

72. Mr. Ludlam to the Secretary of the SPG, March 22, 1725, in "A Series Letter Books," A19:62–63.

73. Stephen Roe to the Secretary of the SPG, December 22, 1741, in "B Series Letter Books," B10:174. For an excellent explanation of how historians have greatly underestimated slave receptivity to Christianity in the colonial period, see Laing, "Heathens and Infidels."

74. Alexander Garden to the Secretary of the SPG, April 9, 1742, in "B Series Letter Books," B10:138.

75. Ibid., B139.

76. Alexander Garden to the Secretary of the SPG, October 10, 1743, in "B Series Letter Books," B10:204.

77. Alexander Garden to the Secretary of the SPG, October 18, 1744, in "B Series Letter Books," B12:119.

78. Secretary of the SPG to Alexander Garden, December 15, 1744, in "B Series Letter Books," B13:349.

79. Alexander Garden to the Secretary of the SPG, September 9, 1750, in "B Series Letter Books," B17:182.

CHAPTER 7: TILL DEATH DO US PART

1. In the case of the orphans, see, for instance, April 29, 1740, in "Minutes of the Vestry, St. Philip's Parish," 51. Examples of all the other types of vestry work described appeared on nearly every page of the vestry minutes.

2. July 17, 1749, in "Minutes of the Vestry, St. Philip's Parish," 143.

3. Ibid., 92, 98.

4. November 18, 1745; August 8, 1737; October 16, 1754; October 9, 1749; August 12, 1754, in ibid., 145.

5. *South Carolina Gazette,* June 21, 1742.

6. October 12, November 5, 1740, and July 6, 1741, in "Minutes of the Vestry, St. Philip's Parish," 56; Salley, *Register of St. Philip's Parish,* 266.

7. August 8, 1737, in "Minutes of the Vestry, St. Philip's Parish," 16–17.

8. Nelson, *Beauty of Holiness,* 295.

9. December 8, 1742, in "Minutes of the Vestry, St. Philip's Parish," 92.

10. November 20, 21, 1740, in ibid., 58–59.

11. December 31, 1740, in ibid., 66.

12. January 6, 173[5], in ibid., 12–14.

13. November 27, 1738, in ibid., 39.

14. December 20, 1742, in ibid., 92.

15. November 5, 1744, in ibid., 109.

16. June 1, 1747, in ibid., 125.

17. Byrd, "First Charles Town Workhouse," 40. See also Lockley, "Rural Poor Relief."

18. Alexander Garden to the Bishop of London, South Carolina, Charles Town, November 8, 1732, in Williams, "Letters to the Bishop of London" (April 1977): 146.

19. Williams, "Letters to the Bishop of London" (October 1977): 296.

20. Alexander Garden to the Bishop of London, South Carolina, Charles Town, September 6, 1737, in Williams, "Letters to the Bishop of London" (October 1977): 289.

21. Alexander Garden to the Bishop of London, South Carolina, Charles Town, July 24, 1731, in Williams, "Letters to the Bishop of London" (October 1977): 141–42.

22. G. Phenney to Bishop Gibson, New Providence, April 14, 1725; Joseph Gegg to Bishop Gibson, Gloucester, September 20, 1725; Affidavits of Edward Leae, bricklayer, and Thomas Sackerson before W. Fairfax, January 9, 1728; Samuel Lawford to Bishop Gibson, South Carolina, January 27, 1728; Samuel Lawford, undated; Thomas Curphey to Bishop Gibson, undated, all in Fulham Papers at Lambeth Palace Library, London, 15:33–34, 39–40, 54–55, 56, 57, 60–61.

23. Alexander Garden to Bishop Gibson, Charles Town, S.C., April 28, 1730, in Fulham Papers at Lambeth Palace Library, London, 68–69.

24. J. Winteley to Bishop Gibson, Charles Town, July 20, 1728, in Fulham Papers at Lambeth Palace Library, London, 9:220–21.

25. Brian Hunt to the Bishop of London, London, September 8, 1729, in Fulham Papers at Lambeth Palace Library, London, 9:237–38.

26. Alexander Garden to the Bishop of London, South Carolina, Charles Town, May 24, 1725, in Williams, "Letters to the Bishop of London" (April 1977): 127–28.

27. Alexander Garden to the Bishop of London, April 20, 1731, in Fulham Papers at Lambeth Palace Library, London, 9:138.

28. Alexander Garden to the Bishop of London, Charlestown, April 18, 1734, in Williams, "Letters to the Bishop of London" (July 1977): 219–20, 222.

29. Bolton, *Southern Anglicanism,* 47–48.

30. Charles Boschi to the Secretary of the SPG, October 30, 1745, in "B Series Letter Books," B12:112.

31. Kelsey, "Swiss Settlers," 86.

32. Alexander Garden to the Bishop of London, South Carolina, Charlestown, May 4, 1724, in Williams, "Letters to the Bishop of London" (April 1977): 125; Alexander Garden to the Bishop of London, South Carolina, Charlestown, October 24, 1736, in Williams, "Letters to the Bishop of London" (April 1977): 242.

33. June 8, 1736, in "Minutes of the Vestry, St. Philip's Parish," 18.

34. Alexander Garden to the Bishop of London, South Carolina, May 4, 1724, in Williams, "Letters to the Bishop of London" (April 1977): 126, 136; Alexander Garden to the Bishop of London, South Carolina, November 24, 1729, in Williams, "Letters to the Bishop of London" (October 1977): 296, 301, 306.

35. McCandles, *Slavery, Disease, and Suffering,* 51. For an excellent analysis of the effects of disease on the daily lives of Anglican ministers, see Wood, "Constant Attendance."

36. Alexander Garden to the Bishop of London, South Carolina, November 13, 1734, in Williams, "Letters to the Bishop of London" (July 1977): 231–32.

37. August 15, 1748, in "Minutes of the Vestry, St. Philip's Parish," 137.

38. See, for instance, April 19, 1742, in "Minutes of the Vestry, St. Philip's Parish," 81.

39. May 21, 1739, and February 27, 1738, in "Minutes of the Vestry, St. Philip's Parish," 33.

40. Calhoun, Zierden, and Paysinger, "Geographic Spread," 199, 201, 205; Higgins, "Charles Town Merchants and Factors," 210, 211; Stumpf, "South Carolina Importers," 5.

41. Gunderson, *To Be Useful to the World,* 47; Anzilotti, *In the Affairs of the World,* 73–74. John Brickell, who wrote *Natural History of North-Carolina,* noted of settlers in North Carolina that a woman still single past the age of twenty was considered a "stale Maid" (31).

42. "Minutes of the Vestry, St. Philip's Parish," 177.

43. This tradition of ingrained deference to the elites has been beautifully explained in Wood, *Radicalism of the American Revolution,* esp. 11–42.

44. Dalcho, *Historical Account of the Protestant Episcopal Church,* 167–70.

45. Ibid., 170–71.

46. Nelson, *Beauty of Holiness,* 212.

47. April 10, 1754, in "Minutes of the Vestry, St. Philip's Parish," 190; Dalcho, *Historical Account of the Protestant Episcopal Church,* 171–73.

48. May 3, 1753, and October 29, 1753, in "Minutes of the Vestry, St. Philip's Parish," 181, 187.

49. Ibid., 189, 195.

50. Alexander Garden to the Bishop of London, Eton, June 23, 1755, in Williams, "Letters to the Bishop of London" (October 1977): 313.

51. Ibid.

52. Alexander Garden to the Bishop of London, South Carolina, Charles Town, May 4, 1724, in Williams, "Letters to the Bishop of London" (October 1977): 125.

53. Manigault, Jervey, and Webber, "Peter Manigault's Letters," 149.

54. Mr. Whaley to Mr. A. D. Stubbs, in "A Series Letter Books," A13:496.

55. "[Last Will and Testament of Alexander Garden]."

56. Smith, *Cautious Enthusiasm,* 93, 98; Little, *Origins of Southern Evangelicalism;* Bolton, *Southern Anglicanism.*

57. Alexander Garden to the Bishop of London, South Carolina, Charlestown, December 29, 1748, in Williams, "Letters to the Bishop of London" (October 1977): 306.

58. The best source on this topic remains Bonomi, *Under the Cope of Heaven,* 1986.

59. Finke and Stark, "How the Upstart Sects Won America."

60. Nonetheless evidence that his congregation grew in the 1740s and 1750s— the vestry kept adding pews, and Anglicans finally built St. Michael's Church in Charles Town in the early 1750s to house the crowds—overwhelms any suggestion that Garden lost followers due to evangelicalism.

61. Heyrman, *Southern Cross.*

62. Ramsay, *History of South Carolina,* 1:dedication. Ramsay signed the preface of this book in 1808.

63. Ramsay, *History of South Carolina,* 2:256.

64. Ibid., 8, 11.

65. Dalcho, *Historical Account of the Protestant Episcopal Church,* 105, 128.

66. Tiffany, *History of the Protestant Episcopal Church,* 232–34; Cross, *Anglican Episcopate.*

67. Billingsley, *Life of the Great Preacher,* 134; Tyerman, *Life of Whitefield,* 364, 396. Another important work ignored Garden altogether: Baird, *Religion in America.* The mid-twentieth-century Whitefield biographer Albert Belden likewise dismissed Garden's controversy with Whitefield as "comparatively unimportant"; see Belden, *George Whitefield,* 100.

68. Pennington, "Reverend Alexander Garden" (December 1933), 194; Pennington, "Reverend Alexander Garden" (March 1934), 54.

69. Keen, "Problems of a Commissary," 138, 155. See also the work by the Episcopalian instructor Addison, *Episcopal Church.*

70. Dallimore, *George Whitefield,* 1:511, 514, 517, 519.

71. Ross, *Origins of American Social Science;* Haskell, *Emergence of Professional Social Science;* Novick, *That Noble Dream.*

72. For an excellent rendition of this process of secularization of the academy, see Marsden, *Soul of the American University.*

73. Miller, *New England Mind,* vii, viii.

74. Sweet, *Story of Religion,* 43; Braurer, *Protestantism.*

75. Olmstead, *History of Religion.*

76. Bridenbaugh, *Mitre and Sceptre;* Polishook, "Review of *Mitre and Sceptre.*"

77. Ahlstrom, *Religious History.*

78. See, for instance, the preface to Banner, *Century of American Historiography.*

79. Heimert, *Religion and the American Mind,* 35, 92; Heimert and Miller, *Great Awakening Documents,* 46.

80. See, for instance, Woolverton, *Colonial Anglicanism,* 193; Lovejoy, *Religious Enthusiasm,* 200; Stout, *Divine Dramatist,* 111; Fraser, *Charleston,* 70; Lambert, *Pedlar in Divinity,* 175, 176; Gaustad and Schmidt, *Religious History,* 104–5; Laing, "Very Immoral and Offensive Man," 24; Goodwin, "Anglican Reaction," 357; Morgan, "George Whitefield"; Holifield, *Theology in America,* 86; Mahaffey, *Preaching Politics,* 81, 94, 95; Kidd, *Great Awakening,* 121, 256; Mahaffey, *Accidental Revolutionary,* 53, 59, 60. There are a few notable exceptions. See, for instance, the mixed depiction of Garden, including his controversy with Whitefield and his steady and well-received leadership of the Anglican church, in Bolton, *Southern Anglicanism;* Fraser, *Charleston.*

81. Klingberg, *Appraisal of the Negro,* 107, 111.

82. Comminey, "Society for the Propagation of the Gospel," 363; Glasson, *Mastering Christianity,* 123. See also Monaghan, *Learning to Read and Write;* Mahaffey, *Preaching Politics;* Sundue, "Confining the Poor to Ignorance"; Watson, "Good Will Come of This Evil."

# Bibliography

"The A Series Letter Books, 1702–1737," n.d. American Material in the Archives of the United Society for the Propagation of the Gospel, 1635–1812, British Online Archives. http://www.britishonlinearchives.co.uk.

Addison, James Thayer. *The Episcopal Church in the United States, 1789–1931.* New York: Scribner, 1951.

Agnew, Jean-Christophe. "Main Currents in American Cultural History." In *A Century of American Historiography*, edited by James M. Banner Jr., 39–51. Boston: Bedford/St. Martin's, 2010.

Ahlstrom, Sydney E. *A Religious History of the American People.* New Haven, Conn.: Yale University Press, 1972.

Allardyce, Colonel James, LL.D., ed. *Records of Old Aberdeen, MCLVII–[MCMIII].* Aberdeen: New Spalding Club, 1895.

Allison, Gregg R. *Historical Theology: An Introduction to Christian Doctrine.* Grand Rapids, Mich.: Zondervan, 2011.

Amussen, Susan Dwyer. *Caribbean Exchanges: Slavery and the Transformation of English Society, 1640–1700.* Chapel Hill: University of North Carolina Press, 2007.

Anderson, Peter John, ed. *Officers and Graduates of University and Kings College Aberdeen, MVD–MDCCCLX.* Aberdeen: New Spalding Club, 1903. http://books.google.com/books/reader?id=PBw9AAAAYAAJ&printsec=frontcover&output=reader&pg=GBS.PA220.

———, ed. *Roll of Alumni in Arts of the University and King's College of Aberdeen, 1596–1860.* Aberdeen: University of Aberdeen, 1900. https://play.google.com/books/reader?id=HCYBAAAAYAAJ&printsec=frontcover&output=reader&authuser=0&hl=en&pg=GBS.PR5.

Anzilotti, Cara. *In the Affairs of the World: Patriarchy and Power in Colonial South Carolina.* Westport, Conn.: Greenwood Press, 2002.

"The B Series Letter Books, 1702–1786," n.d. American Material in the Archives of the USPG, 1635–1812, British Online Archives. http://www.britishonlinearchives.co.uk.

Baird, Robert. *Religion in America.* New York: Harper, 1844.

Banner, James M. Jr. *A Century of American Historiography.* Boston: Bedford/St. Martin's, 2010.

Beasley, Nicholas M. *Christian Ritual and the Creation of British Slave Societies, 1650–1780.* Athens: University of Georgia Press, 2009.

Bebbington, David. *Evangelicalism in Britain: A History from the 1730s to the 1980s.* London: Unwin Hyman, 1989.

Belden, Rev. Albert D., B.D. *George Whitefield—the Awakener: A Modern Study of the Evangelical Revival.* London: Sampson Low, Marston, n.d.

Bellows, Barbara L. "Eliza Lucas Pinckney: The Evolution of an Icon." *South Carolina Historical Magazine* 106, no. 2/3 (July 2005): 147–65.

Benedict, Philip. *Christ's Churches Purely Reformed: A Social History of Calvinism.* New Haven, Conn.: Yale University Press, 2002.

Berkin, Carol. *First Generations: Women in Colonial America.* New York: Hill and Wang, 1996.

Berson, Joel. "How the Stono Rebels Learned of Britain's War with Spain." *South Carolina Historical Magazine* 110, no. 1/2 (April 2009): 53–68.

Bertie, David. *Scottish Episcopal Clergy, 1689–2000.* Edinburgh: T & T Clark, 2000.

Billingsley, Rev. A. S. *The Life of the Great Preacher, Reverend George Whitefield, "Prince of Pulpit Orators," with the Secret of His Success and Specimens of His Sermons.* Philadelphia: P. W. Ziegler, 1878.

Birnie, C. W. "Education of the Negro in Charleston, South Carolina, prior to the Civil War." *Journal of Negro History* 12, no. 1 (January 1927): 13–21.

Bolton, S. Charles. *Southern Anglicanism: The Church of England in Colonial South Carolina.* Contributions to the Study of Religion 5. Westport, Conn.: Greenwood Press, 1982.

Bonomi, Patricia U. *Under the Cope of Heaven: Religion, Society, and Politics in Colonial America.* New York: Oxford University Press, 1986.

Bowie, Karin. "Popular Resistance, Religion and the Union of 1707." In *Scotland and the Union, 1707–2007,* edited by T. M. Devine, 39–53. Edinburgh: Edinburgh University Press, 2008.

Braurer, Jerald C. *Protestantism in America: A Narrative History.* Philadelphia: Westminster Press, 1953.

Breen, T. H. *The Marketplace of Revolution: How Consumer Politics Shaped American Independence.* Oxford: Oxford University Press, 2004.

Brickell, John, M.D. *The Natural History of North-Carolina.* Dublin: James Carson, 1737.

Bridenbaugh, Carl. *Mitre and Sceptre: Transatlantic Faiths, Ideas, Personalities, and Politics, 1689–1775.* New York: Oxford University Press, 1962.

Brinsfield, John Wesley. *Religion and Politics in Colonial South Carolina.* Easley, S.C.: Southern Historical Press, 1983.

British History Online, British History. "'The "New Pretended" Council and Assembly of S. Carolina to the Council of Trade and Plantations,' Dec. 24." *Calendar of State Papers Colonial, America and West Indies, Volume 31.* http://www.british-history.ac.uk/report.aspx?compid=74081, accessed February 7, 2017.

Brown, P. Hume, M.A., LL.D. *The Register of the Privy Council of Scotland, A.D. 1633–1635.* 2nd ed. Vol. 5. Edinburgh: H. M. General Register House, 1904.

Bull, Kinloch. "Barbadian Settlers in Early Carolina: Historiographical Notes." *South Carolina Historical Magazine* 96, no. 4 (October 1, 1995): 329–39.

Burke, Sir Bernard, C.B., LL.D. *A Genealogical and Heraldic History of the Landed Gentry of Great Britain & Ireland*. 5th ed., vol. 1. London: Harrison, Pall Mall, 1875. http://books.google.com/books/about/Burke_s_Genealogical_and_Heraldic_Histor.html?id=ZNEKAAAAYAAJ, accessed February 7, 2017.

Bushman, Richard L. *The Refinement of America: Persons, Houses, Cities*. New York: Knopf, 1992.

Butler, Jon. "Enthusiasm Described and Decried: The Great Awakening as Interpretive Fiction." *Journal of American History* 69, no. 2 (September 1982): 305–25.

———. *The Huguenots in America: A Refugee People in New World Society*. Cambridge, Mass.: Harvard University Press, 1988.

Butler, Lindley S. "The Early Settlement of Carolina: Virginia's Southern Frontier." *Virginia Magazine of History and Biography* 79, no. 1 (January 1, 1971): 20–28.

Byrd, Michael D. "The First Charles Town Workhouse, 1738–1775: A Deterrent to White Pauperism?" *South Carolina Historical Magazine* 110, no. 1/2 (April 2009): 35–52.

"The C Series Letters, 1635–1812," n.d. American Material in the Archives of the United Society for the Propagation of the Gospel, 1635–1812, British Online Archives. http://www.britishonlinearchives.co.uk.

Cadbury, Henry J., ed. "An Early Quaker Anti-Slavery Statement." *Journal of Negro History* 22, no. 4 (October 1937): 488–93.

Calhoun, Jeanne A., Martha A. Zierden, and Elizabeth A. Paysinger. "The Geographic Spread of Charleston's Mercantile Community, 1732–1767." *South Carolina Historical Magazine* 86, no. 3 (July 1985): 182–220.

Carney, Judith A. *Black Rice: The African Origins of Rice Cultivation in the Americas*. Cambridge, Mass.: Harvard University Press, 2001.

Cashin, Edward J. *Beloved Bethesda: A History of George Whitefield's Home for Boys, 1740–2000*. Macon, Ga.: Mercer University Press, 2001.

Central Intelligence Agency. "Country Comparison: Death Rate." *The World Factbook*. https://www.cia.gov/library/publications/the-world-factbook/rankorder/2066rank.html, accessed May 21, 2014.

Chalmers, Lionel. *An Account of the Weather and Diseases of South Carolina*. London: Edward and Charles Dilly, 1776.

Chauncy, Charles, D.D. *Dr. Chauncy's Sermon Cautioning against Enthusiasm*. Boston: J. Draper, 1742.

Childs, St. Julien R. "The Petit-Guerard Colony." *South Carolina Historical Magazine* 43, no. 1 (January 1942): 1–17.

Christie, John W., ed. "Newly Discovered Letters of George Whitefield 1745–1746, Part III." *Journal of the Presbyterian Historical Society* 32, no. 4 (December 1954): 241–71.

Church of Scotland. *Acts of the General Assembly of the Church of Scotland, 1638–1842*. Edinburgh: Edinburgh Printing & Publishing Co., 1843. http://archive.org/details/actsofgeneralassoochur.

Coclanis, Peter A. "Death in Early Charleston: An Estimate of the Crude Death Rate for the White Population of Charleston, 1722–1732." *South Carolina Historical Magazine* 85, no. 4 (October 1984): 280–91.

————. "The Hydra Head of Merchant Capital." In *The Meaning of South Carolina History*, edited by David R. Chesnutt and Clyde N. Wilson. 1–18. Columbia: University of South Carolina Press, 1991.

————. "The Sociology of Architecture in Colonial Charleston: Pattern and Process in an Eighteenth-Century Southern City." *Journal of Social History* 18, no. 4 (Summer 1885): 607–23.

Cohen, Hennig. *The South Carolina Gazette*. Columbia: University of South Carolina Press, 1953.

Comminey, Shawn. "The Society for the Propagation of the Gospel in Foreign Parts and Black Education in South Carolina, 1702–1764." *Journal of Negro History* 84, no. 4 (Autumn 1999): 360–69.

Conforti, Joseph A. *Saints and Strangers: New England in British North America*. Baltimore, Md.: Johns Hopkins University Press, 2006.

*Conveyance Books ["Charleston Deeds"] Vols. G–K (1934–1935 Copies)*. Conveyance Books, 1719–1776, .S 372001. South Carolina, Public Register, n.d.

Cooper, Thomas, M.D., LL.D., ed. *The Statutes at Large of South Carolina*. Vol. 3. Columbia, S.C.: A. S. Johnston, 1838.

Cordingly, David. *Under the Black Flag: The Romance and the Reality of Life among the Pirates*. New York: Random House Trade Paperbacks, 2006.

Cozma, Codrina. "John Martin Bolzius and the Early Christian Opposition to Slavery in Georgia." *Georgia Historical Quarterly* 88, no. 4 (Winter 2004): 457–76.

Cross, Arthur Lyon. *The Anglican Episcopate and the American Colonies*. Harvard Historical Studies. New York: Longmans, Green, 1902.

Dalcho, Frederick, M.D. *An Historical Account of the Protestant Episcopal Church in South Carolina*. Vol. 1. Charleston, S.C.: E. Thayer, 1820.

Dale, Thomas. "The Correspondence of Thomas Dale, M.D. from Charleston, S.C. 1731–1736. British Museum MS 4304." MS, n.d. South Caroliniana Library, University of South Carolina, Columbia.

Dallimore, Arnold. *George Whitefield: The Life and Times of the Great Evangelist of the 18th Century Revival*. Vol. 1. Edinburgh: Banner of Truth Trust, 1970.

————. *George Whitefield: The Life and Times of the Great Evangelist of the 18th Century Revival*. Vol. 2. Edinburgh: Banner of Truth Trust, 1980.

Davis, Harold E. *The Fledgling Province: Social and Cultural Life in Colonial Georgia, 1733–1776*. Chapel Hill: University of North Carolina Press, 1976.

Devine, T. M. *Scotland's Empire and the Shaping of the Americas, 1600–1815*. Washington, D.C.: Smithsonian Books, 2003.

————. *The Scottish Nation: A History, 1700–2000*. New York: Viking, 1999.

Dinnie, Robert. *An Account of the Parish of Birse, Historical, Statistical and Antiquarian; Also, Brief Notices of the Surrounding Parishes*. Aberdeen: Lewis Smith, 1865. http://books.google.com/books/about/An_Account_of_the_Parish _of_Birse.html?id=DWkLAAAAYAAJ.

Dobson, David. *Scottish Emigration to Colonial America, 1607–1785*. Athens: University of Georgia Press, 1994.

"Documents Concerning Mrs. Samuel Thomas, 1707–1710." *South Carolina Historical and Genealogical Magazine* 5, no. 2 (April 1904): 95–99.

"Documents Concerning Rev. Samuel Thomas, 1702–1707." *South Carolina Historical Magazine* 5, no. 1 (January 1904): 21–55.

Donegan, Kathleen. *Seasons of Misery: Catastrophe and Colonial Settlement in Early America.* Philadelphia: University of Pennsylvania Press, 2014.

Douglass, John E. "Power of Attorneys: Formation of Colonial South Carolina's Attorney System, 1700–1731." *American Journal of Legal History* 37, no. 1 (January 1993): 1–24.

Duffy, John. "Yellow Fever in Colonial Charleston." *South Carolina Historical Magazine* 52, no. 4 (October 1951): 189–97.

Dunn, Richard S. *Sugar and Slaves: The Rise of the Planter Class in the English West Indies, 1624–1713.* Chapel Hill: University of North Carolina Press, 1972.

Durnbaugh, Donald F. *Fruit of the Vine: A History of the Brethren 1708–1995.* Elgin, Ill.: Brethren Press, 1997.

Edelson, S. Max. "Clearing Swamps, Harvesting Forests: Trees and the Making of a Plantation Landscape in the Colonial South Carolina Landscape." *Agricultural History* 81, no. 3 (Summer 2007): 381–406.

Edgar, Walter. *South Carolina: A History.* Columbia: University of South Carolina Press, 1998.

Edgar, Walter B., and Louise N. Bailey, eds. *Biographical Directory of the South Carolina House of Representatives.* Vol. 2. Columbia: University of South Carolina Press, 1977.

Enright, Brian J. "An Account of Charles Town in 1725." *South Carolina Historical Magazine* 61, no. 1 (January 1960): 13–18.

Finke, Roger, and Rodney Stark. "How the Upstart Sects Won America: 1776–1850." *Journal for the Scientific Study of Religion* 28, no. 1 (March 1989): 27–44.

Franklin, Benjamin. *The Autobiography of Benjamin Franklin.* Edited by Philip Smith. Mineola, N.Y.: Dover Publications, 1996.

Fraser, Walter J. *Charleston! Charleston! The History of a Southern City.* Columbia: University of South Carolina Press, 1991.

Frey, Sylvia R., and Betty Wood. *Come Shouting to Zion: African American Protestantism in the American South and British Caribbean to 1830.* Chapel Hill: University of North Carolina Press, 1998.

Friedlander, Amy, ed. "Commissary Johnston's Report, 1713." *South Carolina Historical Magazine* 83, no. 4 (October 1982): 259–71.

Gallay, Alan. *The Formation of a Planter Elite: Jonathan Bryan and the Southern Colonial Frontier.* Athens: University of Georgia Press, 2007.

———. *The Indian Slave Trade: The Rise of the English Empire in the American South, 1670–1717.* New Haven, Conn.: Yale University Press, 2002.

———. "The Origins of Slaveholders' Paternalism: George Whitefield, the Bryan Family, and the Great Awakening in the South." *Journal of Southern History* 53, no. 3 (August 1987): 369–94.

Gamble, Thomas, Jr. *Bethesda, an Historical Sketch of Whitefield's House of Mercy in Georgia, and of the Union Society, His Associate and Successor in Philanthropy.* Savannah, Ga.: Morning News Print, 1902.

Gambrill, Florence, ed. "St. Bartholomew's Parish as Seen by Its Rectors, 1713–1761." *South Carolina Historical Magazine* 50, no. 4 (October 1949): 173–203.

Garden, Alexander. *The Doctrine of Justification According to the Scripture, and the Articles, and Homilies of the Church of England, Explained and Vindicated. In a Letter to Mr. A. Croswell of Groton, in New England. Being a Reply to the Said Mr. Croswell's Answer to Mr. Garden's Three First Letters to Mr. Whitefield. With a Postscript.* Charleston, S.C.: Printed by Peter Timothy, 1742.

———. "Letter from Rev. Alexander Garden." In *The New England Historical and Genealogical Register,* edited by George A. Gordon, 390–92. Boston: New England Historic Genealogical Society, 1900.

———. *Regeneration, and the Testimony of the Spirit, Being the Substance of Two Sermons.* Charleston, S.C.: Printed by Peter Timothy, 1740.

———. *Six Letters to the Rev. Mr. George Whitefield.* Boston: Printed by T. Fleet, 1740.

———. *Take Heed How Ye Hear.* New York, 1742.

Gardner, Robert C. *Baptists of Early America: A Statistical History, 1639–1790.* Atlanta: Georgia Baptist Historical Society, 1983.

Gaustad, Edwin S., and Leigh E. Schmidt. *The Religious History of America: The Heart of the American Story from Colonial Times to Today.* Rev. ed. New York: HarperOne, 2002.

Gillies, John. *Memoirs of the Rev. George Whitefield.* Middletown, Pa.: Hunt, 1841.

Gingrich, Kurt. "'That Will Make Carolina Powerful and Flourishing': Scots and Huguenots in Carolina in the 1680s." *South Carolina Historical Magazine* 110, no. 1/2 (April 2009): 6–34.

Glasson, Travis. "'Baptism Doth Not Bestow Freedom': Missionary Anglicanism, Slavery, and the Yorke-Talbot Opinion, 1701–1730." *William and Mary Quarterly* 67, no. 2 (April 2010): 279–318.

———. *Mastering Christianity: Missionary Anglicanism and Slavery in the Atlantic World.* Oxford: Oxford University Press, 2012.

Goetz, Rebecca Anne. "Religious Diversity and the Coming of Christianity in the Prerevolutionary South." *Journal of Southern Religion* 14 (2012). http://jsreligion.org/issues/vol14/goetz.html.

Goff, Philip. "Revivals and Revolution: Historiographic Turns since Alan Heimert's *Religion and the American Mind.*" *Church History* 67, no. 4 (December 1998): 695–722.

Golden, R. M. *The Huguenot Connection: The Edict of Nantes, Its Revocation, and Early French Migration to South Carolina.* Dordrecht, Netherlands: Kluwer Academic, 1988.

Goodwin, Gerald J. "The Anglican Reaction to the Great Awakening." *Historical Magazine of the Protestant Episcopal Church* 35, no. 4 (1996): 343–71.

Gragg, Larry. *Englishmen Transplanted: The English Colonization of Barbados, 1627–1660.* Oxford: Oxford University Press, 2003.

Greene, Donald. "Latitudinarianism Reconsidered: A Review Essay." *Anglican and Episcopal History* 52, no. 2 (June 1993): 159–74.

Greene, Jack P. "Colonial South Carolina and the Caribbean Connection." *South Carolina Historical Magazine* 88, no. 4 (October 1, 1987): 192–210.

Griffin, Edward M. *Old Brick: Charles Chauncy of Boston, 1705–1787.* Minneapolis: University of Minnesota Press, 1980.

Grigg, Susan. "Toward a Theory of Remarriage: A Case Study of Newburyport at the Beginning of the Nineteenth Century." *Journal of Interdisciplinary History* 8, no. 2 (Autumn 1977): 183–220.

Gunderson, Joan R. *To Be Useful to the World: Women in Revolutionary America, 1740–1790.* Chapel Hill: University of North Carolina Press, 2006.

Hart, Emma. *Building Charleston: Town and Society in the Eighteenth-Century British Atlantic World.* Charlottesville: University of Virginia Press, 2010.

Haskell, Thomas L. *The Emergence of Professional Social Science: The American Social Science Association and the Nineteenth-Century Crisis of Authority.* Urbana: University of Illinois Press, 1977.

Hawkins, James Barney IV. "Alexander Garden: The Commissary in Church and State." Ph.D. diss., Duke University, 1981.

Heimert, Alan. *Religion and the American Mind: From the Great Awakening to the Revolution.* Cambridge, Mass.: Harvard University Press, 1966.

Heimert, Alan, and Perry Miller, eds. *The Great Awakening: Documents Illustrating the Crisis and Its Consequences.* The American Heritage Series. Indianapolis, Ind.: Bobbs-Merrill Educational Publishing, 1967.

Henchman, Nathanael. *Reasons Offered by Mr. Nathanael Henchman, Pastor of the First Church of Christ in Lynn, for Declining to Admit Mr. Whitefield into His Pulpit.* Boston: Printed by Timothy Fleet, 1745.

Henderson, G. D., B.D., D.Litt. *Mystics of the North-East, Including Letters of James Keith, M.D., and Others to Lord Deskford and Correspondence between Dr. George Garden and James Cunningham.* Aberdeen: Third Spaulding Club, 1934.

Henderson, John Alexander. *History of the Parish of Banchory-Devenick.* Aberdeen: D. Wyllie, 1890.

Heyrman, Christine Leigh. *Southern Cross: The Beginnings of the Bible Belt.* Chapel Hill: University of North Carolina Press, 1997.

Higgins, W. Robert. "Charles Town Merchants and Factors Dealing in the External Negro Trade 1735–1775." *South Carolina Historical Magazine* 65, no. 4 (October 1964): 205–17.

Higgs, Robert, and H. Louis Stettler III. "Colonial New England Demography: A Sampling Approach." *William and Mary Quarterly* 27, no. 2 (April 1970): 282–94.

Hill, Harvey. "The Law of Nature Revived: Christianity and Natural Religion in the Sermons of John Tillotson." *Anglican and Episcopal History* 70, no. 2 (June 2001): 169–89.

Hoffer, Peter Charles. *When Benjamin Franklin Met the Reverend Whitefield: Enlightenment, Revival, and the Power of the Printed Word.* Baltimore, Md.: Johns Hopkins University Press, 2011.

Holcomb, Brent H. *South Carolina Marriages, 1688–1799*. Baltimore, Md.: Genealogical Publishing Co., 1980.

Holifield, E. Brooks. *Theology in America: Christian Thought from the Age of the Puritans to the Civil War*. New Haven, Conn.: Yale University Press, 2003.

Hoppit, Julian. "The Myths of the South Sea Bubble." *Transactions of the Royal Historical Society*, 6th series, 12 (2002): 141–65.

Howe, George, D.D. *History of the Presbyterian Church in South Carolina*. Vol. 1. Columbia, S.C.: Duffie and Chapman, 1870.

Hutchinson, J., ed. "The Private Character of Admiral Anson. By a Lady." Gale Group, 2006. http://galenet.galegroup.com/servlet/ECCO.

Isaac, Rhys. *The Transformation of Virginia, 1740–1790*. Chapel Hill: University of North Carolina Press, 1982.

Jackson, Harvey H. "Hugh Bryan and the Evangelical Movement in Colonial South Carolina." *William and Mary Quarterly* 43, no. 4 (October 1986): 594–614.

Keen, Quentin Begley. "The Problems of a Commissary: The Reverend Alexander Garden of South Carolina." *Historical Magazine of the Protestant Episcopal Church* 20 (June 1951): 136–55.

Kelsey, R. W. "Swiss Settlers in South Carolina." *South Carolina Historical and Genealogical Magazine* 23, no. 3 (July 1922): 85–91.

Kenney, William Howland III. "Alexander Garden and George Whitefield: The Significance of Revivalism in South Carolina, 1738–1741." *South Carolina Historical Magazine* 71, no. 1 (January 1970): 1–16.

Kidd, Thomas S. *The Great Awakening: The Roots of Evangelical Christianity in Colonial America*. New Haven, Conn.: Yale University Press, 2007.

Kidd, Thomas S., and Barry Hankins. *Baptists in America: A History*. New York: Oxford University Press, 2015.

Kierner, Cynthia A. *Beyond the Household: Women's Place in the Early South, 1700–1835*. Ithaca, N.Y.: Cornell University Press, 1998.

Kingwell, Mark. "Politics and Polite Society in the Scottish Enlightenment." *Historical Reflections* 19, no. 3 (Fall 1993): 363–87.

Klein, Lawrence E. "Politeness and the Interpretation of the British Eighteenth Century." *Historical Journal* 45, no. 4 (2002): 869–98.

———. *Shaftesbury and the Culture of Politeness: Moral Discourse and Cultural Politics in Early Eighteenth-Century England*. Cambridge: Cambridge University Press, 2004.

Klingberg, Frank J. *An Appraisal of the Negro in Colonial South Carolina: A Study in Americanization*. Washington, D.C.: Associated Publishers, 1941.

———. *The Carolina Chronicle of Dr. Francis LeJau, 1706–1717*. Berkeley: University of California Press, 1956.

Kopperman, Paul E. *Sir Robert Heath, 1574–1649: Window on an Age*. London: Boydell and Brewer, 1989.

Laing, Annette. "'Heathens and Infidels'? African Christianization and Anglicanism in the South Carolina Low Country, 1700–1750." *Religion and American Culture* 12, no. 2 (Summer 2002): 197–228.

———. "'A Very Immoral and Offensive Man': Religious Culture, Gentility and the Strange Case of Brian Hunt, 1727." *South Carolina Historical Magazine* 103 (January 2002): 6–29.

Lambert, Frank. *Inventing the "Great Awakening."* Princeton, N.J.: Princeton University Press, 1999.

———. *"Pedlar in Divinity": George Whitefield and the Transatlantic Revivals.* Princeton, N.J.: Princeton University Press, 1994.

Landers, Jane. "Gracia Real de Santa Teresa de Mose: A Free Black Town in Spanish Colonial Florida." *American Historical Review* 95, no. 1 (February 1990): 9–30.

Lane, G. Winston, Jr. "Economic Power among Eighteenth-Century Women of the Carolina Lowcountry." In *Money, Trade, and Power: The Evolution of Colonial South Carolina's Plantation Society,* edited by Jack P. Greene et al., 322–43. Columbia: University of South Carolina Press, 2001.

Langford, Paul. *A Polite and Commercial People: England, 1727–1783.* New Oxford History of England. Oxford: Clarendon Press, 1989.

"[Last Will and Testament of Alexander Garden]." In *Will Books (copies), 1733–1774,* OO: 1752:–56:525–26. S 213027. Columbia, S.C.: Secretary of State, Recorded Instruments, n.d.

Lesser, Charles H. "Barbados." In *The South Carolina Encyclopedia,* edited by Walter Edgar, 47–48. Columbia: University of South Carolina Press, 2006.

———. "Lords Proprietors of Carolina." In *The South Carolina Encyclopedia,* edited by Walter Edgar, 566–68. Columbia: University of South Carolina Press, 2006.

———. "Yeamans, Sir John." In *The South Carolina Encyclopedia,* edited by Walter Edgar, 1056–57. Columbia: University of South Carolina Press, 2006.

Lewis, Kenneth E. "The Metropolis and the Backcountry: The Making of a Colonial Landscape on the South Carolina Frontier." *Historical Archaeology* 33, no. 3 (1999): 3–13.

Ligon, Richard. *A True & Exact History of the Island of Barbadoes Illustrated with a Map of the Island, as Also the Principal Trees and Plants There, Set Forth in Their Due Proportions and Shapes, Drawn out by Their Several and Respective Scales. Together with the Ingenio That Makes the Sugar, with the Plots of the Several Houses, Rooms, and Other Places, That Are Used in the Whole Process of Sugar Making . . . All Cut in Copper /by Richard Ligon, Gent.* London: Printed, and are to be sold by Peter Parker . . . and Thomas Guy . . . , 1673. http://archive.org/details/mobot31753000818390.

Little, Thomas J. *The Origins of Southern Evangelicalism: Religious Revivalism in the South Carolina Lowcountry 1670–1760.* Columbia: University of South Carolina Press, 2013.

Littlefield, Daniel C. "Charleston and Internal Slave Redistribution." *South Carolina Historical Magazine* 65, no. 4 (October 1964): 93–105.

Lockley, Tim. "Rural Poor Relief in Colonial South Carolina." *Historical Journal* 48, no. 4 (December 2005): 955–76.

Loftfield, Thomas C. "Creolization in Seventeenth-Century Barbados: Two Case

Studies." In *Island Lives: Historical Archaeologies of the Caribbean*, edited by Paul Farnsworth, 207–33. Tuscaloosa: University of Alabama Press, 2001.

Lovejoy, Arthur O. *The Great Chain of Being: A Study of the History of an Idea.* Cambridge, Mass.: Harvard University Press, 1936.

Lovejoy, David S. *Religious Enthusiasm in the New World: Heresy to Revolution.* Cambridge, Mass.: Harvard University Press, 1985.

MacFarlane, William. *Genealogical Collections Concerning Families in Scotland, Made by Walter MacFarlane.* Edited by James Toschach Clark. Vol. 2. Publications of the Scottish History Society. Edinburgh: Edinburgh University Press, 1900. https://archive.org/stream/scothistorysoc34scotuoft#page/n1/mode/2up.

MacMaster, Richard K. *Land, Piety, Peoplehood: The Establishment of Mennonite Communities in America, 1683–1790.* Kitchener, Ontario: Herald Press, 1985.

Macmillan, Donald. *The Aberdeen Doctors: A Notable Group of Scottish Theologians of the First Episcopal Period, 1610–1638 and the Bearing of Their Teaching on Some Questions of the Present Time.* London: Hodder and Stoughton, 1909. http://archive.org/details/aberdeendoctorsnoomacm.

Mahaffey, Jerome Dean. *The Accidental Revolutionary: George Whitefield and the Creation of America.* Waco, Tex.: Baylor University Press, 2011.

———. *Preaching Politics: The Religious Rhetoric of George Whitefield and the Founding of the New Nation.* Studies in Rhetoric and Religion 3. Waco, Tex.: Baylor University Press, 2007.

Manigault, Peter, Elizabeth Heyward Jervey, and Mabel L. Webber. "Peter Manigault's Letters." *South Carolina Historical and Genealogical Magazine* 33, no. 2 (April 1932): 148–53.

Marietta, Jack D. *The Reformation of American Quakerism, 1748–1783.* Philadelphia: University of Pennsylvania Press, 1984.

Marsden, George M. *The Soul of the American University: From Protestant Establishment to Established Nonbelief.* New York: Oxford University Press, 1994.

McCandles, Peter. *Slavery, Disease, and Suffering in the Southern Lowcountry.* Cambridge Studies on the American South. Cambridge: Cambridge University Press, 2011.

McCrady, Edward. *An Historic Church: The Westminster Abbey of South Carolina.* Charleston, S.C.: Lucas and Richardson Co. Printers and Engravers, 1897.

McInnis, Maurie D. "Conflating Past and Present in the Reconstruction of Charleston's St. Philip's Church." In Alison Hoagland and Kenneth A. Breisch, eds., *Constructing Image, Identity, and Place,* 39–53. Perspectives in Vernacular Architecture, vol. 9 (Knoxville: University of Tennessee Press, 2003).

*Perspectives in Vernacular Architecture* 9 (2003): 39–53.

Merrens, H. Roy, and George D. Terry. "Dying in Paradise: Malaria, Mortality, and the Perceptual Environment in Colonial South Carolina." *Journal of Southern History* 50, no. 4 (November 1984): 533–50.

Michie, Rev. John Grant, M.A., ed. *The Records of Invercauld, MDXLVII–MDCCCXXVIII.* Aberdeen: New Spalding Club, 1901. http://books.google.com/books?id=S1shAQAAMAAJ&dq=the+records+of+invercauld&source=gbs_navlinks_s.

Miller, Perry. *The New England Mind: The Seventeenth Century.* New York: Macmillan, 1939.

Miller, Randall M. "Roman Catholicism in South Carolina." In *Religion in South Carolina,* edited by Charles H. Lippy, 82–102. Columbia: University of South Carolina Press, 1993.

"Minutes of the Vestry, St. Philip's Parish, 1732–1755. From the Original in Possession of St. Philip's Episcopal Church, Charleston, S.C." Typescript. Columbia, S.C., 1939.

Monaghan, E. Jennifer. *Learning to Read and Write in Colonial America.* Amherst: University of Massachusetts Press, 2005.

Moore, Caroline T., ed. *Abstracts of the Wills of the State of South Carolina.* 3 vols. Columbia, S.C.: R. L. Bryan, 1964.

Morgan, David T., Jr. "George Whitefield and the Great Awakening in the Carolinas and Georgia, 1739–1740." *Georgia Historical Quarterly* 54, no. 4 (Winter 1970): 517–39.

Morgan, Philip D. *Slave Counterpoint: Black Culture in the Eighteenth-Century Chesapeake & Low Country.* Chapel Hill: University of North Carolina Press, 1998.

Myers, Ken. *Roger Lundin on Biographies and Humility.* Mars Hill Audio Journal. https://marshillaudio.org/catalog/volume-79, accessed August 3, 2015.

Nash, Gary B. *The Urban Crucible: The Northern Seaports and the Origins of the American Revolution.* Abridged. Cambridge, Mass.: Harvard University Press, 1986.

Nash, R. C. "Trade and Business in Eighteenth-Century South Carolina: The Career of John Guerard, Merchant and Planter." *South Carolina Historical Magazine* 96, no. 1 (January 1995): 6–29.

Nellis, Eric. *Shaping the New World: African Slavery in the Americas, 1500–1888.* North York, Ontario: University of Toronto Press, 2013.

Nelson, Louis P. *The Beauty of Holiness: Anglicanism and Architecture in Colonial South Carolina.* Chapel Hill: University of North Carolina Press, 2008.

Noll, Mark A. *American Evangelical Christianity: An Introduction.* Oxford: Blackwell, 2001.

Novick, Peter. *That Noble Dream: The "Objectivity Question" and the American Historical Profession.* New York: Cambridge University Press, 1988.

Olmstead, Clifton E. *History of Religion in the United States.* Englewood Cliffs, N.J.: Prentice-Hall, 1960.

Olwell, Robert. *Masters, Slaves, and Subjects: The Culture of Power in the South Carolina Low Country, 1740–1790.* Ithaca, N.Y.: Cornell University Press, 1998.

Pennington, Edgar Legare. "The Reverend Alexander Garden." *Historical Magazine of the Protestant Episcopal Church* 2 (December 1933): 178–94.

———. "The Reverend Alexander Garden." *Historical Magazine of the Protestant Episcopal Church* 3 (March 1934): 48–55.

———. "The Reverend Thomas Morritt and the Free School in Charles Town." *South Carolina Historical and Genealogical Magazine* 32, no. 1 (January 1931): 34–45.

Peterson, Mark A. "The Selling of Joseph: Bostonians, Antislavery, and the Protestant International, 1689–1733." *Massachusetts Historical Review* 4 (2002): iv, 1–22.

Pinckney, Eliza Lucas. "Eliza Lucas Pinckney to Mary Bartlett, [1742]." In *The Papers of Eliza Lucas Pinckney and Harriott Pinckney Horry Digital Edition,* edited by Constance Schulz. Charlottesville: University of Virginia Press, 2012. http://rotunda.upress.virginia.edu/PinckneyHorry/ELP0116. Accessed February 7, 2017.

Pitcairn, Dr. Archibald. *The Whole Works of Dr. Archibald Pitcairn, Published by Himself. Wherein Are Discovered, the True Foundation and Principles of the Art of Physic. With Cases and Observations upon Most Distempers and Medicines.* Edited by George Sewell, M.D., and J. T. Desaguliers, D.D., F.R.S. 2nd ed. London, 1727. https://play.google.com/books/reader?id=GFYwAAAAYAAJ&printsec=frontcover&output=reader&authuser=0&hl=en&pg=GBS.PP10.

Polishook, Irwin H. "Review of *Mitre and Sceptre.*" *Journal of Southern History* 29, no. 1 (February 1963): 117–18.

Ramsay, David, M.D. *History of South Carolina, from Its First Settlement in 1670 to the Year 1808.* 2 vols. Newberry, S.C.: W. J. Duffie, 1858.

Ramsey, William L. "'Something Cloudy in Their Looks': The Origins of the Yamasee War Reconsidered." *Journal of American History* 90, no. 1 (June 1, 2003): 44–75.

*Record Book Independent or Congregational Church 1730–1796 Charleston County, Copied from the Original MS in the Possession of Independent or Congregational Church, Charleston, S.C.* Microfilm. Columbia, S.C.: Works Progress Administration, 1940.

Rivers, Isabel. *Reason, Grace, and Sentiment: A Study of the Language of Religion and Ethics in England, 1660–1780.* Cambridge: Cambridge University Press, 1991.

Roberts, Justin, and Ian Beamish. "Venturing Out: The Barbadian Diaspora and the Carolina Colony, 1650–1685." In *Creating and Contesting Carolina: Proprietary Era Histories,* 49–72. Columbia: University of South Carolina Press, 2013.

Rogers, George C., Jr. *Charleston in the Age of the Pinckneys.* Columbia: University of South Carolina Press, 1980.

Roper, L. H. *Conceiving Carolina: Proprietors, Planters, and Plots, 1662–1729.* New York: Palgrave Macmillan, 2004.

Ross, Dorothy. *The Origins of American Social Science.* Cambridge: Cambridge University Press, 1991.

Salley, A. S., Jr., ed. *Register of St. Philip's Parish, Charles Town, South Carolina, 1720–1758.* Charleston, S.C.: Walker, Evans and Cogswell, 1904.

Salmon, Marylynn. *Women and the Law of Property in Early America.* Chapel Hill: University of North Carolina Press, 1986.

Schmidt, Leigh E. "'The Grand Prophet,' Hugh Bryan: Early Evangelicalism's Challenge to the Establishment and Slavery in the Colonial South." *South Carolina Historical Magazine* 87, no. 4 (October 1986): 238–50.

Schulz, Constance, ed. *The Papers of Eliza Lucas Pinckney and Harriott Pinckney Horry Digital Edition.* Charlottesville: University of Virginia Press, Rotunda, 2012. http://rotunda.upress.virginia.edu/PinckneyHorry.

Scott, Hew. *Fasti Ecclesiae Scoticanae: The Succession of Ministers in the Church of Scotland from the Reformation; Synods of Fife, and of Angus and Mearns.* Vol. 1. Edinburgh: Oliver and Boyd, 1925. https://openlibrary.org/books/OL7133412M/Fasti_ecclesi%C3%A6_scotican%C3%A6.

———. *Fasti Ecclesiae Scoticanae: The Succession of Ministers in the Church of Scotland from the Reformation; Synods of Fife, and of Angus and Mearns.* Vol. 5. Edinburgh: Oliver and Boyd, 1925. https://openlibrary.org/books/OL7039322M/Fasti_ecclesi%C3%A6_scotican%C3%A6.

Scott, Kenneth. "Sufferers in the Charleston Fire of 1740." *South Carolina Historical Magazine* 64, no. 4 (October 1963): 203–11.

*Selected Pages Relating to South Carolina from Library of Congress Transcripts of the Papers of the SPG in Foreign Parts, Copies of Letters Received.* Microfilm. 19–26 vols. Series A, 1724–35. Vol. 19, n.d.

*Selected Pages Relating to South Carolina from Library of Congress Transcripts of the Papers of the SPG in Foreign Parts, Copies of Letters Received.* Microfilm. 19–26 vols. Series A, 1724–35. Vol. 21, n.d.

Sensbach, Jon. "Early Southern Religions in a Global Age." In *The American South and the Atlantic World,* edited by Brian Ward, Martyn Bone, and William A. Link, 45–60. Gainesville: University of Florida Press, 2013.

Severens, Martha R. "Johnston, Henrietta de Beaulieu Dering." In *The South Carolina Encyclopedia,* edited by Walter Edgar, 508. Columbia: University of South Carolina Press, 2006.

Shaffer, E. T. H. *History of Bethel Presbyterian Church: From the Founding in 1728 Down to the Present Time—1928.* Walterboro, S.C: Press and Standard, 1928.

Shields, David S. *Civil Tongues and Polite Letters in British America.* Chapel Hill: University of North Carolina Press, 1997.

Simpson, Archibald. "Archibald Simpson Diary, 1754–1761," n.d. South Carolina Historical Society, Charleston.

Sirmans, M. Eugene. "Politics in Colonial South Carolina: The Failure of Proprietary Reform, 1682–1694." *William and Mary Quarterly* 23, no. 1 (January 1966): 33–55.

Smith, Craig. "'Great Reformation in the Manners of Mankind': Utopian Thought in the Scottish Reformation and Enlightenment." *Utopian Studies* 16, no. 2 (Summer 2005): 221–45.

Smith, Henry A. M. *The Baronies of South Carolina.* Charleston: South Carolina Historical Society, 1931.

———. "Sir John Yeamans, an Historical Error." *South Carolina Historical and Genealogical Magazine* 19, no. 3 (July 1, 1918): 152–56.

Smith, Lisa. *The First Great Awakening in Colonial American Newspapers.* Lanham, Md.: Lexington Books, 2012.

Smith, Mark M. "Remembering Mary, Shaping Revolt: Reconsidering the Stono Rebellion." *Journal of Southern History* 67, no. 3 (August 2001): 513–34.

Smith, Samuel C. *A Cautious Enthusiasm: Mystical Piety and Evangelicalism in Colonial South Carolina.* Columbia: University of South Carolina Press, 2013.

Snyder, Christina. *Slavery in Indian Country: The Changing Face of Captivity in Early America*. Cambridge, Mass.: Harvard University Press, 2010.

Soderland, Jean R. *Quakers and Slavery: A Divided Spirit*. Princeton, N.J.: Princeton University Press, 1985.

Spurr, John. "'Latitudinarianism' and the Restoration Church." *Historical Journal* 31, no. 1 (March 1988): 61–82.

Stout, Harry S. *The Divine Dramatist: George Whitefield and the Rise of Modern Evangelicalism*. Library of Religious Biography. Grand Rapids, Mich.: William B. Eerdmans, 1991.

Stuart, John, ed. *Selections from the Records of the Kirk Session, Presbytery, and Synod of Aberdeen*. Aberdeen: Spalding Club, 1846. http://books.google.com/books?id=cGUuAAAAMAAJ&dq=selections+from+the+Records+of+the+Kirk+Session&source=gbs_navlinks_s.

Stumpf, Stuart O. "South Carolina Importers of General Merchandise, 1735–1765." *South Carolina Historical Magazine* 84, no. 1 (January 1983): 1–10.

Sundue, Sharon Braslaw. "Confining the Poor to Ignorance? Eighteenth-Century American Experiments with Charity Education." *History of Education Quarterly* 47, no. 2 (May 2007): 123–48.

Sweet, William W. *The Story of Religion in America*. Grand Rapids, Mich.: Baker Book House, 1973.

Thornton, John K. "African Dimensions of the Stono Rebellion." *American Historical Review* 96, no. 4 (October 1991): 1101–13.

Tiffany, Charles C. *A History of the Protestant Episcopal Church in the United States of America*. New York: Christian Literature Co., 1895.

Towles, Louis P. "Goose Creek Men." In *The South Carolina Encyclopedia*, edited by Walter Edgar, 384–85. Columbia: University of South Carolina Press, 2006.

Towner, Lawrence W. "The Sewell-Saffin Dialogue on Slavery." *William and Mary Quarterly* 21, no. 1 (January 1964): 40–52.

Townsend, Leah. *South Carolina Baptists: 1670–1805*. Baltimore, Md.: Genealogical Publishing Co., 1978.

Tyerman, Rev. L. *The Life of the Rev. George Whitefield*. Vol. 1. New York: Anson D. F. Randolph, 1877. https://play.google.com/books/reader?id=MVdIAAAAYAAJ&printsec=frontcover&output=reader&authuser=0&hl=en&pg=GBS.PR3.

Underwood, James Lowell, and W. Lewis Burke, eds. *The Dawn of Religious Freedom in South Carolina*. Columbia: University of South Carolina Press, 2006.

Upton, Dell. *Holy Things and Profane: Anglican Parish Churches in Colonial Virginia*. New Haven, Conn.: Yale University Press, 1997.

Van Ruymbeke, Bertrand. *From New Babylon to Eden: The Huguenots and Their Migration to Colonial South Carolina*. Columbia: University of South Carolina Press, 2006.

Vickery, Amanda. *Behind Closed Doors: At Home in Georgian England*. New Haven, Conn.: Yale University Press, 2009.

Waller, Maureen. *1700: Scenes from London Life*. New York: Four Walls Eight Windows, 2000.

Waterhouse, Richard. *A New World Gentry: The Making of a Merchant and Planter Class in South Carolina, 1670–1770*. New York: Garland, 1989.

Watson, Shevaun E. "'Good Will Come of This Evil': Enslaved Teachers and the Transatlantic Politics of Early Black Literacy." *Journal of College Composition and Communication* 66, no. 1 (September 2009): 66–89.

Wax, Darold D. "'The Great Risque We Run': The Aftermath of Slave Rebellion at Stono, South Carolina, 1739–1745." *Journal of Negro History* 67, no. 2 (Summer 1982): 136–47.

Webber, Mabel L., ed. "Presentment of the Grand Jury, March 1733/34." *South Carolina Historical and Genealogical Magazine* 25, no. 4 (October 1924): 193–95.

Weir, Robert M. *Colonial South Carolina: A History*. Columbia: University of South Carolina Press, 1997.

Weis, The Reverend Frederick Lewis, Th.D. *The Colonial Clergy of Virginia, North Carolina, and South Carolina*. Boston: Society of the Descendants of the Colonial Clergy, 1955.

Welsh, William Jeffrey, David Curtis Skaggs, and Donald K. Enholm. "In Pursuit of the 'Golden Mean': A Case Study of Mid-Eighteenth-Century Frontier Anglican Preaching." *Anglican and Episcopal History* 57, no. 2 (June 1988): 176–98.

Wheatley, Phillis. "An Elegiac Poem on the Death of that celebrated Divine, and eminent Servant of Jesus Christ, the Reverend and Learned Mr. George Whitefield." In *Heaven the Residence of the Saints*, edited by Ebenezer Pemberton (Boston: 1771). Massachusetts Historical Society, Collections Online. http://www.masshist.org/database/viewer.php?old=1&item_id=823. Accessed February 7, 2017.

White, Shane, and Graham White. *The Sounds of Slavery: Discovering African American History through Songs, Sermons, and Speech*. Boston: Beacon Press, 2005.

Whitefield, George. *George Whitefield's Journals*. Edinburgh: Banner of Truth Trust, 1998.

———. *Letters of George Whitefield for the Period 1734–1742*. Edinburgh: Banner of Truth Trust, 1976.

———. *Select Sermons of George Whitefield, Formerly of Pembroke College, Oxford and Chaplain to the Countess of Huntingdon, with an Account of His Life by J. C. Ryle, and a Summary of His Doctrine by R. Elliott*. Edinburgh: Banner of Truth Trust, 1997.

———. *Three Letters from the Reverend Mr. G. Whitefield*. Philadelphia: Printed and sold by Benjamin Franklin, 1740.

Whittemore, Henry. *The Heroes of the American Revolution and Their Descendants: Battle of Long Island*. New York: Heroes of the Revolution, 1897.

Williams, George W., ed. "Letters to the Bishop of London from the Commissaries in South Carolina." *South Carolina Historical Magazine* 78, no. 1 (January 1977): 1–31.

———, ed. "Letters to the Bishop of London from the Commissaries in South Carolina." *South Carolina Historical Magazine* 78, no. 2 (April 1977): 120–47.

————, ed. "Letters to the Bishop of London from the Commissaries in South Carolina." *South Carolina Historical Magazine* 78, no. 3 (July 1977): 213–42.

————, ed. "Letters to the Bishop of London from the Commissaries in South Carolina." *The South Carolina Historical Magazine* 78, no. 4 (October 1977): 286–317.

Winston, Lane G., Jr. "Economic Power among Eighteenth-Century Women of the Carolina Lowcountry." In *Money, Trade, and Power: The Evolution of Colonial South Carolina's Plantation Society,* edited by Jack P. Greene, et al, 322–43. Columbia, S.C.: University of South Carolina Press, 2001.

Witzig, Fred. "Beyond Expectation: How Charles Town's 'Pious and Well-Disposed Christians' Changed Their Minds about Slave Education during the Great Awakening." *South Carolina Historical Magazine* 114, no. 4 (October 2013): 286–315.

————. "The Great Anti-Awakening: Anti-Revivalism in Philadelphia and Charles Town, South Carolina, 1735–1745." Ph.D. diss., Indiana University, 2008.

Wood, Bradford J. "'A Constant Attendance on God's Alter [*sic*]': Death, Disease, and the Anglican Church in Colonial South Carolina, 1706–1750." *South Carolina Historical Magazine* 100, no. 3 (July 1999): 204–20.

Wood, Gordon S. *The Radicalism of the American Revolution.* New York: Vintage Books, 1991.

Wood, Peter H. *Black Majority: Negroes in Colonial South Carolina from 1670 through the Stono Rebellion.* New York: W. W. Norton, 1974.

Woolverton, John Frederick. *Colonial Anglicanism in North America.* Detroit: Wayne State University Press, 1984.

The World Bank. "Death Rate, Crude (per 1,000 People) | Data | Table." http://data .worldbank.org/indicator/SP.DYN.CDRT.IN, accessed May 21, 2014.

Yonge, Francis. *A Narrative of the Proceedings of the People of South-Carolina, in the Year 1719: And of the True Causes and Motives That Induced Them to Renounce Their Obedience to the Lords Proprietors, as Their Governors, and to Put Themselves under the Immediate Government of the Crown.* London: Printed in the year 1726.

# Index

Aberdeen, University of, 19, 21

Ahlstrom, Sydney, 183

Anabaptists, 13, 88, 152

Andrew (slave school teacher), 143, 150, 155–57

antirevivalism, 117, 122–24, 127, 145–46, 148–50

Bahamas, 44–45, 121, 163, 165

Baptists, 10–13, 15, 17, 84, 87–88, 98, 176–77

Barbados, 14, 16–17, 22, 24, 45; Barbadian Adventurers, 4–5, 7; Church of England in, 3–4, 16; early colonization of, 2–4, 6, 14, 22, 189n8, 190n24; slavery in, 2, 5, 6, 25, 60, 131, 152, 156, 157; Society for the Propagation of the Gospel involvement in, 152, 156

Boone, Thomas, 37, 62–63, 65–67, 74

Boschi, Charles, 70, 82, 98, 166

Bridenbaugh, Charles, 183

Bull, William Tredwell, 15, 26, 29, 31–32, 34, 40–41, 44, 45, 106

Bryan, Hugh, 101, 147, 150–51

Calvinism, 90–95, 114, 116, 144–45, 166, 185

Catholicism, 9, 14–15, 21, 75, 91–92, 94, 110, 113, 117, 120

Cawood, Gibbon, 43–45, 69, 72

Charles Town, 8, 12, 14, 16, 25–27, 29, 33, 35–36, 49, 116, 149, 150, 177; Free School in, 72, 77, 138, 141, 143; Garden as resident of, 9, 28, 37, 64, 122, 168; layout of, 34–36; polite society in, 37, 53, 56–57; slavery in, 6, 39–40, 55, 79, 124, 137, 146, 155; Whitefield's involvement with, 96, 100–101, 125

Chauncy, Charles, 123–24

Christ Church Parish, 27, 41–42, 52, 61–66, 68, 73–74, 162

Church of England, 4, 9–12, 15–18, 28–29, 45, 53, 122, 154, 158, 176–77; bishop of London, 10–11, 15–16, 30–31, 41–42, 44–45, 100, 132, 139–40, 142, 150, 162–67; establishment, 4, 10–18, 147, 154, 177; politeness and, 61, 74–79, 81, 97, 114–16; slavery and, 80–81; wardens and vestry of, 13, 16, 28, 30–32, 36, 41, 52, 62–68, 74–75, 77, 80, 158–62, 168, 172–73

Congregationalism, 9–10, 13–14, 80, 84, 87, 105, 108, 127, 152

Croswell, Andrew, 91, 93–94

Dalcho, Frederick, 16, 34, 170, 180

Dale, Thomas, 56–57

Dallimore, Arnold, 181

Durand, Levi, 68, 73–74

Dutartre family, 118–19, 122

evangelicalism, 84–89, 119, 123–24, 127, 144, 148, 175, 178; critiques of polite society, 101–5, 108, 110, 114, 126, 129–30, 133, 135, 147, 154; critiques of slavery, 129–30, 133–34, 138, 147–54

French Huguenots, 13, 35, 37, 48, 132

Fulton, John, 66–68, 70, 73–75, 82

Gallay, Alan, 8, 148
Garden, Alexander: ancestry and
    origins of, 19–24; appointment as
    commissary of, 41, 45; arrival in
    Charles Town of, 25–26, 31; death
    of, 174–75; education of, 19; election
    as rector of St. Philip's Church of,
    31–33; health and appearance of, 26,
    27, 173–74, 166–67; marriage and
    family of, 37–38, 40, 43, 45–51, 169,
    174–76; ministry of, 9–10, 18–19,
    36, 41, 97–99, 158–62, 166–68; end
    of, 169–73; in North Carolina and
    Bahamas, 163–65; theological views,
    85–95, 112–16; polite society and,
    37, 61, 70–71, 74–75, 77–79, 81–82,
    102, 104, 114–16, 146, 151–54, 169,
    171; slavery and, 38–40, 52–53,
    55, 129–30, 133, 135, 137–42, 150,
    151–53, 155–57, 168; wealth of,
    70–71. *See also* slave school
Garden, Anne (daughter of Alexander),
    20, 38, 174–75
Garden, Benjamin (son of Alexander),
    38, 174
Garden, George, 20–22
Garden, John (son of Alexander), 38,
    174–75
Garden, Martha (daughter of Alexan-
    der), 38, 169, 174–75
Garden, Martha (wife of Alexander),
    20, 37–38, 40, 43, 46–50, 70–71, 169,
    175–76
Garden, Mary (daughter of Alexan-
    der), 38, 175
Georgia, 57, 71, 79, 101, 129, 135–37,
    144, 148–49, 151–52
Great Anti-Awakening, 116–18, 149
Great Awakening, 12, 84, 86–88, 91, 97,
    99–100, 102–3, 123–24, 128–30, 133,
    138, 148–52, 175
Guy, William, 29, 30, 36, 71, 72, 120,
    142, 150, 163

Harry (slave school teacher), 143, 150,
    155–57
Hasell, Thomas, 30–31, 36, 72, 142, 150
Heimert, Alan, 184–85
Hill, Charles, 37, 43
Hunt, Brian, 43–45, 52, 68–70, 72–75,
    82, 165–66, 179

Judaism, 9, 113, 170
Johnson, Gov. Robert, 26, 29–32
Johnston, Gideon, 11, 16, 29, 41
Johnston, Henrietta, 48–50

Keen, Quentin, 181
Klingberg, Frank, 186

Leslie, Andrew, 105, 107, 166
Ligon, Richard, 3

Marston, Edward, 14, 28–29, 31–32
Miller, Perry, 183, 185
Moore, James, 14, 31–32
Morritt, Thomas, 41–43, 167

Native Americans, 6–8, 10, 15, 25, 37,
    84, 105, 110, 124, 130, 135, 140, 155
Native American slave trade, 14, 40, 52.
    *See also* Yamasee War
New Birth, 85, 88–91, 95–96, 101, 112,
    115, 123, 135
North Carolina, 75, 136, 163

Pennington, Edgar, 181
polite society, 53, 56–62, 64, 67, 70,
    77–78, 99, 129, 143–44, 149–51, 158;
    Church of England and, 74–79, 81,
    97, 114–16; entertainment and, 58,
    103–4, 107–8, 117, 126, 135; evan-
    gelical critiques of, 101–5, 108, 110,
    114, 126, 129–30, 133, 135, 147, 154;
    race and, 53, 59–62, 83, 124, 130,
    152–54, 177; wealth and, 57–58, 59,
    71, 81, 109
Presbyterianism, 9–10, 13–14, 17, 21,
    23–24, 27, 44, 62, 73, 80, 84, 88, 123

Proprietors of Carolinas, 4–5, 9, 11, 13–14, 18, 31, 37, 154
Protestant Episcopal Church, 176–77, 181
Puritanism, 17–18, 88, 183

Ramsay, David, 179–80
Revolution of 1719, 8–9, 11, 30, 31, 32
Revolutionary War, 84, 151, 178

St. Bartholomew's Parish, 15, 65, 69–70
St. George's Dorchester Parish, 13, 32, 43, 69, 72, 80, 155, 160
St. James Goose Creek Parish, 29, 33, 71–72, 131, 155
St. John's Berkeley Parish, 43, 52, 68, 74, 146–47
St. Philip's Church, 18, 24, 28–31, 68–69, 96–98, 101, 125–26, 135, 151, 158, 160–61, 168, 173–74, 176; description of, 33–34, 36, 45, 56, 96, 98, 109
Stono Rebellion, 55, 106–7, 129–30, 138, 149, 152, 154
Schmidt, Leigh E., 147–48
Second Great Awakening, 86, 99, 176–77, 180
slavery, 2, 4, 5–8, 10, 12, 25, 34, 37–40, 52, 54–56, 59–61, 67, 70–71, 76, 77, 124, 168–69; education of, 69, 130–59; resistance of, 106–7, 134, 139–40, 155–57; trade, African, 38–40, 44, 79–83; trade, Indian, 6–8, 14, 37, 52
slave school, 130–32, 135, 138, 141, 143–44, 150–53, 155–57, 180, 186
Smith, Josiah, 87, 108, 127, 173

Society for the Propagation of the Gospel (SPG), 10–11, 28–31, 48, 77, 102, 130–32, 152, 153, 156, 167
*South Carolina Gazette,* 49–50, 54, 59–61, 100, 106, 130, 138, 145–46, 149, 169,
Spanish Florida, 54, 105–6, 117
Sweet, William, 183

Thomas, Samuel, 130, 132, 152
Thompson, Thomas, 69–70, 75
Tiffany, Charles C., 180
Tillotson, John (Archbishop of Canterbury), 19, 88, 95, 104, 114, 129–30
Tyerman, Luke, 181

Vernod (Varnod), Francis, 10, 43, 72, 80, 143, 155

Whitefield, George, 20, 86, 105, 109, 123–25, 141, 144–50, 171, 178; critiques of polite society, 101–4, 108, 151; critiques of slavery, 129–30, 133–38, 140, 148, 150–53; preaching style and sermons, 84, 87–88, 96–101, 108, 125–26; relationship with Garden, 84, 94, 96–97, 100, 102, 104, 109–14, 116, 118–22, 125–28, 130, 138–40, 143–45, 162, 180–81, 184–86; theological beliefs, 88–90, 94–95, 116
Winteley, John, 52–53, 61–68, 70, 73–75, 82, 165–66, 179

Yamassee War, 7–8, 15–17, 24–25, 36–38, 40–41, 46, 52, 57, 60, 69, 79, 178
Yeamans, Sir John, 4–5

www.ingramcontent.com/pod-product-compliance
Lightning Source LLC
Chambersburg PA
CBHW070928150426
42812CB00049B/1574